T0305400

Big Brands Are Watching You

MARKETING SOCIAL JUSTICE
AND DIGITAL CULTURE

Francesca Sobande

UNIVERSITY OF CALIFORNIA PRESS

University of California Press
Oakland, California

© 2024 by Francesca Sobande

Library of Congress Cataloging-in-Publication Data

Names: Sobande, Francesca, author.
Title: Big brands are watching you : marketing social justice and digital
    culture / Francesca Sobande.
Description: Oakland, California : University of California Press,
    [2024] | Includes bibliographical references and index.
Identifiers: LCCN 2023041710 (print) | LCCN 2023041711 (ebook) |
    ISBN 9780520387065 (cloth) | ISBN 9780520387072 (paperback) |
    ISBN 9780520387089 (epub)
Subjects: LCSH: Branding (Marketing)—Political aspects. | Social
    justice—Economic aspects. | Mass media—Influence.
Classification: LCC HF5415.1255 S633 2024 (print) |
    LCC HF5415.1255 (ebook) | DDC 658.8/27—dc23/eng/20231002
LC record available at https://lccn.loc.gov/2023041710
LC ebook record available at https://lccn.loc.gov/2023041711

33   32   31   30   29   28   27   26   25   24
10   9   8   7   6   5   4   3   2   1

Contents

Figures

Preface

The world is on fire.

As I write these words, heat waves are surging, and wildfires are blazing across many places. In the United Kingdom (UK), hottest days on record keep rising (and rising, and rising . . .). In the United States (US), more than one hundred million Americans have been under heat warnings in recent weeks. The climate crisis is not imminent—it's *here* and it's roaring. As well as being ravaged by *global warming* (now deemed *global boiling*)—a term that cannot possibly capture the ferocity of changing temperatures and environmental conditions—the world is feeling the effects of scorching political climates and the cold-hearted decisions of cruel governments.

The current state of politics in the UK and the US has emerged from the embers of histories that are still here and include the ravages of racial capitalism, colonialism, and various wars. My time sifting through material at the Library of Congress Main Reading Room and at the Smithsonian Institution Archives involved reading many remnants of the history of advertising in the UK and the US. That analysis served as a reminder of how global politics has always been a main character in consumer culture's unfolding plot, whether in the form of brands altering their advertising strategy to account for the impact of wars and crises or marketers negotiating with political figures in a plea to share a stage with them.

Undoubtedly, political spheres have always been heated, and many of the pressing issues that the world is facing right now are far from being new, from the erosion of reproductive rights to the societal normalization of antiblackness. However, the combined impact of digital developments, the currents of contemporary consumer culture, and the recent decisions of governments have fueled the flames of politics and policing in ways that are particular to the present day. The UK government's well-documented and ongoing efforts to prohibit public protests are likely to affect the nature of future forms of community organizing. Some brands (e.g., Big Tech) may opportunistically frame digital platforms as the preeminent sites of social protest, and others may accelerate their efforts to portray consumerism as an act of resistance.

The temperature of these times is stifling and sobering, but as always, hope burns eternal. My account of the relationship among consumer culture, social justice, and digital culture might be interpreted as featuring (too) many critiques, from my discussion of facets of influencer culture and white sincerity to critical portrayals of the nexus of nation-branding and self-branding. However, such critiques should not be mistaken for a dismissal of beneficial aspects of digital culture and influential activist efforts that occur in market settings. Also, my critiques should not be confused for a fatalistic lack of hope about the future. To me, critique is generative. Critique *is* hope. Critique is part of how we turn questions that keep us up at night into analysis and action that might contribute to changes that we hope to see happen in the future.

When I started this book, I did not know exactly where it would go, but I knew that I wanted to write about branding, digital culture, and social justice, in a way that did not skirt around naming

Figure 1. "Press the button to experience a sense of agency" sign, Edinburgh, Scotland, 2018. Photo by author.

issues of oppression, morality, and structural forces such as racial capitalism. To draw on the resonant words of Sam, an advertising director whom I interviewed as part of this work, I did not want to find myself simply "softening social justice to DEI [diversity, equity/equality, and inclusion]." Between now and 2024, when this book will be published, the sands of social justice, digital culture, and consumer culture will no doubt have shifted, as they are always in motion. Although I cannot predict all the changes that lie ahead in these interconnected elements of life, one thing is certain: Big Brands are (and will keep) watching you (watching *them*).

Acknowledgments

I often find that the acknowledgments section of my writing is noticeably brief. This is never because of a lack of people I seek to acknowledge and express my gratitude to. Rather, there are so many people I want to thank that I find myself pulled toward a few words that might speak to them all in some way. This time is different, though. In this moment I find myself moved toward writing something slightly longer than I tend to, as part of how I thank those who have been involved in this process and all who have supported me for many years.

First, thank you to my beautiful mum, whose love of reading is no doubt what sparked my own. I could write pages upon pages on her brilliance, creativity, and love, and the open-hearted way that she is there for many people. Were it not for how she has always encouraged me to embrace my own mind, I would never have found my feet as an author.

Since I was wee, my mum and dad supported how I played and experimented with writing, from reading my never-ending stories as a child to celebrating my published work. They did so while lovingly telling me that I have nothing to prove to anyone—words that I often return to when working through bouts of doubt and when in the deep end of self-scrutiny. Sure, humility is important as a writer, but so is writing in ways that are free of a preoccupation with forms of approval and validation.

At home with my parents, debates, laughter, and discussions were served up with warmth alongside dinner, and no question that I asked was ever deemed to be silly or small. My parents taught me to keep asking, keep reading, keep writing, keep searching, keep loving, and keep living in ways that are true to who I am. Thank you, *always*, mum and dad.

Thank you to my dear friends and loved ones who move through this world in ways that are a constant source of love, hope, and inspiration. I appreciate all that we share and the many moments of being and dreaming together that are part of our lives. Love you, Kit.

Thank you to Michelle Lipinski (senior acquisitions editor, University of California Press), whose continued encouragement and guidance was at the center of this book's emergence and progression. Were it not for Michelle's generous advice, patience, and support, I know that I would not have found my way to, and through, writing this book.

Thank you to Dr Anthony Kwame Harrison for such detailed, considerate, and encouraging reader feedback. Thank you to the anonymous reader as well, who offered very helpful, clear, and constructive comments that no doubt shaped the book.

Thank you to members of staff at the Library of Congress Main Reading Room and at the Smithsonian Institution Archives. From the moment that I emailed an enquiry about accessing resources in both spaces in Washington, D.C., I received extensive help.

Thank you to everyone who kindly agreed to be interviewed as part of this research, as well as everyone who took the time to complete my survey on marketplace experiences.

Thank you to music! As far back as I can remember, I have written while listening to music. The soundtrack of this book is expansive but particularly features the songs of Bloc Party, Funeral for a Friend, and the exquisite *Succession* soundtracks by Nicholas Britell.

Thank you to spring, whose arrival always brings with it a renewed sense of hope, the beauty of blooms, and the reminder of all that grows from seeds that were/are planted.

Finally, thanks to *you* for reading this book!

1 Setting the Scene

SOCIAL JUSTICE FOR SALE

In the summer of 2022, I found myself in Washington, D.C., a day after the Supreme Court of the United States (SCOTUS) overturned the landmark *Roe v. Wade* (1973) decision. June 24, 2022, marked the grim reversal of nearly five decades of a SCOTUS ruling that the US Constitution generally protects the liberty to choose to have an abortion. In response to the overturning of *Roe v. Wade*, reproductive rights organizers and reproductive freedom activists continued to mobilize with conviction and a commitment to equity and justice. In contrast, many brands made meager moves to affirm abortion rights advocacy—or to at least *appear* to be interested in these matters.

A flurry of news updates and social media posts had alerted me to which brands were simply wading into "the discourse of the day" and which were doing more than sharing a statement about yet *another* devastating "moment in history." Editorial pieces pointed to various views on what brands should (not) do next. Writing for the industry-oriented website and publication *Marketing Week*, Tanya Joseph

Figure 2. "DEAR SCOTUS, FUCK AROUND AND FIND OUT" sign, Washington, D.C., 2022. Photo by author.

(2022) suggests that "Roe v Wade is not just a US issue, nor can brands assume it doesn't affect them. Now is the time to stand up for your workers' and consumers' rights." In the months prior to June 2022, Amanda—a UK journalist with seventeen years of industry experience—spoke to me about the potential for brands to take a stance on reproductive rights and a host of activist issues.

Amanda, who is a woman of "mixed" Black heritage, does "a lot of social commentary, I would probably call it pop psychology and then pieces on diversity, racism, inclusion, that kind of thing and then on the other side is beauty trends and all that wellness type of writing." Amanda described brand responses to reproductive rights issues this way:

> I think it depends on, in some ways, the size of the brand and the objectives of the brand. If you commit to being an activist, then you

will generally . . . the opposition, or whatever, of the cause that you are supporting . . . will *not* be your customer. So, I think you do start off losing a certain demographic. Again, it would depend on who you're targeting, like if you're pro-abortion in terms of pro-women's choice or just pro-choice, then there'll be people that aren't, and you would lose those people as customers.[1]

As highlighted by the Black feminist media studies work of Timeka N. Tounsel (2022, 2), "Commercial entities market their goods and services by stitching them into the imagined lifestyles of their target consumers." Additionally, such commercial entities do this by connecting their goods, services, and overall image to certain social, political, and moral positions that they perceive as being upheld by their intended audience. Amanda's observations emphasize that the stance of brands on social and political issues is typically strategically aligned with their approach to target marketing. Put differently, brands tailor their stance, and how they communicate it, in ways that correspond with the perceived preferences and positions of their intended audiences—including, in some situations, the preferences and positions of their employees. My interest in these matters has led to me exploring facets of the relationship between morality and marketing, as well as the dynamic between activism and branding. Consequently, my book considers how morality is (re)defined in the marketplace.

I examine how brands struggle to be moral arbiters while drawing on digital culture and marketing and negotiating messages of supposed "social justice" (e.g., messages about addressing structural inequalities and intersecting oppressions). As such, my work is

---

1. As Amanda alludes, although some of the media, public, and political discourse regarding abortion and reproductive rights focuses on the experiences of women (e.g., by framing reproductive rights as being an issue of women's rights), it is not only cisgender women who will be denied legal access to abortions due to the overturning of *Roe v. Wade*. Trans men, nonbinary people, and individuals who are gender nonconforming can, and do, get pregnant. Accordingly, it is vital that the work of reproductive justice organizers and reproductive freedom activists be inclusive of the experiences of individuals with a wide range of gender identities and expressions, and such work must account for the intersecting nature of forms of oppression, including sexism, racism, colorism, transphobia, classism, ableism, misogyny, homophobia, and xenophobia.

shaped by Tressie McMillan Cottom's (2020) extensive research and writing, including "Where Platform Capitalism and Racial Capitalism Meet: The Sociology of Race and Racism in the Digital Society," which "puts forth that there are two turns in the political economy of race, ethnicity, and racism: networked capital that shapes a global racial hierarchy that varies across spatial geographies and the privatization of public and economic life" (441).

My work, past and present, is seeded and molded by critical race and digital studies (Hamilton 2020). This includes the formative research of internet studies scholar Safiya Umoja Noble (2018), which has been crucial to my understanding of, and subsequent work about, the digital lives of Black women in Britain (Sobande 2020). Noble's (2018) work on race, gender, technology, and the internet continues to impact many aspects of critical digital studies and informs elements of my understanding of the workings of power, agency, and oppression in different digital spaces. As I have highlighted in my previous writing, Noble's (2018) multifaceted work has been central to my ability to learn about and research a range of matters related to digital culture, injustice, and media— including, most recently, the digital self-branding practices of Black and Asian people working in the UK's creative and cultural industries (Sobande, Hesmondhalgh, and Saha 2022). Overall, while my book does not include an in-depth discussion of the particularities of algorithmic issues and their oppressive impacts, it is approached with an awareness of such forces that Noble (2018) has critically analyzed with clarity and impact, as discussed in chapter 3. More than that, my book, and the research that led to it, was made possible because of such expansive critical race and digital studies, including *The Intersectional Internet: Race, Sex, Class, and Culture Online* (Noble and Tynes 2016), and the research, writing, and digital alchemist work of Moya Bailey (2021) in *Misogynoir Transformed: Black Women's Digital Resistance*, which is crucial to understanding digital culture, technology, and connected structural conditions, experiences of collectivity, and expressions of creativity.

The extant studies and work that my book draws on also include Naomi Klein's (2000) pivotal account *No Logo: No Space, No Choice, No Jobs*, which tackles the "New Branded World" and "The Triumph of Identity Marketing," among other topics. However, there have been numerous national and global shifts in the decades since then—not least the effects of the ongoing coronavirus (COVID-19) pandemic, which have amounted to such a tumultuous situation that it is now termed a state of "permacrisis." These societal changes and continued times of crises have significantly impacted branding practices, consumer culture, digital culture, activism, messages of morality, and their overlaps. Thus, mindful of the insights in *The Voice Catchers: How Marketers Listen In to Exploit Your Feelings, Your Privacy, and Your Wallet* (Turow 2021), in this book I account for the long history of how brands *watch* people and people watch them, while also grappling with recent changes to how these power relations unfold.

As companies in the US began stating their support for employees seeking to access abortion services in the summer of 2022, the limitations of their corporate communications and concepts of care were criticized and called out. There have been numerous comments about the hypocrisy of companies that have anti-abortion board members and staff. Many people also have voiced concerns about how employers might use the overturning of *Roe v. Wade* as an opportunity to ramp up surveillance of the health, reproductive activity, and privacy of employees—all under the guise of helping them to access abortion services. As existing scholarship explains, the surveillance approaches of various brands involve them using voice surveillance technology which is part of "the spiral of personalization that drives much of twenty-first century marketing" (Turow 2021, 11). In addition to strategically listening to you, as my title states, *Big Brands Are Watching You*—whether by tracking your shopping (Turow 2017), enlisting the oppressive power of algorithms (Noble 2018), or tracing your digital footprints.[2] Accordingly, a through line that connects the themes covered in my book is analysis of how brands watch people and how people watch brands (watching *them*).

The response of brands to the overturning of *Roe v. Wade* is just one of many examples of the complex dynamics between branding, activism, social injustices, and politics. By analyzing other examples of brand practices and brand positionings (e.g., Ben & Jerry's, Brew-Dog, Levi's, Lush, Tony's Chocolonely), pop culture activity (e.g., the When We Were Young music festival), and issues of oppression (e.g., the force of racial capitalism), my book spans a wide range of pressing topics. Although each chapter deals with a different overarching theme, what they all have in common is a connection to questions and concerns regarding the role of brands and messages of morality in the marketplace and in the diverse societies that they are part of. As prior scholarship has noted, "moralism was a touchstone of the pre- and post-Brexit debate in the UK and the Trump election in the US" (Lentin 2020, 97), and moralism continues to be implicated in much contemporary public and political discourse in both places. So I turn my attention to this topic by focusing on morality in the marketplace.

From critically considering the history of nation-branding to scrutinizing the social construct of "culture wars," I detail the interrelated state of branding practices and political actions in this current moment. *Big Brands Are Watching You* draws on in-depth analysis of six research interviews with media, marketing, and retail experts, as well as four hundred responses to a survey on perceptions of alleged brand "woke-washing" and the relationship between consumer culture and activism. While the demographic of survey respondents

---

2. The title of my book is adapted from the slogan "Big Brother is watching you," featured in George Orwell's dystopian novel *Nineteen Eighty-Four*, and relates to an ominous and omnipresent fictional character and symbol (Big Brother). I also chose this title because it marks a continuation of my thinking about forms of watching, gazing, glancing, and looking that can be part of experiences of digital culture and consumer culture, some of which I considered in "Watching Me Watching You" (Sobande 2017).

was varied, most of the responses (n = 172) were from white British people, and the majority of the four hundred responses were from people 26–35 years old, closely followed by those 36–45 years old. Therefore, the research survey responses particularly highlight the perspectives of people who are often referred to as being part of the generationally defined demographics of Gen Z (born 1997–2012), Millennials (born 1981–96), and Gen X (born 1965–80). In addition to being informed by survey responses, my book is based on analysis of an abundance of archived material (e.g., Library of Congress and Smithsonian Institution Archives) and pop culture representations. The discussions and chapters ahead are also brought to life by reflecting on aspects of my own experiences (e.g., at the Museum of Brands exhibition in London and at the Tony's Chocolonely superstore in Amsterdam). Along with this analysis, the pages that follow feature some of my ponderings on the process of doing this work, including descriptions of my time spent in archives in Washington, D.C. Consequently, while my book is an account of how Big Brands are watching you and are marketing "social justice" and digital culture, it is also an invitation to consider different ways of doing, writing about, and reflecting on research. This scaffolding chapter introduces foundational concepts, theories, themes, and contextual details that are threaded throughout my book and provides an overview of the bricolage of experiences and research that has informed this work.

BEYOND BINARIES: ACTIVISM AND ADVERTISING

Many brands steer clear of commenting on social and political issues and pride themselves on their alleged neutrality. However, the number of those that take a very different approach has noticeably increased since the days of US ice-cream manufacturer Ben & Jerry's being deemed one of very few brands to take a stand on issues of injustice (Haig 2011; Kunda 2020; Littler 2008; Sobande 2019a).

Moreover, as Ben & Jerry's (2019) states on its website, "Systemic racism and criminal justice reform are big issues for a business to take on, but we've been advocates for social justice and equity throughout our 40 year history." Essentially, Ben & Jerry's is often framed as a "first mover" in terms of its decision to make its business model and ethos one that places social, political, and environmental issues at the center. Nowadays, many brands are eager to attempt to replicate such an approach and to tap into the zeitgeist, but they often lack the reputation and the grasp of social and political issues to cultivate a brand image that could be comparable to Ben & Jerry's.

Moving beyond simply focusing on Ben & Jerry's, while acknowledging the significance of what it is deemed to stand for, my book analyzes brand examples to critically examine the contemporary coupling of activism and advertising. This involves moving beyond a simplistic binary notion of the latter without diluting distinct differences between the two. Principles of activism and advertising are often at odds with each other. Still, there are times when there appears to be a dialogue between aspects of activism and advertising that cannot simply be characterized as adversarial or something to solely be suspicious of (Mukherjee and Banet-Weiser 2012). What I mean by this is that it is important to understand the relationship between brands and urgent social and political issues—including the dynamic between activism and advertising—as a fraught and fast-moving one that is at once filled with friction and alliances (Banet-Weiser 2018). Just as "coming to a definition or understanding of digital technology is an iterative process dependent on changes in technology, usage, history, and theory" (Hess 2017, 3), so too is the process involved in defining or understanding social justice and activism.

For example, mere minutes after the public announcement that SCOTUS had overturned *Roe v. Wade*, people were posting well-meaning instructions to immediately "delete your period tracking apps," to try to protect the privacy of menstrual and reproductive activity. But does such well-meaning advice, which focuses on individual choices, amount to collective social justice efforts? Online writing that emerged during that time included discussion of the nexus of digital rights advocacy and reproductive rights activism (Slupska and Shipp 2022), as well as writing that praised certain brands for appearing to commit to supporting the fight for reproductive justice and freedom. Some people highlighted how data and use of social media are weaponized as part of the erosion of reproductive rights, while others urged individuals to think twice before tweeting on this topic and advised them to turn to "better" online platforms to "protect" themselves. At that time, I had headed to Washington, D.C., for a Race in the Marketplace (RIM) Research Network Re-Union in nearby Arlington, Virginia, where I was with other scholars, marketing practitioners, and activists who address critical issues regarding race and the marketplace, including issues of bodily autonomy, power, and agency.[3]

In between conversations at the RIM Re-Union, I caught glimpses of US press and pop culture reacting to the overturning of *Roe v. Wade*—sometimes in ways that accounted for the racial, and outright *racist*, politics of the rolling back of reproductive rights. As mainstream media and political reporting on the SCOTUS decision played out, so too did independent and grassroots coverage emphasizing that the reversal of reproductive rights stems from imperialist, white supremacist, capitalist patriarchy (hooks 1984)—a system within which Black people's bodily autonomy has *always* been obstructed by political and legislative institutions. Relatedly, the insightful work of journalism and media studies scholar Meredith D.

3. The RIM Research Network is an international and transdisciplinary research network dedicated to knowledge production on the historic, contemporary, and future interactions of race in the marketplace through scholarship and practice. In addition to being a vital source of research related to the topics of race and racism in the marketplace, RIM is a scholarly community of people whose encouragement and friendship has been central to the trajectory of my research and writing. RIM's "come as you are" ethos has always heartened me and has been a source of much support, particularly when I first began to do academic research. Were it not for meeting members of the RIM Network at the inaugural RIM Forum at American University in Washington, D.C., in 2017, I would not be the researcher, writer, and person that I am today. In fact, attending the 2022 RIM Re-Union in Arlington was one of the main sources of inspiration that kept me going while working on this book during several difficult years. Thank you to RIM and everyone who is part of such a welcoming space. More information about RIM can be accessed at www.rimnetwork.net/.

Clark (2020, 89) affirms the significance of "discursive accountability practices," which "are the creations of Black counterpublics that are conspicuously absent from the American public imaginary." Clark (2020) contends that the oppressive American public imaginary "holds a lofty vision of newspaper op-ed pages, radio shows, town-hall meetings, and the like as forums of debate where a multiplicity of discursive publics are equally empowered to engage in debate and the free expression of ideas. This simply isn't so." Hence the creation of Black "digital accountability praxis" (Clark 2020, 88), including online posts that critically outline what activist and academic Loretta J. Ross and historian and curator Rickie Solinger (2017, 2) refer to as being "the powerful role of colonialism and white supremacy in determining reproductive destinies." Informed by Clark's (2020) work, in addition to a wealth of scholarship from critical studies of race and the marketplace, and specifically, *Black media experiences*, I examine how the attitudes and actions of brands in the US and the UK have become part of conversations about "wokeness," "cancel culture," "publics," and mediated and marketed expressions of politics and morality.

The tapestry of televised responses to the overturning of *Roe v. Wade* in the days that followed it included the Black Entertainment Television (BET) Awards 2022 "In Memoriam" section of the night, which dramatically opened with a black screen that featured the striking and capitalized words "ROE v. WADE" in white lettering (Aniftos 2022). Elsewhere, advertisements by the nonprofit organization Planned Parenthood rapidly responded to the SCOTUS overturning and contributed to the momentum of pushback against it. Some celebrities spoke out about the ruling, while the silence of others spoke volumes (Ng 2022). Some individuals took to the streets to protest, while various people's activism was less public in nature but no less impactful. The day after the derisive decision of SCOTUS, many brands watched and waited (and then watched some more) before carefully commenting on what ensued or before choosing to keep their voices down (Daniels 2022; Kho 2022; Robinson

2022; Alcántara 2022). Yet in the months leading up to the overturning of *Roe v. Wade*, some brands had decided to comment on this issue sooner rather than later.

Reporting for global media platform and marketing website *The Drum*, Kendra Clark (2022) notes: "A number of brands that recently introduced policies to expand employees' access to reproductive care in light of restrictive state-level legislation like Texas's Senate Bill 8 have remained mum on the leaked US Supreme Court draft opinion indicating that *Roe v. Wade* is poised for reversal. However, a small contingent of brands are voicing support for abortion rights—and putting their money where their mouth is." Many brand responses to activism and community organizing are symptomatic of the sticky position of brands in the context of neoliberal racial capitalist societies, where consumption is often mistaken for, or actively (re)presented as, social action.

Sometimes it seems as though social justice is for sale (Rosa-Salas and Sobande 2022), and that "commodity activism" (Littler 2008; Mukherjee and Banet-Weiser 2012) has expanded to such an extent that activism is societally assumed to entail a form of consumerism. Then again, some businesses (e.g., Ben & Jerry's) have appeared to express their support of activism in ways that align with their well-established values, without portraying themselves as corporate saviors, or at least without predominantly being viewed as such. As Rebecca Stewart (2020) reports for *The Drum*, "where other brands posted a black square on their Instagram grid [in response to racism and in support of Black Lives Matter (BLM)] or faced a backlash from consumers over 'tone deaf' watered down declarations that seemed incongruous to their past behavior, Ben & Jerry's did not come to play." When reflecting on this, questions about morality in the marketplace arise, such as who and what drives the moral positions that brands espouse, and how is digital culture implicated in this? Such questions are considered throughout my book.

Many brand responses to activism and social movements exist within an ecology of branding and marketing activities that have been associated with the notion of being "woke"—invested in addressing racism and a myriad of social injustices (Dowell and Jackson 2020; Kanai and Gill 2020; Sobande, Kanai, and Zeng 2022). Some of this industry activity has also been dubbed "woke-washing," which can refer to how brands (mis)use matters of social injustice—particularly Black activism—to manage and improve their own images (Sobande 2019a, 2022a). As my book addresses, woke-washing is sometimes used to describe the actions of brands that are perceived as framing themselves as supporters of certain grassroots movements and collective organizers, but that do not do anything substantial to aid such work. The expression "woke-washing" stems from critical discussions about the relationship between brands and social justice issues in a contemporary context that has been shaped by a surge in the global visibility of the BLM social and political movement. Although the concept of woke-washing can be engaged in generatively critical ways, it can be an unproductively ambiguous term that at times obfuscates the specific issues, individuals, and collective movements that brands frame themselves as supporting. So when discussing the concept of woke-washing, it is vital to specify and reflect on who and what is being referred to, why, and with what impact.

If brands exist because of capitalism and its racist, colonial, and oppressive roots, and if "race is constitutive of organizational foundations, hierarchies, and processes" (Ray 2019, 26), is it possible to regard brand woke-washing as anything other than another cynical process that keeps commercial organizations going? Oscillating between critical discussion of terms such as woke-washing and the brand practices that they are sometimes used in reference to, I call for more attention to be paid to context—from the political context(s) within which the term operates, to the scholarly context(s) that theorizing on woke-washing and morality ping-pongs back and forth between.

Debates and discussions pertaining to woke-washing have surged in recent years. They have moved from peripheral digital spaces to the heart of many marketing industry and academic conversations that attempt to unpack the corporatization of collective organizing, such as the commercialization of LGBTQIA+ Pride and Black History Month events. In an article for *Quartz*, senior reporter Sarah Todd (2020) poses the question on many people's minds: "If everybody hates wokewashing, why do companies still do it?" As Todd's piece demonstrates, the answer to this is far from being simple, but perhaps also the answer to this has changed since 2020. Besides the potential for brands to accrue profit based on perceptions of their interest in social justice issues, as is discussed in this book, the reasons for the rise of woke-washing also relate to the idiosyncrasies of digital culture and the boiling over of the contemporary sociopolitical climate, including the rise of "pejorative discourses of identity politics" (Richmond and Charnley 2022, 2).

My work affirms that the market logic that underlies much advertising and, as a result, woke-washing, is simultaneously molded by the hegemony of whiteness and the marketability of "difference," such as commodified signifiers associated with Black and "mixed-race" identities, but which are (re)presented through the oppressive lens of structural "white sight" (Mirzoeff 2023). Even when marketing—whether it is deemed woke-washing or not—does not depict white people, the dominance of whiteness can play into the parameters within which the marketing is made and within which meanings are ascribed to it (Thomas, Johnson, and Grier 2023). Structural whiteness in the UK and the US does not disappear just because a marketing campaign is populated with Black and brown faces. Nor does the whiteness that pervades many forms of popular and consumer culture pause because a brand claims to be invested in antiracism. The structurally white gaze that guides many marketing and branding strategies may not always be visible, but its unmistakable presence can still be felt and fathomed. Hence the need to critically analyze how power and meaning-making takes shape in the marketplace, including how scholarly work can be entangled with a proprietorial "white sight" (Mirzoeff 2023) and racial capitalism.

"WOKENESS" AND MORALITY: MEANING-MAKING IN THE MARKETPLACE

The term *woke*—which originates from Black American activism, writing, consciousness-raising, and culture—is now frequently used by many non-Black individuals and institutions as a reductive and often plainly racist proxy for anything/anyone not racialized as white. I am critical of the casualness with which woke is used to allude to matters regarding race, racism, and Black lives, in ways that fundamentally are at odds with caring about Black people and that foreground the perspectives of anyone *but* them. I recognize that the word *woke* has become part of political jibing in the UK and the US and is frequently used to dismiss views and people associated with leftist positions but has also been used pejoratively by some who identify with or are identified as leftists (Richmond and Charnley 2022). However, to reduce such issues of the warping of woke to amounting to a "culture war" would be to fall into the trap of perceiving it as a purely polarizing term, as opposed to acknowledging that its appropriation by predominantly white media, marketplace, and political spheres (which run the full political gamut) also serves other functions.

I argue that the label *woke* and its derivatives are often used in ways that reflect the proprietorial pulse of whiteness—from academia to the advertising industry. So present-day pejorative uses of *wokeness* are emblematic of "the racial politics of the Western episteme" (Towns 2022, 9), which is an oppressive context within which "Whiteness is a credential" (Ray 2019, 26) and is equated with expertise and authority, including the brazen entitlement to declare what wokeness is while dismissing it. Amid its many controversial framings, the concept of wokeness and commentary on it have become marketable (e.g., the cottage industry of "woke marketing") and tethered to capitalist notions of expertise, as well as the Western currency of "white sincerity": capital that can be accrued by white people and organizations racialized as white (Ray 2019), who are perceived as having sincere and "good" intentions even if such supposed sincerity involves self-servingly speaking "for" (aka *speaking over*) Black people. Many commercial organizations and marketing industry professionals frequently use the term *woke* in ways that obfuscate its genesis and confuse capitalist activities and corporate spin with collective racial justice work and grassroots liberationist efforts. The fact that the Chartered Institute of Marketing (CIM) (2020) in the UK published an article on "when brands go woke" illustrates that the term has entered the lexicon of the corporate world. Within marketing industry conversations, woke-washing has sometimes been typified in ways that dilute the digital dimensions of its DNA, including how brands have become more attuned to, but have also reframed, digital forms of activism, "social media call outs" (Clark 2020, 88), and the overall societal impact of Black digital creativity and communications. Therefore, my book pays attention to how digital culture and its racial politics function in ways that are implicated in current uses and understandings of the term woke, the notion of woke-washing, and the semantics therein.

When interviewed as part of research for my book, Aaron—a white man who is a journalist with ten years of experience and is based in the UK—spoke in detail about contemporary uses of the term woke and adjacent expressions:

> "Cancel culture" and "woke," often there's an inherent negative association with them. The idea of being socially aware is often portrayed as "woke" to people who think it's not necessary almost, I suppose. They kind of view it as a pejorative term, that comes with quite a lot of baggage and is pretty loaded. Again, it's that stereotyping . . . this kind of "woke"/"gammon" dichotomy, I suppose, which is interesting.[4] And so that idea of "woke," I think, is quite a loaded term now. I don't actually know if I ever thought it was used without a kind of raised eyebrow, or

---

4. In addition to being a word used to describe a traditional pork steak meal, *gammon* is a tenuous term that has gained traction in certain British political, media, and digital spheres over the last decade. The term is typically—although not exclusively—used in reference to the flushed face of a person voicing political perspectives that are associated with a right-wing position and bigoted views.

at least my memory has been so telescoped by just everything happening at five thousand miles an hour, that it's now difficult to remember a time when it [woke] was ever not used like that.

As the words of Aaron allude to, the meanings and associations that have been ascribed to the concept of wokeness in recent years include those that "uncritically stem from an understanding of the term that is tethered to its [white] mainstream appropriation as an expression of disdain that is used to disapprove of something and/or someone" (Sobande 2022a, 41). Building on this point and the illuminating work of Michael Richmond and Alex Charnley (2022) on "identity politics," the subsequent chapters explore a variety of examples of brands implicated in the "culture wars" and taking part (for better or worse) in social advocacy.

Aaron's words during his interview emphasize that notions of wokeness—and the commonly accompanying concept of "cancel culture"—are often associated with political polarity: "You have people who feel they are socially conscious and aware. People that are often left-wing or centre-left in terms of their political belief, thinking that people on the opposite side of the political spectrum are non-reformist pigs who throw around words like 'woke' at them as kind of insulting."

Just as social analysis and cultural politics scholar Jo Littler (2008, 3) argues that "different perspectives that are taken on the subject of CSR [corporate social responsibility]" do not "map neatly onto a simple left/right political grid," notions of wokeness cannot be comprehended by merely focusing on a reductive left/right binary. Often "wokeness emerges from a murky mixture of rhetorics that invoke individualist empowerment, resilience, and success" (Prins 2022, 104), in ways tied to neoliberal notions of productivity and progressiveness. Along these lines, when interviewed, Aaron alluded to the reality that beyond how wokeness and cancel culture are thrown around as pejorative terms are complicated power and political relations that are cloaked by the clickbait culture of consumerism. Such power dynamics include, but are not limited to, those present in "scholarly contortions of 'woke-washing' which appear to be imbedded in an intention to defend brands, while establishing individuals' expertise in 'woke marketing' or while claiming to 'guard' against criticism of corporate social initiatives (CSIs) and business ethicists" (Sobande 2022a, 40).

Wary of the potential of inadvertently reinforcing whitewashed understandings of the marketplace and notions of wokeness, I use woke-washing critically and with ambivalence, including to assert that advertising activities referred to as woke-washing are ultimately bound to "neoliberal racial capitalism" (Ransby 2018, 117). The terms woke-washing and *woke capitalism*, alone, cannot capture the insidious power relations that relate to how brands engage with, or disengage from, issues of social injustice and histories of oppression. When we begin with an analytical starting point built upon the critical idea that capitalism can never *be* "woke," we move beyond surface level discussions about inequality and the marketplace and toward a more rigorous analysis that resists the idea that liberation can be realized through consumer culture.

In recent years, the concept of woke-washing—brands simultaneously pursuing and performing wokeness—has been taken up in ways that yield ineffective and oppositional perspectives of profit-making, politics, and their pairing. Ambiguous analyses of the marketplace have oversimplified the workings of wokeness and the notion of woke-washing and have seldom critically scrutinized the racial politics of consumer culture and the academic spheres that comment on it. At times, "'woke' becomes visible as aspirational corporate culture aligning itself with social justice values; 'woke' is a desirable brand identity packaging socially progressive affects in consumer form" (Sobande, Kanai, and Zeng 2022, 4). Also, just as cultish language involves terms that once had a positive meaning being "recast to signify something threatening" (Montell 2021, 6), the notion of being woke has been reframed in numerous ways that have resulted in wielding the word as a dismissive expression and a catchall phrase. Turning to aspects of Amanda Montell's (2021) *Cultish: The Language of Fanaticism*, I consider why and how elements of contemporary discourse on wokeness appear to reflect a tacit acceptance of morality being (re)defined in the marketplace.

My research survey yielded a range of responses that capture some of the different ways that people perceive woke-washing, as well as the different ways that brands comment on and/or contribute to social justice work:

> A brand can easily respond or contribute to social justice especially if they have enough wealth and have an ulterior motive such as approval. Whilst it appears beneficial from the surface, it is unlikely to be the case. One example is that companies can easily change their logo for Pride month to show they stand for Pride and the LGBT community but it is also likely that large companies employ people with homophobic and transphobic views regardless.
>
> —South Asian (gender undisclosed), UK (18–25 years old)

> I don't really have a problem with that if there is a genuine interest in and concern about a topic. And, also, that it is appropriate for the brand to comment on a given topic. There are things in the world that still need to change, and brands do have a platform which they could use to make others aware of such things. What I do not like is when brands jump on to a current topic for the sake of being perceived as relevant or trendy. Or when a serious subject is trivialized into some form of pop culture that can be nicely marketed, but then loses its original meaning or intent.
>
> —mixed-race woman, UK (36–45 years old)

While wokeness is considered throughout my book, I approach this matter in a way that accounts for how terms such as woke-washing are still relatively insular, in the sense that many people are not familiar with them. This was indicated by survey responses such as the following, which are suggestive of different degrees of awareness, and perspectives, of the concept in the UK:

Never heard of it [woke-washing]! I think a woke is someone who is a bit of a wimp and unable to make their own decisions without influencers and advertisers telling them what to think.
—white woman, UK (46–55 years old)

Never heard of it, but i think it is when a brand uses marketing to take a stance regarding social issues to make a profit
—white man, UK (36–45 years old)

I hadn't heard of it before but I think it's a good term. I see it to mean brands that present themselves as socially/politically progressive and engaged in current events but are actually insidious and responsible for poor labour conditions, donations to conservative "charities," etc.
—white woman, UK (18–25 years old)

Not exactly familiar, but I know what woke is, so I would understand it as re-writing history through a woke lens? Or possibly creating an agenda/campaign with a woke angle.
—white non-binary person, UK (age undisclosed)

I've never heard of "woke washing". Maybe selling ice cream in rainbow colours as though the company is identifying with LGBTQ+ ?? Because it's "on trend[.]"
—white woman, UK (46–55 years old)

In contrast with many of the comments made by UK survey respondents, several US survey respondents offered explanations of their understanding of woke-washing, which highlighted that this was not a term that they were new to. Some of those comments also alluded to people's perceptions of wokeness being connected to the concept of cancel culture. As one person bluntly put it when describing what they believe woke-washing means:

It means getting rid of people who have issues.
—white man, US (36–45 years old)

Although based on the results of this survey there appears to be more exposure to the notion of woke-washing in the US than in the

UK, the majority of the four hundred people whom I surveyed had not heard of the term woke-washing before. This is a reminder of the fact that concepts and terms that are common within certain academic and industry spaces may not be as widely used as is sometimes assumed. Then again, since embarking on writing this book, societal use and visibility of the word *woke* has risen, with Google Trends indicating that searches of the term in the US peaked in spring 2023.

A scholarly preoccupation with wokeness can result in accounts of contemporary branding practices that play into the problematic and predominantly conservative notion of "culture wars." So throughout this book I critically contextualize concepts such as wokeness, cancel culture, culture wars, and scholarly analysis of them, *hopefully*, without overstating their relevance to present-day brands and profit-making and without wielding wokeness to position myself as the arbiter of it. Woke-washing may be best understood as more of a buzzword and timely expression than a term that will endure and enter most spheres of public life. But messages of morality, which are entangled with discourse on wokeness in the marketplace, have a long and steeped history that my book reckons with.

A BRICOLAGE APPROACH: FROM ARCHIVES TO EXHIBITIONS

Politics, morality, and marketing have collided and combined in a multitude of ways, for many decades. On the day after the overturning of *Roe v. Wade*, while wondering about how the notion of wokeness might be invoked as part of discussions that followed, I walked past the windows of an assortment of D.C. shops, bars, and restaurants that had declared their pro-choice position and their dismay at the actions of SCOTUS. As my eyes scanned the sprinkling of statements, symbols, and signs that businesses had chosen to display, I paused to ponder the different ways that politics has been implicated in advertising and markets throughout history. Accordingly, I headed to the Smithsonian Institution Archives and the Library of Congress Main Reading Room. There I learned more about the history of advertising and politics in the US and the UK—including their interconnections and tensions.

During my time in D.C. in 2022, I immersed myself in reading about the climate of capitalism and global relations from the 1940s to the 1990s, while I considered what had (not) changed since then. I thought about all that had led to a point in time that Littler (2008, 2) documented in the early 2000s, when "ethical consumption, fair trade, consumer protests, brand backlashes, green goods, boycotts and downshifting" had finally become "familiar consumer activities—and in some cases, are almost mainstream." I also noted how the development of digital technologies and the trends spawned by them in recent years had impacted the course of consumer culture. Overall, the methodology of the research at the helm of my book is based on embracing bricolage—in terms of both using a diverse range of research methods and analyzing a diverse range of marketing material, artifacts, and representations.

Recalling the rise of brand backlashes and efforts to hold advertisers accountable, while at the Library of Congress Main Reading Room I sifted through folders of correspondence between British advertising icon David Ogilvy and a cast of characters from the industry, politics, and media in decades gone by. I noted the frequency and capitalization of terms such as "Big Boys," "high powered bunch," "The Ladies," and "ad man," all of which revealed much about the gender politics of those times. I studied photographs and ephemera from the launch and development of advertising groups and organizations, wondering what it was like to be one of relatively few women involved in them, let alone what it was like to be the only Black woman there. Pouring over the details of black-and-white depictions of boardroom meetings, I identified raced and gendered power relations on display and surveyed the semiotic subtleties of body language, style, and facial expressions.

I examined attempts to advertise the UK in the US and the US in the UK—observing the use of telling phrases such as "a very Scotch Scotsman." I smiled at naïve questions in 1950s letters that queried why Scotland might want to set itself apart from the UK, while I revisited more contemporary writing about how "some of the constituent parts of the United Kingdom are already establishing their own, distinct nation-brands" (Dinnie 2008, 52). In agreement with Keith Dinnie's (2008, 230) claim that "there is still a widespread misperception that the UK and England are interchangeable terms," it is important to note that even now such terms are sometimes used as though they mean the same. Essentially, nascent forms of nation-branding were on display in the full folders and brimming boxes of papers and pieces of the past that I accessed when analyzing archived material in D.C. To be precise, such nation-branding approaches appeared to dovetail with the development of political issues, wars, and what would become known as globalization and "The Fight for the Global Commons" (Klein 2000).

In the months before my time at these US archives, I had interviewed six people about the relationship between advertising and activism. Over Zoom calls during the COVID-19 crisis, I heard from journalists, brand strategists, business development managers, advertising directors, and retail experts who spoke candidly about consumer culture, digital culture, and social justice. Additionally, prior to and after inspecting archived material in D.C., I analyzed media and marketing representations, from televised pop culture depictions of corporations (e.g., *Industry, Partner Track, Severance, Succession*, and *The Bold Type*) to publicity surrounding the platinum jubilee pudding competition, which was part of societal celebrations of Queen Elizabeth II's seventy years as head of state in the UK. It was during that time that I also surveyed people about their thoughts on social justice and brands in the US and the UK, spending hours analyzing which brands they praised, which brands they criticized, and how all of that linked to ideas and assumptions about advertising, activism, and morality (e.g., "I really don't like large conglomerates run by billionaires who are actively destroying our planet and exploiting people—e.g. amazon, Tesla, etc.").

By the summer of 2022, while working my way through archived boxes of papers and images in D.C., I was reminded of the importance of accounting for the history of advertising when analyzing present-day consumer culture. Among archive collections that I studied were folders of writing about the Smithsonian Institution's Center for Advertising History, which was "housed in the Archives of the National Museum of American History in Washington D.C. With the goal of documenting major trends and developments since the advent of electronic media, the Center selectively acquires materials, papers, and oral histories that illuminate modern advertising history." Such efforts on the part of the center involved them working "with agencies and corporations to compile detailed case studies of successful national campaigns" (American Association of Advertising Agencies 1992, 11), including for Campbell's soup, Marlboro, Nike, Pepsi-Cola, and Cover Girl makeup.

The significance of the Smithsonian Institution's Center for Advertising History is apparent when reading statements from the early 1990s, such as, "Advertising has a central place in American history, but until recently, America didn't have a central place for advertising history" (American Association of Advertising Agencies 1992, 11). While thinking about similar activity in the UK, I reflected on the Museum of Brands (2020a) in London and its promotional material, which confidently states that "we have all grown up with brands, forming close bonds with our favourite sweets, crisps, breakfast cereals and even washing powders." As outlined on the Museum of Brands website, over "fifty years ago consumer historian Robert Opie began to unravel the fascinating story of how consumer products and promotion had evolved since Victorian times. By 1975 Robert had enough material to hold his own exhibition, The Pack Age, at the Victoria & Albert Museum." The Museum of Brands (2020a) provides an overview of how the work of Robert Opie developed: "In 1984 he opened the first museum devoted to the history of packaging and advertising in Gloucester. In the early 2000s, the collection needed a new home. With the help of global brand agency pi Global and founding sponsors Cadbury, Twinings, Vodafone, Diageo, Kellogg's and McVities, the Museum became a charity in 2002 and opened in Notting Hill, London."

In addition to presenting exhibitions of archived brand and marketing material, through its use of social media the Museum of Brands is demonstrating how digital technology has influenced consumer culture—including experiences of the museum itself, which are documented and promoted using #livingbrands.

During the summer of 2020 the Museum of Brands opened an exhibition, *When Brands Take a Stand*—originally slated for March of that year but delayed due to the COVID-19 pandemic. The exhibition was described as presenting posters, packaging, and TV commercials, and it examined the different ways that brands have responded to social and political issues. According to Chris Griffin, CEO at the Museum of Brands, "We want to amplify the debate around the relationship between brands, people, culture and society, and how these interact with each other. Brands and advertising agencies have a platform to influence, and with that comes responsibility. This initiative dives into these complex relationships" (Museum of Brands 2020b).

Terms such as *amplify* and *elevate* frequently feature in discussions and debates about the role of advertising, marketing, and brands in addressing social issues of inequality and injustice. For example, an *Ad Age* article on racism and the industry includes expressions such as "Elevate Black Voices" (Craft 2020) and professes that "it should go without saying, but one of the first steps in addressing racial inequality in advertising is to ensure that Black and POC [people of color] peers are given the same platform to contribute as their white colleagues have long had the opportunity to do." Yet, as my book considers, and as is elucidated by the vital scholarship of Patricia A. Banks (2022) in *Black Culture Inc: How*

Figure 3. "BLACK LIVES MATTER—BLACK TRANS LIVES MATTER" sign on the side of the Human Rights Campaign building in Washington, D.C., 2022. Photo by author.

Ethnic Community Support Pays for Corporate America, the industry's focus on amplifying and elevating is sometimes symptomatic of its preoccupation with visibility and publicity, as opposed to a commitment to doing work that is essential to tackling systemic forms of oppression.

The Museum of Brands's launch of *When Brands Take a Stand* was preceded by a sharp rise in the number of brands commenting on the BLM political and social movement, issues of antiblackness, and police murdering Black people in the US, such as George Floyd. During such times, Ben & Jerry's responded in ways that resulted in praise. Reporting for *The Drum*, Stewart (2020) writes: "The brand didn't stop at the stark statement. It also issued a series of four 'concrete steps' to dismantle white supremacy, including calling on President Trump to commit the US to a formal process of healing and reconciliation, asking Congress to create a commission to study the effects of slavery and discrimination from 1619 to the present and supporting the Floyd family's call to create a national task force that would draft bipartisan legislation aimed at ending racial violence and increasing police accountability."

The buzz of brand commentary on such issues prompted critique of the hypocrisy of brands that claim to be "anti-racist" and "allies," but whose track records tell a distinctly different and shady story. Terms including *woke-washing* and *woke capitalism*—often outlined in nebulous ways—were in the orbit of such brand responses to racism. Some of this brand activity was indicative of "the affective entanglements of 'wokeness' with whiteness, the valorization of visibility, and neoliberal identity culture" (Sobande, Kanai, and Zeng 2022, 1), which is digitally mediated, and sometimes takes the form of the self-branding practices of influencers who are keen to appear invested in activism. By spring 2022, and with the aim of critically analyzing how "brand activism" is being narrativized, I visited the Museum of Brands and what remained of *When Brands Take a Stand*. Although the museum was different in scope and scale to the Smithsonian Institution's Center for Advertising History, both play an important part in the archiving of advertising in their national locations, also meaning that they may be part of the bigger picture of nation-branding in the UK and the US. For that reason, consideration of the work of the Museum of Brands, and analysis of archived material about the history of advertising in the US, features throughout the chapters of my book.

CONCEPTUALIZING CULTURE: CRITICAL THEORIES OF MEDIA AND MARKETS

When, why, and how are technologies of branding entangled with ideas about, and experiences of, activism, digital culture, morality, and markets? My grasp of this question is formed by embracing aspects of Black media philosophy that "take seriously the racial implications of Western media philosophy's 'we' and 'our'" (Towns 2022, 9)—a "we" and "our" that are typically wedded to whiteness. In the incisive words of Armond R. Towns, who conceptualized Black media philosophy, "Black media philosophy requires recognition of the racial politics of the Western episteme and a complex understanding of the projects that challenge such an episteme" (9). My book brings Black media philosophy into conversation with Black digital studies, critical studies of race in the marketplace, and analysis of the histories of different nations. In turn, I focus on some of the numerous meaning-making processes that are part of experiences of popular culture, politics, messages of morality, and the work of brands.

Rather than "accept that an advertisement's meaning will be precisely determined and encoded during its production, and then decoded by the public in a way that can be accurately predicted," I recognize "the unpredictability of what happens when advertising texts containing unstable cultural content" (Bradshaw and Scott 2018, 12) circulate in consumer culture. I also recognize that some people "deploy advertising texts and products as building blocks of identity, forging a coherent subjectivity that aligns with the imposed parameters communicated through popular culture" (Tounsel 2022, 1). Key changes in recent decades that have affected advertising, activism, and their intermingling include the rise of social media and digital remix culture, which "results in commentary that reflects different public conversations, contestations and concerns about the current state of politics and society" (Sobande 2019b, 153). Focusing on such changes and their impact on branding practices and expectations of them, I critically examine the ongoing ways that big brands are watching you (watching them).

The road to revolution is not paved with brands' "good intentions," but much marketing material appears to claim otherwise. The overturning of *Roe v. Wade* coincided with LGBTQIA+ Pride Month, so during that time there was a mass of marketing material that alluded to many matters related to gender, sexuality, *and* reproductive rights. Allusions to the alleged activist attributes of brands seem to be everywhere, yet actual evidence of such activism is often illusionary if not completely absent. From mission statements that frame brands as freedom fighters to advertising that positions them as altruistic, the message that brands care about social injustice has become a hallmark of twenty-first-century marketing and media (Littler 2008). Put differently, the illusion of "brand activism" has made itself at home in contemporary consumer culture, so what are some of the ways that these issues can be discussed and analyzed without reinforcing simplistic perspectives of what constitutes branding, advertising, and activism? The chapters that follow take up this question and more.

Big Brands are marketing themselves in ways that reflect the politics of marketing *and* the marketing of politics. Hence, I scrutinize attempts to portray brands as purposeful, moral, and even activist, to consider what such activity reveals about the recent history of branding, activism, and geopolitical power relations that the US and the UK are embroiled in. Shaped by the crucial edited collection *Commodity Activism: Cultural Resistance in Neoliberal Times*, I examine how digital developments have impacted dynamics between brands, consumers, and social justice issues, including "the contradictions inherent in grafting philanthropy and social action onto merchandising practices, market incentives, and corporate profits" (Mukherjee and Banet-Weiser 2012, 1). Critical of the rise of claims that "we love purpose-driven brands" (Hieatt 2014, 7), I articulate some of the power dynamics that are masked by notions of "brand purpose." Consequently, I conceptualize the ways that brands negotiate different ideas about, and expectations of, morality.

The expansion of scholarly writing on wokeness, as well as brand activism, cannot be understood without grasping the details of digital culture. Specifically, it is essential to acknowledge and understand the societal significance of *Black* digital culture and "to grapple with how internet, consumer, and celebrity culture is implicated in contemporary understandings and expectations of social justice work" (Sobande, Kanai, and Zeng 2022, 10). Although it features discussion of how institutions have tried to build a bridge between branding and activism, my book is *not* an account of "good or bad" "brand activism," nor is it about what brands should "do better." Instead, *Big Brands Are Watching You* is a critical analysis of the fraught, fluid, yet sometimes firm and even "fruitful" relationship between consumer culture, digital culture, and social justice in the US and the UK. By parsing this I elucidate how such dynamics reflect the entangled histories of these different geocultural locations and their global power(s). Thus, I account for how entwined histories of colonialism, racism, and capitalism (Harris 2021) are apparent in the forms of marketing and branding approaches that tap into social justice rhetoric that may be intended to shield brands from critique.

Shaped by work that affirms "that within contemporary culture it is utterly unsurprising to participate in social activism by buying something" (Mukherjee and Banet-Weiser 2012, 1), the subsequent chapters detail elements of the relationship and differences between what is societally perceived as branding and activism. Moving beyond asserting that all branding efforts and activist attempts are innately antithetical, but also without confusing branding for activism, I consider how the development of influencer culture has molded marketing, activism, and their (de)coupling. In doing so, I call for more critical research on influencer culture that will move beyond a conveniently cursory nod to intersectionality and take to task the pervasiveness of the lens of "white sight" (Mirzoeff 2023) in both the influencer industry and academia.

BOOK BREAD CRUMBS: THE PATH AHEAD

A decade ago a friend of mine who worked in advertising in the UK used to entertain me with stories about the clueless ways that many industry practitioners were attempting to engage and understand the internationally impactful Black American "online phenomenon 'Black Twitter'" (Clark 2014, viii). Over phone calls filled with loose lips and laughter, my friend would regale me with vivid accounts of agencies obnoxiously dismissing the existence and cultural force of Black Twitter: the collective and societal impact of what Black people were saying, doing, and sharing on the microblogging site. In the years since then, numerous agencies and brands have invested in new roles that specifically focus on Black digital audiences, intersectionality, and the construction and maintenance of a brand's Twitter presence and online voice with the intention of appealing to Black people.

Whether it is with the use of Twitter (which was rebranded as X) hashtags or by sharing video-recorded footage on platforms such as Instagram and TikTok, Black women have been creatively harnessing the affordances of digital media as part of many aspects of their lives (Bailey 2021; Gray 2020; Sobande 2020; Steele 2021; Tounsel 2022). However, the ways that brands watch and respond to this are sometimes cause for concern. Analysis at the center of my book offers a critical account of some of these issues, including by turning to the pointed words of media, marketing, business, and retail professionals, who might typically be assumed to lack a critical take on these matters. Inspired by collective efforts to tackle systemic power relations, I have spent much time doing work that critically focuses on structural forms of watching and being watched. So I arrived at writing this book with the aim to author something that would bring together many of my ongoing critical considerations of *who* and *what* brands watch, and *when*, *how*, and *why* they do so. The title of this work may initially be interpreted as ominous—I am a horror film fan, after all. However, as I hope my work conveys, there can be a power in staring back at structural forces that categorize, monitor, surveil, track, and target. There can also be power in naming such processes, critiquing the turning tides of notions of morality in the marketplace, and refusing the ruse of brand activism.

The shelf life of many products may be short, but the complicated relationship between brands and social justice issues is a deeply entrenched one. In the chapters that follow I contend with contradictions at the core of consumer culture. It is vital that analysis of the politics and cultural impact of advertising avoid reinforcing what Bradshaw and Scott (2018, 12) refer to as "reductive understandings of intentionality." Their crucial work features a call for scholars to ensure that their critical analysis of advertising does not treat advertisers and their intentions as a homogenous and fixed entity. As Bradshaw and Scott (2018, 12) put it: "We must avoid imagining a mythical monolith called 'advertisers'. Behind this term are brand managers, account executives, sales managers, copywriters, art directors, television producers, actors, musicians, set designers, casting chiefs, distributors, and multiple others who struggle over the competing objectives, strategies, and designs that clash, mesh, and crystalise into a final campaign. In place of what is often a dense thicket of personal, political, economic, and aesthetic ends, it is simply too reductive to assume that advertising exists for a single goal: to sell stuff."

Taking heed of such words, my understanding of advertisers and their varied intentions is outlined in chapter 2, which draws on the perspectives of interview participants and survey respondents, including by combing through their comments on brands (e.g., the multinational brewery and pub chain BrewDog). Chapter 2 theorizes how morality manifests in the marketplace (e.g., "brands' moral impositions" and "single-use social justice"). Alongside that, the chapter examines parts of the political foundations of the US and the UK marketplace(s), focusing on forms of nation-branding and how marketers construct and court different cultural sensibilities, including during periods of perceived public mourning (e.g., in the aftermath of the death of British monarch Queen Elizabeth II).

As part of my critique of nation-branding and the politics of marketing, chapter 2 discusses the branding activity that surrounded the UK's pudding competition, which was part of its 2022 celebration of the platinum jubilee of Queen Elizabeth II, months before she died. As well as dealing with the nuances of nation-branding, chapter 2 also explores the ways that notions of "the business case for" (*commercial imperatives*) and "the moral case for" (*moral impositions*) are used interchangeably in certain consumer culture contexts. Although the chapter critically discusses the impacts of "racial capitalism" (Robinson 1983), I also reflect on some limitations of this term and its varied uptake in recent years.

My analysis of the relationship between nations and brands features discussion of celebrities' denouncing July 4 (also referred to as American Independence Day) in 2022. Previously, in collaboration with Akane Kanai and Natasha Zeng, in "The Hypervisibility and Discourses of 'Wokeness' in Digital Culture" we have argued that "the iconic 'woke' subjectivities that circulate, the affective circulation of irony, authenticity and what we note as 'white sincerity' require further analysis" (Sobande, Kanai, and Zeng 2022, 4). We have acknowledged "the fluid and increasingly contested nature of notions of 'wokeness' and the need to bring care and clarity to the ways in which 'woke' is operationalized" (Sobande, Kanai, and Zeng 2022, 10). Drawing on that point and bringing chapter 2 to a close is a discussion of the role of white sincerity in celebrity brand responses to social and political issues, such as the part that such responses play in some of the ways that morality is perceived in media and the marketplace.

Chapter 3 continues conversations about the politics of marketing, analyzing how the business of activism, antagonism, and aging connects to and disconnects from various perceptions and experiences of digital culture, social justice, and the work and impact of creators and creatives. I consider various examples of the idolatry and inconsistencies of influencer culture, paying particular attention to the expanding industry of virtual—aka computer-generated imagery (CGI)—influencers. Additionally, I discuss perceptions of the nexus of BLM and influencer culture, while considering the extent to which social movements can be(come) brands. Prior scholarship includes claims about critiques of brands that frame such critiques as amounting to little more than an unjust court of public opinion. However, as I discuss, the power dynamics that shape critiques and their impact are more complicated than that. Thus, chapter 3 considers how Hall's (2013) concept of the "circuit of culture" relates to public discourse regarding antagonism, wokeness, and alleged culture wars.

Chapter 3 also focuses on the portrayal of fictional brands and their corporate culture in the TV shows *Industry*, *Partner Track*, *Severance*, *Succession*, and *The Bold Type*. Following this discussion are my reflections on the role of Big Tech and marketed nostalgia in recent emo trends in consumer culture. Namely, drawing on my experience of attending the When We Were Young (WWWY) music festival in 2022, I discuss how certain subcultures, and the age/stage of life associated with them, are being revisited and reimagined in the process of how Big Brands are watching you. The remainder of chapter 3 unpacks a range of messages of morality in popular culture and the marketing of it, including by considering what the marketing and branding of the Netflix series *You* suggests about the construction of an online brand voice in the age of "social justice" selling.

Finally, chapter 4 synthesizes the key arguments that are the bedrock of my book, while pointing to the always incomplete nature of knowledge and the need for continued curiosity and critique. It does this by journeying through the following sections: "Past the Marketplace of Morality," "Marketing and Moral Arbiters," "Beyond Wokeness as an 'American Import,'" "Vying to Be the Vanguard in the Digital (and Virtual Influencer) Age," and "Watching the Watcher." The tempestuous relationship between digital culture, the marketplace, and social justice has been the subject of much insightful scholarship (Banks 2022; Littler 2008; Mukherjee and Banet-Weiser 2012; Sobande 2020, 2022a). Among such accounts are examinations of brand impression management techniques that hinge on brands' performance of proximity to, or distance from, politics and activism. Extant work has analyzed the far from altruistic attitudes of brands, but rarely has such research focused on the perspectives of consumers, pop culture, and media and marketing practitioners in both the UK and the US, while also analyzing past and present-day media and marketing representations from both locations.

Big Brands Are Watching You is my attempt to bridge gaps between critical studies of branding, consumer culture, digital media, sociology, and the marketization and monetization of morality and social (in)justice. While I examine how the commodification and corporatization of activism has changed during the first quarter of the turbulent twenty-first century, I also consider why, and how, communications in general have shifted during this time. Over the course of four different yet linked chapters, I explore when, why, and how brands in the US and the UK turn to digital tools and trends to align themselves with social justice movements, messages of morality, and notions of nation, while they watch *you* (watching *them*).

2 The Politics of Morality and the Marketplace

Morality is a political matter. Perceptions of who and what constitutes "good and bad" and "right and wrong" are not innate. Instead, they reflect different social norms, cultural conventions, and political struggles that play out in society, including in the form of marketing content, communications, and campaigns. This chapter is grounded in a critical discussion of how morality is (re)defined in the marketplace. Focusing on the relationship between racial capitalism and the whitewashing of morality, I clarify the understanding of morality at the center of this book: my perspective of the racial, gender, and class politics of how morality is positioned in society. While outlining this, I consider why it is that strands of business and marketing scholarship frame morality as a menace and obscure power dynamics involved in how morality functions. I go on to explain sociopolitical components of what I term "brands' moral impositions"—the precarious process by which moral positions are imposed on and/or upheld by brands, including how such positions are responded to by individuals and other institutions.[1] Following my reflections on the relationship between morality, commerce, and scholarly commentaries on it, I turn my attention to nation-branding.

Certain expressions come to characterize countries, states, and cities—"the American dream" in the US, "People make Glasgow" in Scotland, Virginia being "for lovers" (or Ohio, if you're a fan of Hawthorne Heights' music), Dundee's "jute, jam, and journalism," and various places in Europe vying to be the "Venice of the North." Often uttered to paint a positive or playful picture of parts of the world, such phrases can be central to marketing, branding, and political strategies that seek to secure favorable public impressions of the overall identity of a place. Then again, it is not just words that are used to frame geocultural contexts to attract audiences and appeal to specific stakeholders.

Shaped by Melissa Aronczyk's (2013, 3) landmark research in *Branding the Nation*, I account for the power of "the long-standing relationship between the nation-state and the corporation, the two dominant social institutions of the last three centuries." As this chapter details, individuals and institutions use various rhetorical and representational devices in pursuit of a persuasive public image, including when constructing the nation-brands of the UK and the US, or when constructing self-brands that are intended to contrast with the image of a nation. So across the following pages I analyze key aspects of advertising in the UK and the US—including how each country has been narrativized in the other, at points in time between the 1940s and the present day.

The term *politics* is often associated with polarizing propaganda, such as the promotion of ideologies via public messaging and the

---

1. The concept of "coining" theories and terms typically results in knowledge and ideas being treated in possessive ways that involve individualistic forms of credit being attributed and that tend to overlook and undermine the collective nature of knowledge production, including the work of others that preceded the perceived coining of a particular concept or term. For these reasons, rather than regarding my conceptualizing in this book as amounting to any sort of coining, I perceive it as being part of the ongoing form of my research, writing, and theorizing—and as being the outcome of the dialogic nature of knowledge production.

wider work of political parties. However, politics is inclusive of a broad range of activities, even those that circulate within spaces seldom deemed to be political. It has been argued that "everybody wants something different in life: politics examines how it is decided who gets what, when and how" (Lees-Marshment 2004, 6). It is important to note that such decisions and the politics that are part of them are often steered by structural inequalities, which determine who tends to have decision-making powers, how they exercise them, and some of the ways that they are likely to be responded to. Drawing together the themes of power, racial capitalism, morality, nation-branding, and celebrity, the final section of this chapter reflects on the concept of "white sincerity" (Sobande, Kanai, and Zeng 2022), which may be interpreted as also relating to "the 'white comfort' underpinning the dominant approach to racism, which relies on individualized, moral accounts and that sees it as outside of the ordinary, extraneous, and excessive to white self-understandings" (Lentin 2020, 11). In conversation with work on the "'whiteness' of capital" (McBride 2005, 26) and in *Nice White Ladies* (Daniels 2021), I consider how whiteness and the marketability of perceived sincerity collide in the world of self-brands.

While aspects of this chapter are informed by scholarship on political marketing, there are distinct differences between that specific domain and what can be referred to as the politics of marketing. The former tends to describe marketing activity that is explicitly and intentionally attached to certain political parties, governmental entities, and individuals who officially represent nations. But the latter is an expression that encompasses how marketing, by nature, is political. Therefore, as well as capturing connections between party politics, governmental activity, and marketing, the term *politics of marketing* encompasses other examples of how politics manifests in the work of marketers and the marketplace. For these reasons, this chapter also draws on critical marketing and consumer culture studies to examine the ways that the politics of morality, marketing, and celebrity are implicated in how Big Brands are watching you.

RACIAL CAPITALISM AND MORALITY
IN THE MARKETPLACE

Morality's presence in society is archaic. Whether in the form of fables, art, or oral histories, cautionary tales that are meant to encourage or discourage allegedly moral and immoral behaviors have been central to many cultures for centuries. These tales involve messages that uphold certain ideas about morality, such as by alluding to who and what is perceived as "altruistic" and "pure" and who and what is perceived as "evil" and "corrupt." Still, societal perceptions of morality are not fixed, including "how discourses of moralism and morality work to shape ethical consumption" (Littler 2008, 2) and to shape consumer culture more broadly.

Ideas about morality do not emerge in ways free from the influence of power dynamics and oppression, such as the whiteness and Eurocentric nature of much "canonical" work on the philosophy of morality and ethics. To date, it is common for words such as *morality, moralism,* and *ethics* to be discussed as though they are sociopolitically neutral and detached from histories of oppression such as the colonial and racist foundations of the establishment of Western science and many capitalist systems. "[W]ho gets to authoritatively determine what is (and is not) 'morally problematic' and how so-called 'moral purity' functions, is worthy of critical analysis" (Sobande 2022a, 41)—particularly when addressing the nexus of morality, the carceral state, and the punitive societal treatment of Black people and Black epistemologies.

The work of Littler (2008, 12) on radical consumption affirms that "the insight that morality becomes annexed to ideas of the 'good' and 'the noble' through aristocratic practices clearly holds a lot of explanatory power for the way we might talk about the phenomena of patronage and charity today." Elaborating on such research, I affirm that the ways in which morality has become annexed to notions of the "good" and "the noble" include through racist, colonialist, and xenophobic practices that must receive critical attention equal to that paid to the class politics of morality. Black studies, Black radical traditions, and Black Marxist work that tackles the intersections of capitalism, ruling class domination, and racism yield praxis and analytical frameworks that name the oppressive impacts of both the (petit) bourgeois and white supremacy. Inspired by such work, I understand morality as being at once raced and classed. Specifically, moral judgments in society reflect systemic forms of oppression (e.g., racism and capitalism, which result in the pathologization, criminalization, and incarceration of many Black working-class people in both the UK and the US).

Exploring how brands negotiate morality aids understanding of the dynamic between the marketplace, power regimes, and systems of rule. As such, my work is informed by the research and writing of Alana Lentin, including the crucial book *Why Race Still Matters* (2020), which includes the following insightful explanation: "I disagree that it is sufficient or possible to talk about racism without explaining the genealogy of race as a system of rule and revealing this process of continual reproduction. I believe that racism is best understood as beliefs, attitudes, ideas, and morals that build on understandings of the world as racially delineated" (9). As Lentin points out, "we need to work with both concepts – race and racism – because they are reliant on each other," and "while we can and should use race analytically, we should always question its terms" (9, 10). While I recognize that moral judgments in society can reveal much about forms of structural oppression, including racism, I also affirm Lentin's position that the concept of racism has undergone harmful forms of "(re)definition" as something that is "universal, ahistorical and a question of individual morality, rather than being structurally engendered" (25).

Other key perspectives that steer my book include acknowledgment and understanding of the ongoing impacts of racial capitalism in both the UK and the US. Conceptualized and developed by political theorist, historian, and activist Cedric J. Robinson, the term *racial capitalism* has been engaged in various ways in the decades since its inception. In the vital book *Black Marxism: The Making of the Black Radical Tradition*, Robinson's (1983, 2) articulation of racial capitalism includes the following: "The development, organization, and expansion of capitalist society pursued essentially racial directions, so too did social ideology. As a material force, then, it could be expected that racialism would inevitably permeate the social structures emergent from capitalism. I have used the term 'racial capitalism' to refer to this development and to the subsequent structure as a historical agency."

Writing about the legacy of such work, Joshua Myers (2021, 149) describes Robinson's work as having had the effect of "clearing space to understand racism beyond the historical particulars of capitalist development at the same time he was critiquing the idea that the world-system was somehow devoid or untouched by the racisms and nationalisms that characterized western life." Additionally, in the recent work *Black Anarchism and the Black Radical Tradition: Moving beyond Racial Capitalism*, discussion of Robinson's concept of racial capitalism includes this statement, "Europe was never a free and equal society, as racialization and racism permeated reality" (Bagby-Williams and Za Suekama 2022, 6). Anchored in such explanations of racial capitalism and the tenor of Robinson's crucial work, my book accounts for the ways that moral judgments and ideas about value in the marketplace stem from a racial capitalist system that is invested in nationalism too. Aware of the limitations of any notion of racial capitalism that disregards the fact that gender politics are entangled in a racial capitalist system, I take a Black feminist approach to my discussion of such matters.

As critical legal scholar Angela P. Harris (2021, vii) states, "neither the racial nor the capitalism part of the term racial capitalism ought to be taken for granted." Racial capitalism encompasses histories and effects of capitalism that are inextricably linked to the oppressive forces of race, racialization, and racism. Furthermore, "an important strand of the new racial capitalism literature traces the historical role of white supremacy, in the processes of dispossession, extraction, accumulation, and exploitation that are central to today's capitalism" (vii). Such critical work on racial capitalism, including its recognition of the environmental impacts of colonialism, molds my analysis of how morality is (re)defined and negotiated in the marketplace, such as my focus on the racial and class politics of notions of who and what is and is not moral.

Recent and critical scholarship has yielded a different concept, known as *cannibal capitalism* (Fraser 2022), which is intended to address the all-consuming and violent nature of capitalism but arguably does not address its racist foundations and effects in the explicit and nuanced way that theorizations of racial capitalism do. Moreover, at times Fraser's work on cannibal capitalism appears to move away from naming racial oppression in the present day and toward the potentially liberal framings of "racial disparities" and "racial antagonisms," expressions that are less tethered to articulating the systemic nature and harmful impacts of racism and white supremacy. In attempting to bring "together in a single frame all the oppressions, contradictions, and conflicts of the present conjuncture" (Fraser 2022, xv), the concept of cannibal capitalism risks obfuscating the specific nature of, and differences between, how capitalism impacts different people and places around the world.

Similarly, terms such as *woke capitalism* (Rhodes 2022) can function in nebulous ways that result in broad discussions of corporate and public morality, but which dilute a clear focus on specific forms of structural oppression, such as the intersections of racism, capitalism, sexism, ableism, and misogyny. Hence, I remain steadfast in my focus on racial capitalism, but I also acknowledge different framings of contemporary capitalist structures. Naming racial capitalism in critical work during the "permacrisis" of our times can help to ensure that the interdependence of race, racism, and capitalism is understood as being central to how capitalism and concepts of crisis operate, including how brands negotiate morality. While prior work has paired the concepts of racial capitalism and woke capitalism (e.g., Rhodes 2022), it is important to avoid conflating them, due to the former's robust roots in Black and Pan-Africanist traditions and the latter's embrace by neoliberal politics. As I have previously critiqued, scholarly analyses of morality in the marketplace include many accounts that cloud how racism and colonialism functions in all of this (Sobande 2022a). One example is strands of scholarship such as the works of Warren (2022), which focus on the potential stigma that brands face when being perceived as morally problematic. Such work does not seem to critically consider the racial and class(ist) politics of morality in these matters and appears to avoid reference to "white supremacy," opting for the more amorphous expression "racial supremacy." Scholarship on "wokeness" and the perceived "stigmatization of corporations," which lacks any reference to whiteness or racial capitalism, may reinforce revisionist framings of the marketplace as untethered from racism.[2] Scholarship that positions critiques of business ethics and corporate social initiatives as extreme and purist may also reflect an alliance between Big Business and much of the academic study of it—especially in the context of marketized higher education (Klein 2000), where Big Brands may be watching scholars (and their affiliated institutions) watching them.

The concept of *stigma* has been critically engaged in some fruitful ways amid the vast array of consumer, business, and marketing studies scholarship in existence, for example as part of the articulation of hopes "that researchers and practitioners will be mindful of our contributions to marketplace exclusion and stigma in practice. Too often we problematize identities that fall outside societal norms and offer consumption-oriented remedies that purport to "solve" already marginalized identities" (Arsel, David, and Scott 2022, 920). Although the concept of stigma has been drawn on as part of critical research that meaningfully addresses inequalities in the marketplace, on

---

2. In recent years there has been a rise in scholarship on topics such as "wokeness," BLM, decolonial approaches, and the "Global South," but often in ways that ultimately center whiteness, including by foregrounding the perspectives of white individuals and settlers on issues that have an impact on and oppress Black, Asian, and Indigenous people.

other occasions it has served as a go-to term that shifts the focus away from naming specific forms of structural oppression (e.g., racism and classism) and consequently yields opaque analyses of morality and the marketplace. Steeped in the language of business ethics, the work of scholars such as Warren (2022) focuses on the polarizing binary of "morally problematic" and "moral perfectionism," without reflecting on the power regimes that shape who tends to be societally legitimized as a moral arbiter and who tends to be dismissed as an extreme critic. In sum, not all who make moral judgments are treated as equal, but scholarship on morality and the marketplace sometimes fails to contend with this and in turn paints a whitewashed picture of how morality operates.

Much, but not all, work on morality and the marketplace seems to reflect the relative conservatism of many spheres of marketing and business scholarship, which tiptoe around topics such as whiteness, white supremacy, and oppression—instead favoring a framing of morality that is detached from the racist, classist, and colonialist ways that moral judgments have often functioned throughout history. Another example of approaches to scholarship on morality and the marketplace that do not effectively address issues of racism and colonialism is studies of the environmentally damaging effects of consumer culture that do not discuss the reality that "Western racial violence and ecological violence are inseparable developments" (Towns 2022, 21). Such research can result in revisionist accounts of history that paint morality in a painfully postracial light.

In commenting on the whitewashed ways that morality and the marketplace is sometimes discussed and researched, I am not only referring to the omission of how histories of racism and colonialism underpin contemporary marketplace and economic activity. Rather, I am also referring to how racism, xenophobia, and colonialism factors into normative notions of what knowledge is and who knowledge producers are. Turning to the work of Towns, *On Black Media Philosophy* has helped me to clarify some of the ways that whitewashed accounts of morality circulate, including amid scholarly research regarding the marketplace. As Towns (2022, 16) states: "Black studies is not concerned with creating a world of Black heroes that would just replace the white heroes studied in the disciplines; it is not concerned with putting a Black face to white theory; it is not a communications/area studies campaign to teach Black and brown people, both at home and abroad, the benefits of capitalism. It is a full intellectual, epistemological shift in knowledge, one directly articulated to the materialist demands for liberation worldwide."

Shaped by Towns's work and that of Black studies more widely, I argue that the epistemological basis of many societal definitions and defenses of morality in the UK and the US is wedded to whiteness. Such perspectives of morality uphold perceptions of who and what is "moral" and "immoral," including who and what is "legal" and "illegal," in ways that are distinctly influenced by the impacts of racism, colonialism, xenophobia, and white supremacy. As such, I note that framings of morality that do not critically attend to both the racial and class politics that they are premised on tend to work in ways that maintain whiteness and antiblackness (e.g., by policing and dismissing the knowledge, epistemologies, concerns, and lives of Black people, particularly those who are working class).

Although they can operate in ways that outlive generations, normative notions of morality can, and do, change. Individuals' and institutions' views regarding morality are influenced by many different factors, but one of the most pronounced is the impact of significant sociocultural and geopolitical shifts, such as legislative changes and challenges to previously embraced societal norms. Acknowledging that ideas about morality shift is not the same as suggesting that contemporary contentions concerning morality are completely removed from perspectives of morality from the past. Rather, when detailing morality in the present day, it is necessary to account for both the enduring and malleable qualities of it. Put briefly, morality is not something inherent, but its socially constructed nature does not mean that all ideas about morality are in the exact same state of flux.

Certain perspectives on morality (e.g., rooted in religion, law, and the rulings of the nation-state) and adjacent concepts such as normality are more pervasive than others. While ideas about normality, morality, and the associated concepts of ethics and dutifulness were at the forefront of much public discourse long before it, the coronavirus (COVID-19) crisis has stirred such discussions about who and what is reasonable or unreasonable (Sedgman 2023) and who and what is normal or abnormal. Writing about these matters, I have argued that "there is a need for more work that breaks down how racial capitalism, discourses of multiculturalism, and colonialist constructions of 'good citizenry' are implicated in experiences of, and allusions to, care and camaraderie during the COVID-19 crisis" (Sobande 2022a, 8–9). When writing that, I focused on how brands and political entities were creating media and marketing that conveyed messages about the sense of duty and citizenry that was expected of people. Specifically, I analyzed how institutions appeared to promote the moralizing message that people must "keep calm and consume" to supposedly sustain the economy during the crisis. In this chapter I shift my focus to consider how notions of morality are projected, or even imposed, on brands, rather than how brands project or impose expectations on people.

WHO AND WHAT SETS THE MORAL AGENDA

People are a part of brands, and sometimes people are brands. So my analysis of brands' moral impositions accounts for the reality that brands often deal with diverging perceptions of morality among employees and different stakeholders (e.g., within target markets). My use of terms such as *imposed* and *imposition*, as part of how I conceptualize brands' moral impositions, is not intended to engender sympathy for them. Nor is my use of such expressions intended to portray them as passive or to diminish the relative power and agency that brands have. Instead, I use such terms to call attention to the fact that some of the ways that brands engage with matters of morality stem from their facing pressures to do so (e.g., brands responding to the watched watching them back), as opposed to being indicative of their altruism.

While the existing expression "cause-related marketing" (Littler 2008, 3) articulates brands' active engagement with messages and marketing related to specific causes (e.g., social, political, environmental), the expression does not name the nature of any power dynamics that influence this (e.g., how the cause is chosen and who/what compels this choice). My hope is that the imperfect phrase "brands' (or brand) moral impositions" puts the focus squarely on power struggles that are imbued in how brands negotiate morality. Here it is helpful to reflect on the perspectives and experiences of the media, marketing, business, and retail professionals whom I interviewed.

The three journalists I interviewed as part of this research are referred to using the pseudonyms Aaron, Amanda, and Sarah. While all live in the UK, their experiences include working and writing for US publications as well. During each of their interviews, Aaron, Amanda, and Sarah discussed the ineffective ways that brands attempt to make and communicate decisions related to morality and issues of inequality and injustice. Aaron—a journalist—reflected on various moral judgments that have been made in response to brands in recent years. As Aaron's words on woke-washing signal, perceptions of the moral or immoral actions of brands can include impressions of the degree to which their business practices correspond with whom and what they claim to care about:

> I guess the woke-washing thing is an interesting one, right, because . . .
> I don't know, I've not really ever thought deeply about what woke-washing is. I suppose it's this idea of taking a stand around hot-button issues that are kind of within the news agenda, while not necessarily living up to it. I'm trying to think of a good example. BrewDog is probably an old one, but it's the one I think of most commonly, of saying that they are for the people and being a collective, the idea that you can

invest in them and support them and actually you look at a lot of their business practices, and you look at the role of their management, and it's not necessarily as noble an enterprise as you maybe first imagined.

Business scholar Douglas Holt (2016) has observed that "by targeting novel ideologies from crowdcultures, brands can stand out." On a similar note, as is indicated by Aaron's mention of "hot-button issues," brand responses to moral, social, and political issues (and perceptions of those responses) are also influenced by news agendas. Further still, expectations of brands' stances on certain issues are impacted by local, national, and international news agendas, including coverage of party politics and controversial political campaigns. Thus, the concept of brands' moral impositions that I theorize accounts for the potentially imposing force of news agendas and their capacity to steer some expectations of what brands "should" be taking a stance on at different points in time (e.g., a stance on mitigating the spread of COVID-19 and a stance on how they will "support" customers facing the cost-of-living crisis). That said, the extent to which news agendas have power over the moral positioning of brands is impacted by a range of factors, including whether the brands in question are known locally, nationally, and/or globally, in addition to whether the sector that the brands are part of is associated with specific moral, social, and political issues.

Although when discussing brand woke-washing Aaron reflected on whether the example of BrewDog (a multinational brewery and pub chain) might be "an old one," the brand's inclusion in the Museum of Brands' exhibition *When Brands Take a Stand* is indicative of continued interest in the public image and stance of BrewDog. When I visited the exhibition in spring 2022, I noticed that BrewDog-branded merchandise appeared next to Ben & Jerry's Justice ReMix'd ice cream products, on display in a glass cabinet. In its website announcements of Justice ReMix'd, Ben & Jerry's (2019) states that it is launching the products "in partnership with the Advancement Project National Office, a multi-racial civil rights organization that works with local grassroots organizers on racial justice issues. We believe justice should be for everyone, not just the white and wealthy. So we're speaking out in the best way we know of—with a euphoric ice cream flavor—for an end to structural racism in our broken criminal legal system." Seeing the iconicity of BrewDog sitting alongside that of Ben & Jerry's at the Museum of Brands made me think about whether the intended message may have been that both brands have demonstrated a commitment to addressing issues of injustice. The fact that BrewDog is named in the "supporting partners" section of information about the exhibition on the museum's website also evidences the brand's active participation in discussions about how "brands and advertising have the power to influence society" (Museum of Brands 2020b).

A British Broadcasting Corporation (BBC 2022a) episode of the documentary series *Disclosure* about BrewDog reflects the ongoing nature of news coverage of criticism of the brand's business practices and the extent to which they correspond with a proclaimed "punk" ethos. In "The Truth about BrewDog," reporter Mark Daly "investigates the truth behind the beer company's marketing and financial hype, and hears disturbing claims about BrewDog's corporate culture." Other examples of media coverage of the brand include articles reporting that "BrewDog co-founder apologises to ex-staff over 'toxic' working environment" (Davies 2021), following more than sixty staff complaints about the business's culture. Put plainly, BrewDog continues to face public criticism concerning the perceived ethics and overall culture of the business, which has previously been marketed as being unapologetically and playfully punk. Several survey responses convey some of the many critiques of BrewDog and concerns related to its work and labor practices:

> BrewDog [is a brand that I dislike]—bad ethics, poor treatment of workers.
> —white man, UK (26–35 years old)

Brewdog [is a brand that I dislike]—pretentious and the owner is not a very nice person. Targeting of smaller companies with similar naming.
—white person (gender undisclosed), UK (26–35 years old)

However, other survey responses are suggestive of the praise of BrewDog by some people, in addition to being indicative of critiques of influencers (which are discussed in more detail later in this chapter):

Brands certainly can be activists, providing they practice what they preach. For example, BrewDog plant trees for the beers purchased and have a carbon-neutral lager out called Lost, which I think is a great start. It would be great to see brands disassociate themselves from cringeworthy "influencers" like Molly-Mae Hague [who found fame on the UK reality TV show *Love Island*], but I doubt that will happen any time soon.
—white person (gender undisclosed), UK (26–35 years old)

BrewDog's website features a section called "Our Responsibilities," and its website also includes a range of subsections that cover environmental and ethical issues such as information about "sustainability," being "a living wage employer," and BrewDog's "modern slavery statement." As this writing indicates, BrewDog is aware of scrutiny of its brand claims to do with changing, or at least, sustaining, the world. Extant research has explored how and why "corporations are rushing to proclaim their 'ethical' credentials: to show us that they care, and that they are 'socially responsible'" (Littler 2008, 2). Littler's work, which features the pressing question, "Ethics: the new morality?" (9), offers a crucial account of the ways that moralizing and sanctimony manifest in consumer culture contexts. I argue that one person's perception of morality may be another person's perception of sanctimony, so careful attention must be paid to how morality and sanctimony are positioned in the marketplace (and in studies of it). Additionally, attention should be paid to who and what histories tend to be behind the normative positioning of morality and sanctimony, including in the scholarly and industry spheres of "business ethics" and "corporate social responsibility," where specific forms of structural oppression are sometimes deflected by focusing on the language and lens of stigma.

The parameters of both morality and sanctimony are far from being fixed but are sometimes treated as such in narratives that dismiss critiques of the (im)moral stances and actions of brands. When discussing morality, ethics, and the concept of ethical consumption, Littler (2008, 8) discusses provocations that are relevant to ongoing research into morality in the marketplace, including the racial and class politics that mobilizes much moralizing and fear mongering in response to critiques of brands and so-called business ethics: "To take but a few examples: who decides what is ethical about ethical consumption? Who gets to decide what is fair about fair trade? Don't a lot of these practices simply enable corporations to hold up their 'ethical' line as a niche market, while they continue to perpetuate exploitation through their regular range? Is ethical consumption merely a conscience-salving mechanism for the privileged?"

Expanding on Littler's research and accounting for what has changed during the time since it was written, I explore numerous sociopolitical issues and power struggles that contribute to the ways that brands position themselves in relation to moral matters and in relation to what can be termed "competing value systems" (Sedgman 2023, 6). Namely, I examine expectations of moral stances that are directed at brands and the extent to which such expectations may appear to be embraced by brands or imposed on them. Exploring this involves acknowledging different struggles, and sometimes synergies, between the perspectives of brands and the people identified as their customers/audience, as well as different external stakeholders (e.g., press and politicians). Additionally, theorizing what I refer to as brands' moral impositions involves considering the impact of struggles that are internal to brands (e.g., diverging views on morality between different employees and internal stakeholders), which is an aspect of the relationship between branding and morality that requires further analysis.

Countless examples of the work of corporate whistleblowers make clear that the professed values—moral and otherwise—of a brand rarely reflect the values of everyone who works for or is associated with it. In-depth discussion of this dimension of dynamics between brands and morality is mainly beyond the focus of my book, but my awareness of such issues informs how I make sense of brands' moral impositions and the melding of moral and commercial imperatives. It has often been through a Euro-American binary lens of religious versus secular that morality has been considered in critical marketing and consumption studies, or through a lens that focuses on "universal" moral principles (Dunfee 1998), without critically discussing who and what determines the allegedly universal nature of certain moral positions. "More than that, some efforts to undermine critique of brands and capitalism draw on theories of philosophy that, at 'best', don't address race, and at worst, have promoted racist perspectives. As a result, I am reminded of how oppressive notions of morality that treat whiteness as their compass, have been rehashed for centuries" (Sobande 2022a, 42) in ways that maintain the oppression of Black people.

Much of the earlier research on morality and consumer culture did not directly address how racism, white supremacy, and accordant forms of respectability politics mold societal notions of morality (e.g., who is deemed as possessing the capacity to make moral judgments, and why). Critical analysis of these matters is central to my conceptualization of brands' moral impositions, which is guided by the insights of Black media philosophy (Towns 2022) and critical studies of race in the marketplace (Henderson, Hakstian, and Williams 2016; Johnson et al. 2019; Thomas, Johnson, and Grier 2023). On that note, were it not for the creative, impactful, and insightful ways that Black people have used social media in the first quarter of the twenty-first century, some of the statements and stances of brands on racism, white supremacy, and issues regarding morality and oppression would never have come to be.

Then again, "the larger digital economy" (Towns 2022, 119) that the online words, works, and worlds of Black people are part of arguably rests on racial capitalism. Ultimately, it is an economy that has treated images and accounts of the harm, deaths, and murders of Black people as commodifiable content. What I mean by stating all of this is that I recognize (a) the role of Black people's distinct digital presence and impact in the changing landscape of brand responses to social and political injustices (e.g., brand responses to BLM); (b) the oppressive nature of the digital economy that Black people find themselves participating in, even when using digital platforms and processes in ways that are intended to entertain them and enrich their lives; and (c) the need to critically conceptualize and consider brands' moral impositions in a way that attends to both the agency and oppression of Black people—whose online critiques and commentaries influence the actions of many brands, and likely more so than most brands acknowledge.

Relatedly, although claims of the alleged neutrality of news outlets continue to be made by many in society, much evidence suggests that the world of news is far from being a hub of objectivity and impartiality. Indeed, there are differences between the mainstream news landscapes in the UK and the US, but both industries have been identified as spaces within which institutional racism remains a problem, in terms of both hiring practices and the framing of news reports and coverage of events. Thus, if the news agenda plays a part in determining what moral, social, and political issues brands take a stance on, the influence of such an agenda may at times reinforce racist value systems and racist moral judgments. That said, the ways that brands negotiate ideas about morality and expectations of what they comment on is also impacted by digital culture more widely, including, in some cases, Black "digital accountability praxis" (Clark 2020), which conveys a perspective that typically contrasts with that of mainstream media. Hence, it is important to avoid overdetermining the impact of mainstream media—including mainstream news—on the ways that brands negotiate issues of morality.

Critical studies of race in the marketplace offer insights that can contribute to a nuanced understanding of how notions of morality are impacted by structural oppression such as racism, sexism, and classism. Such studies include the essential research of the cofounders of the RIM Research Network, Sonya A. Grier, Guillaume D. Johnson, and Kevin D. Thomas, whose individual and collective work has illuminated the intricacies of how both race and racism impact experiences of a range of marketplace environments and processes (e.g., education, retail, tourism). In an account of how RIM was established, Grier, Johnson, and Thomas (2019, 96) state: "As the three of us discussed our individual experiences at different marketing conferences three things became distinctly clear: (1) there is a general lack of race related research done by academic marketing researchers; (2) when race is broached the focus is typically placed solely on non-white populations; and (3) race-related market research rarely takes on a critical and intersectional perspective. These realizations birthed a vision—the Race in the Marketplace (RIM) Research Network."

The research of Grier, Thomas, and Johnson and that of other scholars who critically take seriously the way that racism and whiteness is implicated in the marketplace is key to the arguments articulated in my book (Crockett 2022; Harrison 2013; Henderson et al. 2016; Jones 2019; Ray 2019; Rosa-Salas 2019). For example, in "Black Skiing, Everyday Racism, and the Racial Spatiality of Whiteness," cultural anthropologist Anthony Kwame Harrison (2013, 316) argues that "in addition to specific structural constraints typically used to explain Black underrepresentation in skiing, there are powerful symbolic forces which work to define and maintain skiing and its associated social spaces as essentially White." Informed by Harrison's insightful research, I consider how both structural and symbolic forces contribute to the often unarticulated yet ever-present whiteness of how notions of morality and associated concepts such as wokeness are understood and engaged with by brands in the marketplace. I also discuss how such structural and symbolic sources shape the way that whiteness colors some of the existing scholarship on the marketplace and/of morality. In addition to being informed by Harrison's (2013) work, my book draws on Victor Ray's (2019, 26) theory of racialized organizations, which explains the ways "that organizations are racial structures—cognitive schemas connecting organizational rules to social and material resources."

Unlike concepts such as "caring capitalism" (Cohen and Greenfield 1997), which the founders of Ben & Jerry's (Ben Cohen and Jerry Greenfield) outlined, the idea of brands' moral impositions rests upon recognition of the ever-present cruelties and inherent carelessness of racial capitalism. So far, my discussion of brands has involved attending to the way that ideas about morality are wielded by power regimes, including those that stem from the intersections of racism and capitalism, which result in individuals and institutions positioned as elite and racialized as white being legitimized as (the only) moral arbiters. But now, by focusing further on discussions catalyzed by COVID-19 and by drawing on other empirical examples (e.g., the perspectives of media professionals, marketers, and consumers), I discuss more of the details of how brands' moral impositions manifest.

MORAL IMPOSITIONS AND COMMERCIAL IMPERATIVES

Extant writing on COVID-19 and morality includes a commentary in the Oxford University Press *Journal of Public Health* by scholar Melanio L. Leal. In the commentary, Leal (2022, 1) poses the question, "Which moral system works better during COVID-19 pandemic?" As part of such writing, different dimensions of "moral obligation" and "moral imposition" are detailed. Focusing on the complexities of COVID-19, Leal (2022, 1) contends that "moral obligation is part of a long history of social development and ethical thinking. It is probably a way of understanding well our duties as citizen without coercion internally or externally. In certain ways, I think, moral obligation can lead people into realizing the important societal values that will contribute to the betterment and advancement of the community." In contrast with how moral obligation is associated with individuals embracing a sense of duty, Leal's notion of moral imposition connotes more controlling, coercive, and concerted actions. As Leal (2022, 1) puts it, "at this time of pandemic, 'controlling' certain action or code of conduct is not helping out in making people understand their moral obligation. This becomes moral imposition." Mindful of Leal's explanation of moral obligation and moral imposition—which seems to position the former as resembling a nudge in comparison to the latter, which is perceived as more of a forceful push—I have analyzed aspects of how brands are mixed up with morality and how people perceive their actions.

My own views on moral obligation and moral imposition depart from Leal's in various ways. For example, while Leal (2022) implies that moral obligation is devoid of coerciveness, I assert that both moral obligation and moral imposition involve structural forms of coercion that are associated with the concept of the social contract. These structural forms of coercion relate to dominant norms and cultural conventions, which carve out societal expectations regarding who has a moral obligation and what that obligation is. Basically, moral obligation and moral imposition may be two sides of the same coercive coin, meaning that morality always involves some form of imposition, as it is not innate but instead is often instructed via socialization processes. Moreover, morality can be forceful and depends on potentially persuasive forms of relationality that involve people determining who and what they perceive to be (im)moral, including who and what they regard as (un)reasonable (Sedgman 2023).

As is indicated by how notions of morality have changed throughout history and across geocultural contexts, the parameters of moral and immoral are socially constructed and shift. So too are the mantras and images of brands that seek to stay relevant and adapt to changing times. In *How Brands Become Icons: The Principles of Cultural Branding*, Holt (2004, 57) states that "nations require a moral consensus to function. Citizens must identify with the nation, accept its institutions, and work towards its betterment. Nations are organized around a set of values that defines what is good and just." Although some sense of moral agreement is essential to how nations function, the culture of competition that typifies capitalism is partly made possible by moral disagreement and disharmony. Accordingly, arguments and antagonisms can sometimes equal money.

As Turow (2008, 3) notes, "It may seem strange to associate the marketplace with a sense of belonging. Yet it has long been true that the marketplace is more than an arena in which people can buy stuff; it is the hub of social life. The complex industrialized American marketplace [and, I argue, the UK marketplace] is no exception. It is hard to think of any part of life that is not continually affected by it." Relatedly, as "genealogies of morality" (Littler 2008, 3) point out, ideas about morality contribute to the establishment of an "us" and a "them," including in ways that brands can benefit from when attempting to stand out from the consumerist crowd and by cultishly carving out a brand identity that fosters feelings of belonging (Montell 2021).

Examples such as Ben & Jerry's—which hires people in roles such as "global head of activism" (Stewart 2020)—are helpful to focus on here. It has been argued that "in a world where many marketers will be all too familiar with red tape and prolonged sign-offs, the brand is in a unique position. Yes, it's a wholly-owned subsidiary of Unilever but its board of directors remains independent" (Stewart 2020). In the 1990s Ben & Jerry's noted that many mainstream businesses were beginning to express interest in the responsibility to society that businesses have, including a responsibility to work in ways that benefit society (and not just businesses) (Cohen and Greenfield 1997). Since then, the number of businesses actively expressing their views on social, political, and moral matters has skyrocketed, as has discussion about the different identities of brands.

By 2022 there were numerous declarations that individuals and institutions in advertising, branding, and marketing had been reckoning with racism in recent years and had been embracing activism in ways that they had not previously considered. Just a few of the many examples of such discourse are these headlines: "5 Key Takeaways from Ad Age's Town Hall on Racism" (Craft 2020); "'It's Not a Marketing Exercise': Ben & Jerry's on Dismantling White Supremacy" (Stewart 2020); "We're Entering the Age of Corporate Social Justice" (Zheng 2020); and "Gen-Z Demand Racial Justice, Not Just Diversity, Equity and Inclusion from Brands" (Bakhtiari 2022). As Zeynep Arsel, David Crockett, and Maura L. Scott (2022, 920) have outlined, "Diversity, Equity, and Inclusion (DEI) has become ubiquitous in public and academic discourse. This is despite ongoing contests over definitions and the lack of a clear consensus about the relative importance (and even the appropriate order) of each component." They offer an insightful explanation of DEI in the context of their account: "For our purposes, diversity refers broadly to real or perceived physical or socio-cultural differences attributed to people and the representation of these differences in research, market spaces, and organizations. Equity refers to fairness in the treatment of people in terms of both opportunity and outcome. Inclusion refers to creating a culture that fosters belonging and incorporation of diverse groups and is usually operationalized as opposition to exclusion or marginalization. Taken together, DEI is typically accompanied by an axiological orientation toward procedural and distributive justice in organizations and institutions" (920).

As the preceding explanation signals, typically there is a perceived connection between forms of DEI work and aims related to "justice in organizations and institutions" (Arsel, Crockett, and Scott 2022, 920). However, as this chapter explores, various perceptions and different critiques of organizational DEI work include interpretations of it as being disconnected from a focus on social justice. Put

differently, sometimes DEI efforts are perceived as working symbi-
otically with social justice struggles, while at other times DEI might
be interpreted as being an obstacle to some social justice and liberationist goals.

Advertising, marketing, and branding have a long history of operating in ways that involve attempting to appeal to specific groups of
people (aka target markets) (Rosa-Salas 2019). Particularly since the
1970s, when germinal forms of audience segmentation and targeted
advertising emerged, brands have been categorizing people into an
expanding range of consumer demographics. As Cottom (2020,
443) notes, "Internet technologies became a dominant tool of capital because of their ability to expand markets and consumer classes."
*The Daily You: How the Advertising Industry Is Defining Your Iden-
tity and Your World* (Turow 2012) provides an illuminating account
of dimensions of the relationship between identity and consumer
culture. More than a decade later, the book's premise remains relevant. However, contemporary discourse on identity and advertising now involves more of an emphasis on the specifics of identity
politics.

Some views that brands espouse allude to specific identities and
social demographics in ways that reflect the continued commercialization of identity politics, including profitable demarcations
between an "us" and a "them" (Klein 2000; Mukherjee and Banet-
Weiser 2012). "For example, through segmentation, or the technique
of classifying people into target markets, marketers craft discourses
about identity which have also historically reflected the existence of
interlocking oppressions" (Rosa-Salas and Sobande 2022, 179). Contortions of identity politics in the marketplace and beyond it include
"conservative propagations of identity politics—a political smear
that has been monopolised by the right, but also has form on the
centre and left" (Richmond and Charnley 2022, 2). As philosophy
scholar Olúfẹ́mi O. Táíwò (2022, 6) observes, "Some expressions of
identity politics are twisted to rebrand old imperial projects, while
others are actively banned by the powers that be."

Essentially, the marketplace is an unequal and oppressive playing field, within which many brands move toward and away from moral positions and (re)presentations of identity politics to try to win the competition of racial capitalism. Accordingly, the critical work of Richmond and Charnley (2022, 6–7) outlines the following: "Identity politics underwent a pejorative turn after the social movements of the 1960s–1980s dispersed and a massive deskilling of industrial labour was facilitated, freeing capital to exploit labour across the world. Rights-based discourses and social justice issues were gradually limited to campaigns within the state or NGOs."

Now, *identity politics* is a term that is often used in ways that are completely unmoored from the grassroots organizing—namely, the Black feminist work (e.g., the extensive work of the Combahee River Collective 1977)—that it was once most associated with. In addition to being uttered as a pejorative, identity politics is an expression that brands have tried to turn to, such as when articulating their stance on certain social, political, and moral issues and when denouncing the stance of others.

While consumer culture, unsurprisingly, continues to uphold capitalist principles, words such as *moral*, *ethical*, *social*, and *political* have taken up residence in this space in the twenty-first century in a way that has sparked some industry shifts. As such, *Ad Age*—"a global media brand that publishes news, analysis, and data on marketing and media"—now has a "regularly updated blog tracking brands' responses to racial injustice." The *Ad Age* initiative is one of a mass of examples of how the advertising industry is trying to keep up with contemporary activism and corporatized versions. Such industry interest in social (in)justice has swelled since the high-profile social and political movement BLM was established in the US in 2013 (Ransby 2018; Taylor 2021). While some people have welcomed recent waves of brands declaring their anti-racist stance, others interpret such actions as gestures that simply symbolize the salability of social justice and brands' capacity to monetize morality and to capitalize on racial capitalism. Furthermore, as Noble (2018,

24) calls for: "Interrogating what advertising companies serve up as credible information must happen, rather than have a public instantly gratified with stereotypes in three-hundredths of a second or less."

For decades, many corporations have made use of CSR programs, "which include social issue marketing, philanthropic efforts, employee volunteer initiatives, and diversity and inclusion work, to build their brands and satisfy customers. Now, consumers and employees are raising the bar" (Zheng 2020). If every brand had the exact same moral position, concepts such as CSR and brand activism—which often serve to distinguish the allegedly "good" brands from the "bad"—would not exist. Again, here it is helpful to acknowledge that there can even be significant variations between the moral positions of individuals working for the same brand, despite the brand's overall image being associated with a specific view of morality and complementing ideologies. Also, brands that have the same parent company may diverge in terms of their moral, social, and political perspectives (e.g., by challenging their parent company). This demonstrates the complexities of brands negotiating morality (aka brands' moral impositions), including different expectations of them, and the problems that brands face when constructing a cohesive public image. Ben & Jerry's decision to sue its parent company (Unilever) to try to prevent the sale of its Israeli business to a local licensee exemplifies this.

The ice-cream and frozen yogurt manufacturer (Ben & Jerry's) claimed that Unilever's planned actions were inconsistent with its own values. This proclamation had the effect of distancing its own moral position (its sense of "us") from that of its imposing parent company (an identified "them"). Hence, as Bradshaw and Scott (2018) affirm, analyses of advertising history need to account for the collective and individual contributions of a range of different market actors—including brands and parent companies—who are often grouped together under the label "advertisers" and "each of whom brings an often deeply different intention" (Bradshaw and Scott 2018, 12).

The concept of brands' moral impositions that I outline through-out this book highlights that expectations of how brands respond to moral matters include expectations imposed on them by other brands, not just those expressed by people typically referred to as consumer groups and external audiences. Often, discussions of the perceived moral (and social and political) stance of a brand center on the assumption that brands simply respond to critiques and concerns voiced by potential or current consumers (e.g., a bottom-up process, whereby "we" watch "them"). The reality is much more complicated and is impacted by power struggles that are internal to brands and/or that exist between them (e.g., horizontal and top-down power dynamics, whereby "they" watch each other).

In the months prior to Ben & Jerry's controversial decision to sue Unilever (a lawsuit that was settled), several people responded to my survey with statements that expressed their thoughts about the brand. In response to the question, "How do you feel about brands commenting on and contributing to social justice work? If possible, please refer to specific examples of brands doing this," someone wrote: "I don't mind so much if they're actually putting their money where their mouth is—I find it deeply annoying & harmful when it's 'woke-washing' as you said, like how Ben & Jerry's go on about how great they are but actively support the apartheid of Palestin-ian people." In contrast, some of the four hundred survey respon-dents praised Ben & Jerry's for commenting on and contributing to social justice work "authentically" and in ways that they believe "strengthens a brand and their customer loyalty":

> Ben & Jerry's is a company, in particular whose social justice work is directly linked to their products. The organization educates and supports causes they believe in. I think Ben & Jerry's is a fantastic example of that brand activism. They've taken stances on BLM, legal-ization of weed, the prison industrial complex, etc. Whether through their social media presence, how they donate profits, etc. their brand has become synonymous with social justice. Patagonia is another example with their environmental work—taking a stance by not

creating company branded merchandise with orgs whose values aren't aligned was a pretty big statement to tech bros.

—Black woman, US (36–45 years old)

There are companies out there that already put some sort of social issue into their company manifesto—like Ben & Jerry's. . . . I suspect it has to be the smaller businesses, though—the ones with enough control in the decisions not to have to bow down only to the might[y] stock holder and their ROI [return on investment].

—white woman, UK (46–55 years old)

One example that comes to mind of brands commenting on social issues is Ben & Jerry's ice cream. I know they have commented on the issues between Israel and Palestine when realistically I think it's not really an issue they need to comment on, though it has no bearing on whether I'll buy it.

—white man, UK (18–25 years old)

Most of the survey respondents who mentioned Ben & Jerry's praised the brand for its efforts to address a range of social and political issues. However, one respondent identified it as a brand that they dislike "because of their support for extreme left wing causes." The different opinions of Ben & Jerry's reflect the fact that perceptions of brands are influenced by political factors, such as the resonance or lack of relatability of a brand's ideological stance on certain issues and its overall perceived moral position.

The ways that brands negotiate ideas and expectations of morality sometimes connect to commodified concepts of identity (politics), resulting in a reductive understanding and response to social and political movements. Insights on this topic are offered by communication scholar Lily Kunda (2020), who examined "the politics of public statements" regarding Ben & Jerry's and BLM:

In a sea of public statements, Ben & Jerry's managed to stand out in comparison to other corporations. Their statement directly addressed systemic racism, offered suggestions for national reform, and promoted additional articles from their website for further education on topics related to the Black Lives Matter movement. In the midst of an abundance of public conversation discussing racial reform, I question what role—if any—do corporate public statements play in the fight against white supremacy? Is verbally saying you support black lives enough when capitalism in itself has been so intertwined with the systems that perpetuate racism in the first place?

In August 2022 Ben & Jerry's and Dutch confectionary company Tony's Chocolonely teamed up as part of a collaboration that combined their brand images, which are linked to terms such as *fairtrade* and *ethics*, and the concept of "caring capitalism." The two brands announced "A Chocolatey Love A-Fair" to describe the creation and launch of a new ice cream, inspired by Tony's Chocolonely. Ben & Jerry's proclaimed that this product was created "to celebrate joining their [Tony's Chocolonely] mission, a mission to end modern slavery in cocoa farming." As well as creating new ice cream, the brands partnered to produce new chocolate bar blends. Descriptions of the products included statements such as "Changing the world has never tasted so good." Copy accompanying images of the blends on Ben & Jerry's website features sentences such as "We tickled each other's taste buds with 2 tasty, new limited-edition bars and 2 tasty, new limited-edition tubs." This collaboration appeared to be yet another example of how ideas about morality and ethics manifest in the marketplace (e.g., in the form of mutually beneficial brand collaborations that draw on the socially conscious image of two brands in similar markets).

When visiting the Tony's Chocolonely superstore and chocolate bar in Amsterdam earlier that year, I was struck by how much literature on display outlined the ethos of the brand in detail. While eating my s'mores-style breakfast and listening to the rain outside, I perused the reading material that was decoratively placed on the table that had become my space for the morning. The literature documented the brand's mission and story in ways that blended bold colored graphics with incisive copy about Tony's Chocolonely's (2021) commitment to address modern slavery. The first chapter of

Tony's Chocolonely Annual FAIR 2020/2021 Report is titled "Our Fight for Equality and Fairness" and features casual expressions such as "Hey there!" Other statements in the opening chapter include "Human rights are not optional," and there is a clear call for "all key players in the chocolate industry . . . to roll up their sleeves and work collectively" in order "to make 100% slave free the norm in chocolate." This writing is followed by bright visual representations of data and descriptions of "Team Tony's," which is referred to using words and phrases such as "outspoken," "willful," "makes you smile," and "entrepreneurial."

As was announced through their Instagram account and website, by December 2022 the Tony's Chocolonely chocolate bar in Amsterdam had closed. The brand's statement on this is yet another example of the ways that the company emphasizes its image as ethical: "Dear choco fans, at Tony we're always looking for ways to tell you about our story and involve you in our mission. Cos, bottom line, that's what it's all about: making 100% slave free the norm in chocolate. But . . . if you want to change the norm in the industry, you sometimes try things that don't have the right effect on your mission. . . . Unfortunately, this is the case for Tony's Chocolate Bar in the Beurs van Berlage. The love, effort, time and money we invested in our Bar, does not result in realizing our mission faster" (Tony's Chocolonely 2022).

Although its brand identity is undoubtedly distinct from Ben & Jerry's—from its use of bold typography to the informality of its friendly yet political tone—Tony's Chocolonely appears to be based on a similar sentiment and style. Anticipating customers' interest in their values, and perhaps attuned to the ways that people watch and scrutinize brands, Tony's Chocolonely seems to lay it all on the table by providing people with the opportunity to read about its origins and ethos while purchasing its products in its superstore and former chocolate bar. It is unsurprising that the word *taste* and variations of it were featured throughout the promotional content that surrounded the pairing of Ben & Jerry's and Tony's Chocolonely.

However, the brands' connection to the concept and experience of taste extends beyond the flavors of their food and includes the public relations palettes of their customers.

Both Ben & Jerry's and Tony's Chocolonely appear to effectively account for their target audiences' preferences regarding the tone and tenor of marketing messages (e.g., which moral, social, and political positions are digestible to their intended consumers). The brands' stances on various matters of morality and injustice, and their explicit endorsement of each other, might be perceived as contributing to their twinned status as brand "tastemakers" in the domains of corporate social initiatives (CSI) and CSR work. Viewing such brands and their actions as amounting to a degree of "taste-making" power does not detract from the potentially significant societal benefits of their work. Two truths can exist at once. Such brands can contribute to efforts to address structural forms of oppression while also benefiting commercially from the appeal of their moral, social, and political stance.

Sometimes referred to as the benchmark(s) against which brands should measure the (in)effectiveness of their own CSI and CSR strategies, Ben & Jerry's, and Tony's Chocolonely can be understood as having an individual and somewhat collective capacity to shape some of the CSI and CSR norms and standards in the orbit of their industries. In this sense, I argue, the title "tastemakers" is applicable to them and can help to highlight that brands themselves can influence expectations regarding the moral stance of (other) brands—via moral impositions (e.g., the combined profile and relative power of Ben & Jerry's and Tony's Chocolonely may compel other brands to reevaluate their own positions and efforts related to matters of morality and injustice).

The advertising and marketing industry's move toward more actively engaging with, or at least acknowledging, certain social and political movements reflects the impact of brands' moral impositions. As well as learning about people's views about Ben & Jerry's via my research survey on brand woke-washing, the research interviews that informed my book brought to light various industry impressions of the brand. When interviewed, Amanda, a beauty and lifestyle journalist and brand consultant in the UK, highlighted the impressive image of Ben & Jerry's when discussing how brands comment on social and political issues:

> I think brands are aware that they need to have a social conscience. I'm a fan of Ben & Jerry's, even though they've been bought but they have control over the company, so I'm a big fan of that brand and their stance politically and the fact that they voice their opinions, but I don't think a lot of brands ever go as far as maybe Ben & Jerry's go. And I think a lot of people do it out of convenience. If something is not going to impact your company, then you'll do it but if it might, then you won't.

As Bradshaw and Scott (2018, 12) note, assessing the intentions of advertisers and brands, "either real or inferred, is central to the formation of the public response" to them and the products and services that they promote. In agreement with this, I acknowledge that such assessments of advertisers' intentions must be understood and contextualized in relation to macro-societal issues, such as the current sociopolitical climate that they are part of and that to some extent determines normative ideas regarding morality and the marketplace. Aaron, whom I also interviewed, addressed some of these matters.

Aaron's decade-long work as a journalist and writer involved covering a wide range of topics, including digital culture. During his interview Aaron described himself as "an independent journalist, who has their own opinions and thoughts, and has, through my social media presence, a moderately vocal point of view on certain things. Like I get gobby about social media, because I feel like it is in parts an area that I know a bit about and, therefore, could comment on stuff." When discussing the actions of brands in response to issues of injustice in society, Aaron said:

> I think I'm very sceptical of it, in large part because . . . it's very difficult to square the concept of a brand being able to speak out with a

united voice over these sorts of things, and there's always the underlying element of they're doing so in order to position themselves in the market, that enables them to have a better portrayal amongst a certain group of customers that will result in them having good business. It always comes down to this idea that it's very difficult to disentangle what could be a well-meaning stance on an issue with the concept that these are money making enterprises who are calculating every single public statement they make, if not necessarily to make the most money but to lose the least money, through impacts of key issues.

Expanding on his thoughts on some of the ways that brands attempt to comment on issues of injustice, Aaron said:

It's kind of virtue signaling, that idea that we are very noble, we are doing good, we are listening to you when, in fact, you know that these things have kind of been stress tested, market tested, and focused grouped to the nth degree. They glue on to these key issues and you see it, I guess, in the media cycle. It will be Ukraine for a while, let's be honest, but they come about every few weeks, every few months, of this is the thing where a brand must be seen to act or not act, and not acting is always bad, so, therefore, you have to put out a statement of platitudes and things like that. It's difficult because they're often huge, intractable societal issues, that you can't expect a brand to solve, and yet we've gone into this weird situation where not attempting to engage in that conversation is seen as terrible.

Although he did not use the words *morality* or *imposition*, Aaron's observations explicitly articulate that the expectations of brands are connected to changing perceptions of which sociopolitical issues of injustice are deemed worthy of attention and support. Acknowledging the messiness of such expectations and brand responses, Aaron stated:

Even things like . . . what you'd hope most people would see as innate, like having a firm stance on the merits of masks, or Covid vaccines, or seeing Black Lives Matter as an objectively good thing, for a brand to take a stance on those things you're always going to alienate some people now in this world, and because of the way that social media kind of amplifies those voices, you can often have such a negative impact as a result of it.

Both Aaron and Amanda spoke about some of the ways that brands have responded to geopolitical issues, including the Russian invasion of Ukraine in 2022. When speaking about how brands attempt to wade into discussions about such issues, Aaron said:

> The perfect example, which we're going through now, which is potentially going to date this, the Russian invasion of Ukraine, there are a lot of brands coming out and talking about how they're making a stand against this. You've got all of these different companies saying we're withdrawing our products that are on sale from Russia, or our services from Russia, or supermarkets saying they won't sell Russian booze anymore, and you think, you've probably already paid for all of that.
>
> And so, to what extent is that actually meaningful versus you just not wanting to be the one holding the parcel when the music runs out, and being the only one that's not doing it, which I admit is a very cynical way of looking at things. It's kind of like you do it not necessarily because you feel principled enough to do so, but because you feel cowardly enough to not get caught as the last person not doing so, I think.

Aaron's words emphasize that brands can feel pressured to navigate various expectations that they declare and demonstrate their moral, social, and political position on many societal issues. He also points out that the motives and potential genuineness of brands' gestures and decisions in response to such pressures may be called into question by many people. Aaron's perspective was echoed by the statements of survey respondents who commented on pressures—impositions—on brands to speak up about issues:

> I feel that it is important. Silence speaks volumes in instances of social justice. Speaking out about the inequality and unfairness of the world is a bold step.
>
> —Japanese American woman, US (26–35 years old)

Amanda's perspective during her interview was similar to but slightly different from Aaron's, as she commented on what she regarded as being distinctly different brand responses and silences concerning political issues and invasions in various parts of the world. As Amanda put it:

> At the end of the day, it's all about making money and so I think often-times brands don't want to lose one stream of customer base by align-ing themselves with one thing over another thing. Obviously, there are lots of brands that do but I think the bigger brands try to be more general around things. I think it's quite interesting obviously now to see what's happening between Ukraine and Russia, and to see the way in which, obviously not big, big brands but how smaller and middling brands are taking a stance on something but won't take a stance on things like Israel and Palestine and things like that.

Amanda's remarks on this delineate an aspect of the politics of marketing—that is, the fact that certain political issues and injustices receive more attention and support from brands than others. This also reflects the politics of morality (e.g., structural and global power relations that impact who and what is regarded as moral and immoral, in and by different geocultural contexts and cultures). When continuing to comment on this, Amanda reflected on the racial politics of marketing and branding decisions, such as how brands might determine who and what to speak up in support of. Amanda said:

> So, I think in general when people choose certain issues to comment on or to help as a brand or even as a person who is a brand, in terms of Ukraine I think one part of me thinks that it's great that you can stand up and say this is wrong or you don't believe in it, and want to help people. But I think that it's also a convenient war to be against because obviously, there are things going on in the rest of the world that don't generally affect us in the same way, or we profit off them, and obviously in terms of race, these are white people and generally in terms of brands, they're mostly owned and run by white people.

Amanda's reference to self-brands ("a person who is a brand") implies that some influencers monetize morality by strategically commenting on issues of injustice in ways that are palatable to a predominantly white audience. Such a perspective might be perceived as alluding to the existence of racial capitalism—a capitalist structure within which colonialism, racism, and nationalism result in institutions ascribing different degrees of "value" (aka capital) to people, places, and political wars. During her interview, Amanda offered detailed reflections regarding brands' disregard of social, political, and global issues that impact people of color:

> It does sadden me because you can see how much of an impact companies/brands/people can have if they want to. So, while I do think it's admirable that people are donating, like Bolt are donating proceeds, so every ride on the car hire app, there's money that goes to Ukraine. . . . I find it a bit offensive, because it's like, what about Yemen and the Palestinians, because it's all about people. There are so many people in the world that need our help and brands can clearly do things but choose not to, but then get behind certain causes and not others. So, I think personally—and white people might not feel the same way—but as a person of color, I think it's really sad to see and it's just a confirmation of institutionalized racism, that brands can do so much if they want to.

Amanda's words are suggestive of a frustration with how the moral, social, and political positions of some brands in the UK and the US appear to involve a concern with addressing issues that predominantly impact white people in detrimental ways. It is not that people such as Amanda are calling for brands to remain silent about what is happening in and to Ukraine. Nor is she dismissing the severity of the situation there. Instead, Amanda is poignantly asking where a comparably vocal brand outcry in response to violent oppression and atrocities in places such as Yemen and Palestine is. When sharing her thoughts on this, Amanda also discussed the contentious term woke-washing, including its connection to matters of morality:

So, I feel like there's two things, the woke-washing, I would think of that in a negative light in terms of . . . a lot of the time brands doing things, or individuals who are brands in and of themselves saying and doing things just because they think they have to, and not really necessarily understanding the reasons as to why they probably should be doing certain things, and oftentimes it feels like there's not a lot of thought behind it and a lack of understanding. So, I think the definition of woke is an understanding of, I suppose in an ideal world, how we should be behaving, what we should be considering in terms of people and cultures and ethnicities but also general morality.

Although brands deciding to speak up or stay silent about certain societal issues and injustices can result in accusations of woke-washing and can yield damaging consequences for brands, such decisions can also help them to establish their brand identity in ways that outweigh negative responses to these choices. Differences and disagreements between the moral, ethical, environmental, social, and political positions of brands have at least partly driven the emergence and expansion of entities such as Corporate Knights, founded in 2002 by Toby A. A. Heaps and Paul Fengler.

As is outlined on its website, "Corporate Knights Inc. (CK) has a media division which includes the award-winning business and society magazine Corporate Knights, and a research division which produces corporate rankings, research reports and financial product ratings based on corporate sustainability performance. Its best-known rankings include the Best 50 Corporate Citizens in Canada and the Global 100 Most Sustainable Corporations." Such rankings would be redundant were it not for clear distinctions between brands' proximity to different moral, environmental, social, and political positions. Acknowledging moral and political disunity as being a defining feature of market activity aids understanding of how brands establish themselves in ways that align with their audience and contrast with their competitors. I therefore scrutinize some of the many power dynamics (e.g., between different brands, between brands and consumers, between race and capitalism) that propel brands' moral impositions—expectations that brands declare and demonstrate certain moral positions and aligned sociopolitical views. The imposition of different perspectives of morality in the marketplace (e.g., regarding racism, political unrest, violent wars, and reproductive rights) contributes to how brands establish their distinct identity and attempt to adapt and/or protect it. Furthermore, I contend that as well as facing pressures to espouse certain moral positions, brands themselves can also foster such pressures (e.g., as "tastemakers" in the spheres of CSI and CSR work). The concept of brands' moral impositions that I propose may help to move the focus away from terms such as *brand stance* and *brand purpose*, which have often foregrounded the agency of brands in ways that muddy the structural forces and power struggles that can compel them to articulate their so-called stance and/or purpose. Expanding on extant research in *The Conquest of Cool: Business Culture, Counterculture, and the Rise of Hip Consumerism* (Frank 1998), my work attempts to make sense of the contemporary ways that brands are negotiating matters of morality while trying to project an image that frames them as one of the "good (aka cool)" brands.

It is useful to again turn to the words of Aaron, who when interviewed offered a detailed description of what the notion of brand purpose can encompass, and why the term itself is often relatively redundant:

> Brand purpose is like one of those weird, horrible business terms, where you often see it as a sentence which is very difficult, because how do you distil anything down into a single sentence, not least the way that a hugely complex business runs and operates in a hugely complex world. It's kind of meant to be that North Star isn't it, of using all the business nonsense words at the minute. . . . My eyes kind of glaze over and this may be just a cynical, journalistic thing, whenever I see brand purpose statements, or anything like that, because you just know they've been workshopped seven ways to whatever. . . . I don't see how a brand can have a purpose.

Aaron's skeptical view seems to resonate with what Mark Ritson (2022) states on the topic of brand purpose for *Marketing Week*: "Marketers, it would appear, are now looking at the grey skies above and acknowledging they might have drunk a little too much from the (100% recycled) bottle of purpose Kool-Aid." As Aaron emphasized during his interview, businesses are run in complex ways that seldom involve the sense of cohesion and unity that they publicly claim to uphold, and businesses' efforts to profess their supposed purpose is sometimes responded to with much criticism:

> A brand can't, in my mind, have a purpose. Because a brand is the 500,000 people that work for it around the world, and so how do you possibly herd all those chickens into one cohesive purposeful statement that is usually a sentence long and doesn't usually have many words that aren't just marketing nonsense in them. I see them all the time and you think, is that really your purpose, is every single employee rowing in that same direction, are they all behind that, or do they disagree, and at what point does it become not purposeful? What proportion of your employees have to non-agree with your brand purpose for it to actually be completely negated, and how strongly do they have to feel against it? Can they just be very indifferent to it, and it still stands?

In agreement with Aaron's take on the shortcomings of the notion of brand purpose, my hope is that the notion of brands' moral impositions can aid critical analysis of brands and morality in the marketplace, but without framing brands via an ineffective binary lens of all powerful or powerless and without simply supplying brands with another term that benefits them.

Some brands choose to take a moral position or stance on a sociopolitical matter in a flippant or noncommittal way. When doing so, brands may make claims and decisions that involve what I regard as being *disposable duties*, which are part of (in)actions that amount to what I refer to as *single-use social justice*. Such terms can connote a lack of care, which certainly is evidenced by the track record of many brands. But my use of the terms disposable duties and single-use social justice is also meant to encompass the short-term nature of duties that brands briefly feel bound to fulfill (e.g., being expected to swiftly speak in support of, or to condemn, social and political movements and moral matters following a related high-profile incident and news coverage of it). It is often the pressure to say or do something right now that brands appear keen to dispose of, by making stand-alone statements or one-time offerings such as a publicized donation.

Throwaway words on social media and impulsive industry roundtables/Q&As may be interpreted as being part of brands' disposable duties—how they attempt to shake off the pressure to say and do something, but without saying or doing something of substance that might shift the racial capitalist status quo. Inspired by the work of Sarah Banet-Weiser (2018) on the economy of visibility, I understand brand responses to moral impositions as being based on the valorization of visibility, which compels brands to focus on being seen to say something. It is also important to understand that brand statements about choosing not to comment on an issue or choosing to disengage from different public platforms complicates these matters, as such statements are situated somewhere between speaking up and staying silent. Focusing on the example of Lush turning away from social media in 2021, I now reflect on when brands pursue forms of disengagement as part of their strategic management of moral impositions, before I then go on to discuss the notion of the softening of social justice in the marketplace.

DISENGAGEMENT AS STRATEGY AND SOFTENING SOCIAL JUSTICE

In autumn 2021 Lush—an international cosmetics retailer that originated in Britain—issued a statement about why it was becoming "anti-social." The statement's simultaneously informal yet potentially sincere tone is evident in sentences such as the following, which suggest that Lush was particularly trying to connect to young people through its decision to log off: "Like so many teenagers have experienced before us, Lush has tried to come off social media, but our FOMO [fear of missing out] was vast, and our compulsion to use the various platforms meant we found ourselves back on there, despite our best intentions."

Lush's decision about social media may have been an effort to distance itself from the culture of online surveillance (e.g., ways of watching you) and harm that other brands are associated with. The statement is sprinkled with gestures to Lush's stance on a range of different issues, such as its pro-vegan position (e.g., "So here we are again, trying to go cold [plant-based] turkey") and its support of people who speak out against various issues of injustice and corruption (e.g., "This time, our resolve is strengthened by all the latest information from courageous whistleblowers"). Via Lush's online statement about why it is not going to be saying much on social media anymore, it ends up saying a lot.

Before stating that "from 26th November 2021 we will be signing out from Facebook, Instagram, Snapchat, Whatsapp and Tik-Tok, until these platforms can provide a safer environment for their users" (Lush 2021), the brand refers to a range of reasons why it will be moving away from social media. These include the following: "bullying, fake news, extremist viewpoints, FOMO, phantom vibrations, manipulative algorithms; an endlessly scrolling stream, leading, we are told, to massively increasing rates of youth suicides, depression, anxiety." The penultimate part of Lush's statement on "becoming anti-social" seems to poke fun at the influencer practice of asking people to "please like, follow, subscribe": "Lush promises not to be completely anti-social. We will do all we can to find new ways to connect, to build better channels of communication elsewhere, as well as using the older tried and tested routes. For now we can still be found on YouTube daily—no need to Click Like, Subscribe or Get Notifications, people can just pop along to check us out when they fancy." The casualness of that part of its statement, paired with the implicit dismissal of influencer culture practices, reflects an approach to online influencing known as "de-influencing." As prior marketing scholarship has explained, "Rather than representing the demise of influencers, de-influencing is an opportunity for them to reassert their original 'guru' role and gain trust through transparency and authenticity. It is a strategy used to protect their influencer role—and future income" (Mardon, Cocker, and Daunt 2023). In the world of influencer culture, de-influencing practices include the posting of negative reviews about products to regain the trust of followers (Mardon et al. 2023), but in the wider world of branding, arguably, de-influencing approaches can include positioning a brand as uninterested in social media and the interconnected commercial and predatory logic that often underpins it.

Unsurprisingly, Lush's decision to disengage from aspects of social media, and to announce this, resulted in a hive of media coverage, which included articles that ask the question, "Lush is quitting social media. The start of a trend?" (Webb 2021). I agree that "the Global Anti-Social Media Policy is a grand title for a high-stakes marketing decision by British cosmetics brand Lush" (Webb 2021)—a business that has faced a litany of publicly documented claims about its allegedly cultish and unfair workplace culture (Kilikita 2021). As the following survey responses indicate, Lush can divide opinion, with some people holding it in high regard and others viewing it as a problem that needs to be addressed:

> [I dislike] companies that suddenly find a new interest and care for trending causes, when they never cared before, eg Lush, M&S. I assume just jumping on a bandwagon for financial reasons.
> —English woman, UK (56–65 years old)

> I would say that Lush, the cosmetics company, is currently my favourite brand. I feel that as a large retailer, they seem genuinely interested in making environmentally conscious decisions (e.g. their biodegradable packaging) and their attempts to take a stance against the use of social media by deleting their platforms. Their products are

not permanent and therefore I do not feel that I am simply purchasing "clutter" when buying from them.

—white Scottish man, UK (26–35 years old)

LUSH created a campaign over covert police officers that lead a "double life," however, the campaign was misinformed and targeted all officers rather than the ones that did this which contributed to the public distrust in the police.

—white British man, UK (18–25 years old)

The comments of someone else whom I interviewed offer another opinion of the company, which is particularly relevant to Lush's decision to become "anti-social." Alessandro, who had worked in the retail sector for nearly a decade in the UK, referred to Lush when sharing his thoughts on dynamics between branding and activism:

The thing about Lush is that, in some regards, they're very much, "activists," in the sense that they do a lot of in-store fundraising, and they're very vocal about being against animal testing and such . . . on the other hand, they're not really pushing the boundary that much. Like it's "activism" to a point. It's kind of like . . . to use the term "bedroom producer," a person in a bedroom being able to make music, there's also a "bedroom activist," and that idea that, "oh, yes, I'm protesting all the time," or whatever. But it's like, all you're doing is you're liking some posts online, but you're not doing anything beyond that. I think there are some brands that maybe push beyond that, but for main, it's [brand activism] a zeitgeist thing. It's like whatever is really taking the online sphere, or even the physical sphere, by storm— brands will latch on to that and be like #BlackLivesMatter and whatever. And it's like, where was that before?

Lush's decision to announce that it was becoming "anti-social" in 2021 may exemplify when no marketing is marketing, in a similar vein to the no logo branding approaches of the early 2000s (Heath and Potter 2006; Klein 2000). Lush's decision may also be perceived as a strategic response to growing consumer cynicism in relation to what brands say and do online. Its statement about ostensibly planning to say less online resulted in Lush being amplified in the press at that time and ultimately platformed the business in a way that tends to be the end goal of marketing and branding activities. Maybe Lush's "anti-social" decision was made as part of efforts to distance it from influencer culture and the assumed harm and vapidness that it is sometimes associated with. Maybe Lush simply wanted to say something, anything, while businesses were fighting to stay relevant at a time when many were being shuttered due to the economic effects of the COVID-19 pandemic. Whatever the reasons for Lush becoming "anti-social," the impacts of its decision include its gaining more visibility and praise, which highlights the potentially positive outcome of brand decisions to disengage (even temporarily) from aspects of social media and digital culture. The competitive nature of the marketplace is such that brands are constantly jostling for attention, so establishing images of themselves as "changemakers," or perceived "culture jammers" (Heath and Potter 2006, 3), is one way that brands try to stand out from the crowd.

Prior writing, including the work of David Hieatt (2014), co-founder of Hiut Denim Co. and The Do Lectures, has focused on how founders and their companies can compel societal change. Contrastingly, I consider who and what compels founders and their companies to pursue change or to pursue an image as a changemaker. I contend that what is typically termed brand purpose and brand stance is the by-product of moral impositions that impact the attitudes, aesthetics, and at times the actions, of brands. Hieatt (2014, 7) states that "for me, the most important brands in the world make you feel something. They do that because they have something they want to change. And as customers, we want to be part of that Change. These companies feel human. The founders tell us how the world could be." I argue that the world and its parts—people, places, processes, and politics—tell brands how they could and should be, but that does not mean that brands always listen. Mindful of this, I now turn to the pseudonymous words of Inaya—a business professional whom I interviewed and who spoke at length about both the morality and neutrality of brands in the financial services sector.

Inaya was born and brought up in the UK to first-generation Pakistani immigrant parents and has worked in financial services for close to a decade. Previously Inaya had done "a few stints in terms of work experience in the public sector and sort of party politics." In her current role, Inaya focused on business development and sales and relationship management. When I interviewed Inaya, one of the key themes that arose during our conversation was the concept of the "moral position" of companies and the (dis)connection between "commercial imperatives," ethics, and morality. Inaya said: "Brands of the future are going to be connecting those three things [activism, social justice, and marketing] along with anything else that they do. Consumers will vote more quickly with their feet." Expanding on her forecasting about the future of branding, Inaya added:

> So, they [consumers] used to vote with their feet anyway, but actually, given how quick digital culture is now, they'll be voting more quickly with their feet. So, they'll be, I guess, leaving brands, going to other brands and so on. Brands can now be built up very quickly, and so there will be a fast-moving pace to all of this. I think that future generations, the next generations, are going to be asking more of businesses around what their practices are in social justice spaces, activist spaces and so on, and I think the companies that don't get onboard with that more quickly are going to be left behind. The ones that will be winning, regardless of what their product is, will be the ones that can demonstrate real activity in that space with meaningful impact.

Inaya shared observations about how financial services brands are attempting to appeal to individuals who are interested in environmental and social issues, but without such brands being forced to take an actual stance on those matters themselves. Such detailed reflections unpack some of the ways that matters of morality are caught up with what companies perceive as being "commercial imperatives" or, as Inaya also put it, a "financial material position":

We've got long-term investments and members are asking, and
younger demographics are asking, where's our money invested and
why is it invested in certain funds? And more and more people are
doing that, so much so that our default investment solutions—essentially where members are invested by default without them having to
choose—is an ESG [environmental, social and governance] default.
And we're not taking a sort of moral position on that, it's not an ethical position that's been taken on that, they've been very clear this is
the financial material position that we're taking on it.

Inaya's words point to the entangled nature of moral and financial
positions in the marketplace, including in sectors such as finance,
where due to an explicit focus on the maximization of profit, tensions between morality and commerce may be most pronounced.

What Inaya shared illuminates the reality that financial services
brands have been observing increased consumer interest in the social
and environmental implications of their investments. However, as
Inaya emphasized, the decisions that financial services brands make
in response to this are decisions rooted in the management of their
reputation and the preservation and pursuit of profit, rather than
being decisions that are intended to convey a specific moral stance.
Thus, although Inaya's employer had to navigate various moral
impositions, such as the concerns of consumers who are seeking
supposedly "ethical" investments, the financial services brand was
not compelled to declare a moral stance itself. The reasons for this
include the perceived value of alleged social and political neutrality
and impartiality, which is a relative norm in this sector and is consistent with how "organizational theory scholars typically see organizations as race-neutral bureaucratic structures," despite the reality
that "organizations are not race neutral" (Ray 2019, 26). Expanding
on the topic of "ethical" investments, Inaya said:

We are doing things right now, and investing in things right now, that
we need to be sure of will not incur regulatory, legal, or reputational
damage 10/15/20 years down the line. That means we can't be

investing in clinical or biological weapons, we can't be investing in fracking. We can't be investing in industries where you've seen structural increases in consumer awareness and structural falls in consumer spending, so things like the tobacco industry you just can't be investing in that. It's not an ethical or a moral position, it's literally a commercial imperative that you have to do that to remove the financial material risk. So, if that's happening in this space, I'm guessing every business, every brand, will be thinking about that from their own perspectives, around what is going to remove that financial material risk. So, it's becoming less of a fashion and it's becoming more of a commercial imperative.

Again, what Inaya said signals that societal concerns related to ethical and moral issues sometimes steer changes to the ways that commercial imperatives are understood and embraced by brands.

Inaya made clear that financial services businesses are expanding their ESG investment portfolios to remain commercially viable, rather than to be perceived as changemakers or as "more moral" than their competitors. On the topic of ethics and the marketplace, as Littler (2008, 1) has articulated, "the specific constellation of anxieties about consumption has combined with the ever-expanding niche markets of neoliberal consumer capitalism to generate an explosion in sales of 'ethical' goods," which now include demand for ESG investments. No matter the number of industry efforts to frame aspects of financial investment services as socially conscious and/or ethical, the recent history of various corporate bailouts is a reminder of the continued greed and recklessness of corporations, including the reality that many corporations absolve themselves of any responsibility to society, even when receiving government (aka taxpayer) financial support during crises.

In the years since Littler's (2008) account of the expansion of what has been termed *ethical consumption*, many brands have courted a range of moral and ethical positions, but sometimes without expressing their own views on them. Returning to the words of

Inaya about the actions of her employer, she highlighted the fuzzy relationship between some moral impositions and commercial imperatives:

> Let's take [the example of] smoking and let's take the financial services industry, or the investment asset management industry. The reason why investing in the tobacco industry poses a financial material risk to investments is because of all of the great work done, all of the moral and ethical sort of judgement work done by society around the impacts of long-term health concerns of smoking and the tobacco industry. It's probably a highly pragmatic and savvy approach for the business to come in and say.... We are an institution and we're a for-profit institution, so we are not taking a moral or ethical judgement here, because maybe we don't have the right to do that, but they're still going to get the benefits of not investing in that, so that's financial material.

After a minute or so of pensive silence, during which Inaya seemed to be carefully considering the similarities and differences between moral and commercial imperatives, she confidently declared:

> Can it happen where they're both so entwined that you can't demarcate, or distinguish them? Yes, absolutely it can happen, and this sort of move to ESG investing is one of them. In my business it has become one and the same in terms of investment approach. It's not questioned, everybody agrees it is the way that it has to be, that things have to be done, and the industry agrees that's the way that things are moving.... [I]t was a commercial imperative to do it and now it's a commercial reality. It's a strategic reality of our business.

Brands such as Inaya's employer may believe that they are disengaging from taking a moral stance. However, regardless of whether they refer to the decisions that they make as being based on a moral imperative, a commercial imperative, or their management of financial material risk, how they strategize this is affected by both morality and capitalism, in ways that brands can never completely control but may still benefit from.

Relatedly, DEI strategist and consultant Lily Zheng (2020) argues that "consumers and employees are now looking for more than Corporate Social Responsibility—they're looking for what I call Corporate Social Justice." This may be true in some cases. However, as with many terms that bring together the language of business and activism, the concept of "corporate social justice" is a shaky one. Detailing the definition of corporate social justice, Zheng (2020) describes it as being "a framework regulated by the trust between a company and its employees, customers, shareholders, and the broader community it touches, with the goal of explicitly doing good by all of them." But given the different and sometimes conflicting interests of stakeholders, it may not be possible for any business to do good by all of them. Mindful of this, and of the perspectives of brand employees such as Inaya, I regard corporate social justice as a concept that may be mainly grounded in the purview of brands and does not capture tensions between the perspectives of different stakeholders, including conflicting concepts of social justice in the marketplace and potentially contradictory concepts of morality and neutrality.

Moving beyond a focus on the financial services sector, Inaya reflected on other examples of brands that have made decisions that appear to relate to issues of inequality, morality, and commerce.

> I remember there was a big thing around Tommy Hilfiger—I don't know if you remember that? Years ago, there was this total . . . there was this chat [unfounded rumor] that Tommy Hilfiger was racist and didn't want Black people to wear his clothes, and it caused a massive backlash. Now, I think he came out with a famous Black celebrity—I can't remember the name—to say I'm not racist and want people to wear my clothing, actually "it's for everyone" and so on. Now, whether he was taking an ethical or moral reason, or a judgement on that . . . he probably was but even if he wasn't, it was a commercial imperative to him. 100% a commercial imperative for him to not ostracize non-white communities, because they would potentially be the ones buying his stock, because it was being used in lots of different spaces.

Figure 4. Martin Luther King Jr. Memorial, Washington D.C., 2022. Photo by author.

Closing her comments on brands such as Tommy Hilfiger—one of the sponsors of the Martin Luther King Jr. Memorial in Washington, D.C. (having donated $6.25 million toward it) (Banks 2022; Cole 2011)—Inaya said:

We can take a moral judgement perspective on it [issues regarding racism], I know what the right thing to do is in terms of racial equality or not, but actually, what I'm trying to say is that it's gone past moral and ethical reasons now. Those people who are the commercial number crunchers are sitting there thinking, this is now a commercial imperative. Social justice will become a commercial imperative that businesses will be marked by in terms of consumers. So, whether they [businesses] believe it or not, they need to get on-board.

Other people whom I interviewed as part of this work spoke of similar issues. Sam—an advertising director—also discussed the rise of ESG concerns across businesses. Sam is a white man who lives in North America but previously worked in Europe and described himself as being "an advertising and media specialist, I guess. I have worked across media agencies and companies that buy ad inventory on behalf of clients, so, for example, TV spots, social media spots, whatever it is, and kind of come up with the right strategies to reach their target consumers on those given platforms, in a way which makes sense for their business and their business goals." Sam, who had been working in advertising communications for over a decade, had experience of being drawn into the DEI work of a wide range of brands. Thus, he shared many examples of how brands are "trying to get it right" when it comes to responding to issues of injustice and inequality, but Sam also indicated that many brands rarely want to "do the work":

DEI is something that became a conversation in lots of agencies, in lots of brands, and I'd say, in my experience, that was happening a lot in the late 2010s, so to speak, and obviously a really big focus on that in the last couple of years, with antiracism because of George Floyd and everything that happened there. What I've noticed are two things of note, which is conversations around social justice movements have kind of morphed into this broader conversation of less specificity and less kind of radical politics. . . . [I]t's all about diversity, equity and inclusion, so it's all around our people, our culture, who works in organizations, and all of that sort of fun stuff. And that's become focused on women and sometimes not even through an intersectional lens, focused on LGBTQ, but, again, maybe not through an intersectional lens.

When reflecting on what Sam said during his interview, I was reminded of episode 7 ("Talking Points") of the now canceled Netflix legal drama *Partner Track*, which I discuss in more detail in chapter 3. Based on the 2013 novel by Helen Wan, the television series *Partner Track* premiered on August 26, 2022, offering ten episodes of lighthearted plots and a dose of commentary on the politics and corporate culture of the legal profession in the US. Focusing on Ingrid Yun's (played by Arden Cho) pursuit of a position as partner at an illustrious legal firm (Parsons), *Partner Track* is punctuated by numerous moments that gesture to issues of inequality, including the intersecting nature of the impacts of racism and sexism, as outlined in foundational critical legal studies on intersectionality (Crenshaw 1989, 1991). A memorable scene in episode 7 involves Ingrid attending a tense meeting with two women who are clients, who take it in turn to proudly profess that "as a company and as people, we put intersectionality front and center"; "it's a priority that we acquire and invest in companies that are socially conscious." The words of these representatives of a fictional brand reminded me of Sam's comments and his concerns about intersectionality and corporate culture, such as his dismay at brands that don't bother to understand intersectionality and treat it merely as an opportunity to attract various consumer demographics.

The two women who speak to Ingrid in the episode 7 scene attempt to communicate that the brand they represent understands and values intersectionality. However, their words may merely reflect the corporatization of intersectionality—a concept that was intended to capture how the intersecting nature of forms of oppression impact Black women and other women of color in ways that the legal system had not adequately acknowledged at the time that Kimberlé Crenshaw authored articles such as "Demarginalizing the Intersection of Race and Sex: A Black Feminist Critique of

Antidiscrimination Doctrine, Feminist Theory and Antiracist Politics" (1989) and "Mapping the Margins: Intersectionality, Identity Politics, and Violence against Women of Color" (1991). Therefore, the episode 7 scene may be more about the marketization of intersectionality than a commentary on how the concept is meaningfully understood by businesses.

As cultural anthropologist and documentary filmmaker Marcel Rosa-Salas and I (2022) argue, a wide range of marketplace institutions make strategic use of what we describe as being allusions to, and illusions of, intersectionality. "By allusions to intersectionality, we mean surface-level or symbolic gestures to intersectionality that do not engage with the wholeness of the concept but also do not actively misrepresent it either. By illusions of intersectionality, we mean statements and actions that completely reframe and misrepresent what intersectionality is intended to convey" (176). Our research on this focused on the actions of advertisers, marketers, and academia.[3] Yet as I examine in more detail in chapter 3, such allusions to and illusions of intersectionality are also present in pop culture depictions of corporate culture, including portrayals of characters and storylines in Freeform's comedy drama *The Bold Type* (2017–21).

Kian Bakhtiari (2022) writes in *Forbes*, "For a long time, the case for diversity and equity was centred around the business case. Most diversity, equity and inclusion (DEI) projects appealed to business leaders and shareholders' desire to increase profits. Now the conversation shifts to social justice and equal access to opportunities."

---

3. Cultural anthropologist and documentary filmmaker Marcel Rosa-Salas and I (2022, 175) have examined "how market logics propelled by gendered racial capitalism and the commercialization of identity politics impact the production of knowledge about intersectionality in the marketing discipline and industry." As part of such work on "hierarchies of knowledge about intersectionality in marketing theory and practice," we provided "a genealogy of how 'intersectionality' has been framed in marketing studies and industry approaches which reflect the entanglements of knowledge production, the politics of representation, and the marketization of social justice. Overall, we contribute to scholarly interventions regarding how intersecting oppressions influence marketing and critical analyses of it, as well as the complex interrelationship between marketing, commercial representation, and discourses of identity, inequality, and structural change" (175).

Figure 5. "I'M NOT A BOSS BITCH. I'M A BOSS, BITCH," advertisement for *The Bold Type*, New York, 2017. Photo by author.

During his interview, Sam commented on how the strategic ambiguity that can be part of industry DEI efforts is not due to a lack of awareness or understanding of social justice issues, but instead is reflective of a lack of will to meaningfully address them:

> The social justice piece has also morphed into, I forget the three letters but like ESG, like environmental sustainability, good corporate citizens contributing to society. Maybe it's just my experience, and where I work, but it's all kind of softened a little bit, become more palatable, more generic, wider and less specific, all kind of, in my opinion, to make it easier for organizations to achieve. Yes, I'd say the

industry has caught up to how bad its reputation is, how bad the reputation of marketing and advertising is when it comes to things like purpose and social justice, kind of that critique that it's all just marketing, all just fake, and I think industry has caught up to that and is actually trying to challenge that.

Although he was unsure of the extent to which changes have been made in the industry, Sam remarked:

I'm sure there are good initiatives happening in lots of places, but has there, in my experience, been 'systemic change' or transformation? No. For me, the biggest enabler of how a brand does or doesn't engage on social justice is who its target audience is, what its existing customer base is, and also what that kind of growth customer base is. For example, retailers and beauty brands, companies which might have a little bit of a younger target audience, a younger customer base, where their growth customer base might be younger consumers, in my experience they tend to embrace social justice movements, DEI, a lot more than other companies, which have a more diverse or an all adult consumer base.

Sam's perspective is consistent with much research on generational differences between the expectations of consumers and the fact that "for some advertising agencies, intersectionality is defined as a heuristic for conceptualizing the identities of the coveted Generation Z youth demographic" (Rosa-Salas and Sobande 2022, 180). That said, Sam's remarks about DEI work sometimes being embraced (and not just criticized) by younger generations highlights that some DEI approaches to marketing and advertising may appeal to generations that are often assumed to be critical of them or to call for more evidence of so-called social justice commitments.

Going into more detail about the ways that brands appear to speak out about social injustices without doing anything of substance to aid efforts to address them, Sam said: "I worked for a large retailer and, following the murder of George Floyd, they decided they were going to post content about it, etc. . . . . [W]hat's the purpose of them posting content, what are they doing beyond posting randomly a couple of pieces of content?" After sighing with frustration over the decisions made by the brand client, Sam said:

> Obviously, they wanted to make sure they were not seeming to ignore the issue, but here's the reality, businesses are always going to be very limited, in my opinion, to make truly big differences to society, but one of the things they can do is they can give money, just give cash to causes. Sure, it's not perfect but, more often than not, that's the closest they can do to making a big cause. But, yeah . . . they posted a couple of pieces of content, there was a bit of a backlash, as ever . . . and, ultimately, they gave some money. That, in my experience, is the classic piece for brands, that they speak a lot, internally at least and with partners, about how much they care about social justice, but . . . in my experience, that social justice has been softened to DEI over the last couple of years.

As Inaya's and Sam's perspectives suggest, across business sectors, brands are framing corporate DEI strategies through the lens and language of social justice. In doing so, such brands might be seeking to reframe market-oriented efforts as being much more socially conscious and impactful than they are. This is symptomatic of the ways that marketplace institutions scoop up terms and ideas with origins in grassroots organizing to engender an image of brands and the marketplace as relatable and more moral—or attuned to changing moral impositions—than is often assumed. In other cases, such as in the financial services sector, brands are grasping for means to maintain an image of sociopolitical neutrality, while watching how societal opinions about various issues shift and impact their business strategy. Mindful of these different and tense ways that brands are shaped by, and seeking to shape, matters of morality, I critically reflect on UK and US nation-branding practices, the histories that have spawned them, and the ways that the British monarchy and celebrity culture are connected to this.

NATION-BRANDING, THE MONARCHY, AND CELEBRITY

The branding of nations (also referred to as nation-branding) has been relevant to critical analysis of marketing and advertising for decades. Such branding practices reflect "the common pressures and possibilities of a globalized and competitive world," including nations' "apparent desire to be recognized and valued in this world under the sign of the brand" (Aronczyk 2013, 3). While conceptualizations of nation-branding have often focused on the actions and strategies of national organizations and institutions, the concept of nation-branding can also be inclusive of the self-branding narratives of individuals—such as how they draw on, or actively push against, the myth and symbolism of nations when platforming themselves. Then again, as Dinnie (2008, 14) points out, "Before looking in detail at the concept of treating a nation as a brand, it is worthwhile to look at some definitions of what is meant by a 'brand'. Such definitions tend to fall into two camps. On the one hand are definitions that focus upon the visual manifestation of a brand. On the other hand, there are deeper definitions that go beyond the visual aspects of a brand and attempt to capture the essence of a brand."

It is an understanding of brands that accounts for but goes beyond the visual that guides my book. Specifically, as this chapter deals with, the component parts of brands include various social and political dimensions that despite being discernible in elements of visual branding do not always take visual, tangible, or public forms.

The word *politics* often connotes the governance of countries and different geocultural connections to political positions. However, politics encompasses a lot more than that, including different strategies and actions intended to bolster the power of certain individuals, groups, and institutions. Thus, the political underpinnings of advertising and brand practices include strategic decisions that are ostensibly made to manage economic and reputational risk but are also informed by contemporary sociopolitical matters, such as the rise in consumers' concern about the ethics of their financial investments.

Although politics and marketing are commonly treated as separate academic disciplines and areas of work, their interconnectedness affects society in many significant ways—from policymaking and consumer trendsetting to the framing of the cost-of-living crisis and the construction of cultural norms. As well as being impacted by types of media and the travel of technological developments, the politics of marketing is influenced by the norms of countries and their histories. This means that critical analysis of marketing can reveal much about the norms and societal narratives that define nations.

Approached from the point of view that politics and marketing are interdependent, I explore elements of nation-branding and nationalistic marketing messages in the UK and the US. This involves examining how such activity unfolds in ways that relate to what scholars Roopali Mukherjee and Sarah Banet-Weiser (2012, 2) refer to as "'commodity activism' in the neoliberal moment, a moment in which realms of culture and society once considered 'outside' the official economy are harnessed, reshaped, and made legible in economic terms." Focusing on the UK and the US in comparative and dialogic ways can yield insights into the complexities of Anglo-American nation-branding activities involving branding practices that are at times mutually beneficial to nations. Acknowledging the benefit of analyzing branding activities in both the UK and the US is not the same as suggesting that these nations are entirely unified in their approach to advertising, politics, and the marketplace.

Furthermore, it is important to account for the fact that as well as being strategically positioned as allies, the UK and the US are sometimes framed as antithetical in ways that promote an exceptional image of one nation at the expense of the other (e.g., unfounded claims that the UK is "less racist" than the US). Thus, my decision to pair analysis of marketing and branding activity in the UK with analysis of marketing and branding activity in the US is built upon an understanding of the differences and similarities between these nations, including the friendship and friction that is part of their past and present. Before discussing contemporary nation-branding examples, it is important to make sense of how the history of advertising has informed present-day branding practices. By *history of advertising* I mean crucial elements of the politics of advertising in the UK and the US in previous decades (1940s–2010s), including how the UK has been advertised in the US and vice versa. Part of the way that I critically consider these matters is by reflecting on the concept and conventions of nation-branding, including "the branding, or rebranding, of Britain in the late 1990s" (Dinnie 2008, 30) and the preceding decades.

In a pivotal account, *Branding the Nation*, Aronczyk (2013, 3) asserts that "using the tools, techniques, and expertise of commercial branding is seen as a way to help a nation articulate a more coherent and cohesive national identity to animate the spirit of its citizens in the service of national priorities, and to maintain loyalty to the territory within its borders." In a similar vein, and by drawing on discourse that surrounds national imaginaries (Hesse 2000), individuals sometimes brand themselves in ways that strategically speak to the iconicity and idiosyncrasies of certain nations and the institutions that they are known for. When analyzing material from the David Ogilvy Collection at the Library of Congress Main Reading Room in Washington, D.C., I encountered numerous exchanges and archived notes that exemplify individualized expressions of nation-branding, national imaginaries, or what might be considered nationalistic forms of self-branding, and which existed long before the age of social media.

The assortment of archived notes that I perused included comments that allude to the capital and currency of Englishness, Scottishness, and Americanness, such as biographies, job recommendations, relationship-building letters, and correspondence that critiqued and contested the use of various words and visuals that might offend nations in the decades during which British advertising icon David Ogilvy's work reigned supreme. A case in point is that when writing about advertising proofs and tearsheets in a November 1959 letter, Ogilvy remarked, "The phrase 'speak American' in the first paragraph may arouse some criticism in London. It would annoy any decent Englishman, but the advert was not addressed to Englishman." Ogilvy's brief comment is just one of many examples of how different cultural norms and concerns about diplomacy and global relations shape the details of advertising, including how the US advertises in the UK and vice versa.

In the 1950s, Big Brands were not able to use social media to watch people and learn about their tastes, preferences, and cultural sensibilities, so individuals such as Ogilvy became their eyes and ears—observing and reporting on social norms and their shifts. Additional evidence of the relationship between advertising, branding, national identities, and national imaginaries can be found in David Ogilvy's ([1963] 2004) autobiography, *Confessions of an Advertising Man*. Even the opening lines of the book signify how assumptions about places and the people from them are part of the conventions of the Anglo-American advertising industry. As Ogilvy notes, "Fourteen years before writing the Confessions, I had gone to New York and started an advertising agency. Americans thought I was crazy. What could a Scotsman know about advertising?" (15). As it would turn out, a lot.

During a humid June morning in 2022, while watching the world react to the overturning of *Roe v. Wade*, I analyzed an assortment of writing at the Library of Congress. I observed how advertisers of the past signaled their national and cultural knowledge when interacting with each other and discussing matters such as "Operation Britain" and the year of "Come to America." Numerous examples of how advertisers have attempted to market the UK in the US, and the US in the UK, include the following suggestions by Ogilvy in a letter dated May 11, 1959. Regarding an upcoming advertising exhibition at the time, Ogilvy wrote: "I would prefer a straightforward, hard-working stand devoted to the theme, 'American Industry Locating New Factories in Scotland'. You would show photographs or preferably movies of the most famous U.S. factories. An articulate spokesman, dressed in a kilt, would be on hand to buttonhole prospects and give them sales literature." The marketable value of kilts, Scottish whisky, and the classed notion of an "articulate [Scottish] spokesman" was also alluded to in other correspondence documented in papers that I looked at in D.C.—demonstrating nascent forms of nation-branding. Additionally, the material about Ogilvy that I studied included evidence of the relationship between depictions of the British monarchy and the British nation-brand (e.g., discussions about a request for the Duke of Edinburgh to appear on television).

In a different letter, dated January 28, 1959, Ogilvy offered a plethora of phrases that could help to promote Britain: "1. Britain Invites You!," "2. The British Are Back!," "3. Here Come the British!," "4. British Fortnight at the Colosseum," and "5. Festival of Britain." Elsewhere in the archived collection is evidence of discussions about Ogilvy's idea to broadcast a program on life in Britain on TV in America, which it was proposed could feature "BBC news footage of great occasions, e.g. Trooping the Colour, the Edinburgh Tattoo." In a separate letter dated December 3, 1958, before signing it off, Ogilvy remarked on the possibility of such broadcasts being something that "would project a valid image of Britain, without undue emphasis on the past. They would stimulate the purchase of British products. They would give Anglo-American relations a most lovely shot in the arm." In sum, the Ogilvy Collection that I studied at the Library of Congress is a cornucopia of correspondence that captures iterations of nation-branding long before more recent examples such as the London 2012 Olympics, which also involved much pronounced marketing of specific regions of the UK.

In the decades since Ogilvy's correspondence, British politics and public life have changed considerably and now "are distinctly shaped by digital spheres. These include online content creation that enables the expression of political and social issues in dialogic and powerful ways, challenging the dominance of discussions led by traditional news outlets and gatekeepers" (Sobande 2019c, 152). Then again, mainstream media such as the BBC still have a significant amount of power, which contributes to forms of nation-branding and political marketing—including through coverage of national celebrations and public mourning related to the British monarchy.

By the 2000s marketing had been "adopted not just by political parties, but by every organisation within the non-profit, political, public or governmental sphere" (Lees-Marshment 2004, 1). The politics of marketing includes marketing activities that are associ-ated with the British monarchy (aka the royal family), which, as Lees-Marshment (2004, 3) notes, "has also succumbed to market forces." Examples of the marketing of the monarchy include the fact that "responding to the nature and demands of its market, the mon-archy designed a popular product: the palace pop party during the 2002 jubilee" (3). It is now more than two decades later, and the monarchy's use of marketing and branding practices has morphed in ways influenced by the uptake of social media and digital mar-keting processes (Clancy 2021; Otnes and Maclaran 2015). These changes culminated in the marketing of the platinum jubilee cel-ebrations in 2022.

These royalist celebrations took place two years after the COVID-19 crisis first surfaced and thus occurred during the ever-present after-math of the disastrous effects of a global pandemic that appeared to exacerbate many existing inequalities. Perhaps those who were involved in planning the platinum jubilee celebrations sincerely believed that what the British people needed during such dark times was a party in support of the queen. However, those costly celebra-tory activities coincided with a cost-of-living crisis (aka ongoing capitalism) that is continuing to run rampant and will no doubt, result in more deaths. In 2022, while activities laced with luxury and excess were being meticulously planned and then executed in aid of the platinum jubilee, many people were (still) turning to food banks and were forced to choose between staying warm or staying fed because of the poverty that they faced. Regardless of the grim realities and social injustices that many people were (and are) experiencing, the platinum jubilee was marked and marketed in myriad ways that involved the creation of media and digital content that confidently conveyed a whimsical yet dutiful tone. What better way to consider connections between consumer culture, the British monarchy, nation-branding, and social (in)justices than to focus on the framing of a jubilee celebration that had consumption at its core?

Perhaps shaped by the global success of television programs such as *The Great British Bake Off*—which some have claimed offers "a window on the nation's soul" (Perkins 2017)—a national pudding competition was chosen to be part of high-profile activities that were part of the UK's celebration of the platinum jubilee. Writing for the *Guardian* about the success of *The Great British Bake Off*, which long predates the platinum jubilee pudding competition, Joanna Moorhead (2021) states:

> Bake Off's success is perhaps the best modern example of the UK's soft power, the nation's ability to create a positive impression abroad. The licensing process ensures each edition is true to the show's original style: when companies abroad pitch for the franchise, they're given the "Bake Off Bible", and any change to the format has to be agreed with Love Productions.
>
> It explains, too, why for some Bake Off has the cloying scent of "soft empire" about it: all that twee Britishness, with a set modelled on a tented village fete: and it's either exported directly, in its UK version, or slightly adapted to fit a different country and culture.

When witnessing the whirlwind of media and press activity related to the platinum jubilee pudding competition, I found myself rereading Moorhead's (2021) take on *Bake Off*. I noticed parallels between the soft power that the TV show is imbued with and the unabashed patriotism and orchestrated image of the nation that propelled the platinum jubilee celebrations. Building on my recent writing on mediated depictions and discourses of food, particularly baking (Sobande 2022a, forthcoming), I began to examine the significance of how the platinum jubilee pudding competition was being framed and consumed. Previously I have considered "what the rise (pun intended!) of banana bread and its online documentation during the crisis suggests about elements of the racial, gender, and class politics of notions and experiences of productivity and rest" (Sobande 2022a). But here I consider connections between baking, consumer culture, and the construction of Britain's nation-brand, including via the marketing of its monarchy.

Before continuing with this analysis, it is worth clarifying that I agree with sociologist Laura Clancy's (2021, 29) understanding of "the monarchy as a corporation to distinguish from existing work that considers monarchy as brand." As Clancy asserts, brands operate externally and involve a focus on public-facing messages. While the British monarchy makes use of branding practices and marketing strategies to maintain certain types of public visibility, as the detailed work of Clancy (2021, 30) makes clear, "to understand the monarchy's material practices, we must consider its complex historical, economic, political, social and cultural infrastructures, infrastructures often rendered invisible behind royal spectacle." Given that my book focuses on Big Brands, it is that royal spectacle that I examine here, while accounting for the complexities of what Clancy discusses, including differences between the branding practices of the monarchy and its overall construction and control as an institution.

Media coverage of the platinum jubilee pudding competition in 2022 included a one-hour celebratory special on the BBC, *The Jubilee Pudding: 70 Years in the Baking?* The TV special documented elements of the competition to find a winning pudding, which the British public would then be encouraged to make as part of platinum jubilee celebrations of their own. On its iPlayer website, the BBC (2022b) describes the celebratory special as follows: "Five exceptional home bakers create an extraordinary pudding fit for the Queen in a national competition, hoping to be crowned winner of the jubilee pudding, and go down in history." A tweet by BBC Food

(2022) reiterates this messaging, infused with references to royalty and the dutifulness that citizens are expected to express: "ALL HAIL THE WINNING PUDDING! Outcompeting 5,000 competition entries, this regal delight will go down in history as the OFFICIAL Queen's Platinum Jubilee pudding. We can't wait to see this being made around the country over the Jubilee weekend!"

The platinum jubilee pudding competition was publicized in many ways, including via online and playful content, such as with the use of the following copy, which was featured on the UK government's official platinum jubilee website (previously available at www.platinumjubilee.gov.uk): "Steamed or baked? Layered or rolled? Pie or crumble? The British pudding comes in all shapes and sizes and now the #PlatinumPudding competition was launched in 2021 to find a dessert dedicated to Her Majesty The Queen." As well as featuring these words, the UK government's official platinum jubilee website included calls to action, such as "Join the Platinum Jubilee story on social media using #HM70 AND #PlatinumJubilee." That statement is a reminder that Big Brands—including nation-brands—are watching you (watching them). More than that, such copy about the jubilee may be interpreted as signaling the expectation that (good) British citizens should publicly praise the monarchy, and as became apparent following the queen's death in September 2022, should publicly mourn monarchs, too.

At a time when there were numerous public calls for more meaningful and national forms of memorializing in response to the COVID-19 crisis, the death of Queen Elizabeth II became the focus of many brands, including national media. In the immediate aftermath of the queen's death, countless brands issued online statements, created new signage, and found other ways to mark a period of perceived national mourning for the monarch. Witnessing brands—commercial and otherwise—declaring their condolences and quickly offering up products to memorialize the queen, I reflected on the marketing of mourning and the commodification of grief. To be clear, I was thinking critically about the significance of brands communicating statements about mourning a monarch (and encouraging others to express such sentiments), having ignored public calls for more recognition of the magnitude of mourning and grief that people were (and are) dealing with during the COVID-19 crisis. While it is beyond my book's scope, future work on the power and politics of the marketing of mourning may result in insights related to who and what brands deem worthy of mourning and what this suggests about societal issues of inequality, injustice, and morality in the marketplace.

Unlike the somber tone of brand responses to the death of Queen Elizabeth II, platinum jubilee promotional content often featured a more casual tone. Content included social media posts that called for people to respond with their own content about the occasion, which is also indicative of how the monarchy has become "subject to citizen opinion" (Lees-Marshment 2004, 5) and a consumer trend of "Royal Fever" (Otnes and Maclaran 2015). Additional examples of how the world of the monarchy rubs up against that of consumer and popular culture includes the successful Netflix historical drama series *The Crown*, featuring actors portraying members of the royal family. The ongoing series, which has a fandom that spans many countries, is further evidence of how the UK's nation-brand and its component parts (e.g., British royalty) are marketed to a global audience with the use of digital culture (e.g., streaming services) (Clancy 2021). Since the days of Ogilvy and other advertising professionals pontificating about whether members of the British monarchy might deign to appear on TV, a lot has changed, and not only in terms of how technology has developed.

The platinum jubilee celebrations occurred little more than a year after the Duchess of Sussex—a "biracial" American woman named Meghan Markle—famously sat down with iconic media personality Oprah Winfrey to publicly discuss her ostracization by the British monarchy. The much meme-ified conversation involved Meghan Markle sharing anecdotes about an unnamed member of the royal family who speculated about the physical features and skin color of her child Archie before he was born. The Oprah interview took place after the media spectacle that surrounded the decision by the Duke and Duchess of Sussex (Prince Harry and Meghan Markle) to relocate to the US, due to the scrutiny that the couple faced both by and beyond the monarchy. The discussion between Meghan Markle and Oprah Winfrey and its viral circulation online symbolize some shifts with regard to power dynamics between the British monarchy, mainstream media, popular culture, and, I argue, aspects of nation-branding.

During the televised Oprah interview, with each word that Markle publicly shared about her negative reception by some of the royal family and extreme harassment by the British press came a deluge of social media responses that the monarchy could not control or contain. Some such content positioned the US as less racist than the UK, while other content made the inverse claim. Some people took to Twitter to defend Markle, while others tweeted to convey the view that no member of the monarchy—Markle included—was defensible. This social media discourse included the creation and circulation of content I deem as being part of the phenomenon that is digital remix culture, such as memes and GIFs that "can shed light on British political and social attitudes, particularly those that previously people may have primarily, or only, shared in private" (Sobande 2019c, 154). No matter the differences between the perspectives that were expressed online in response to Markle's interview with Oprah, they all had one thing in common: their presence points to how digital culture and social media have become inextricably enmeshed with public discussion about the monarchy and consequently about the UK and its image on a global stage.

Returning to the example of the platinum jubilee pudding competition, while the competition was often framed in a light-hearted manner at the time it was underway, the promotion of it also included messages that were undoubtedly serious in tone. Such messages were made up of signs, symbols, and (sub)texts that reveal how aspects of nation-branding are interlinked with the images of a range of brands—including those of celebrities and the iconicity of the British monarchy. A prime example of this is how some promotional material related to the platinum jubilee pudding competition publicized British brands such as Fortnum & Mason, an upmarket department store located in Piccadilly, London. Fortnum & Mason's website featured a section dedicated to the platinum jubilee pudding competition, which the UK government's platinum jubilee website linked to, signposting where people could find out more about the prizewinning recipe. Statements on Fortnum & Mason's part of its website that focused on the platinum jubilee pudding competition included reference to "the famous faces on our judging panel" and repetition of the word *victorious* when describing the winning recipe for Lemon Swiss Roll and Amaretti Trifle, created by Jemma Melvin. Images that featured alongside text on Fortnum & Mason's website section on the jubilee pudding included a photograph of the competition finalists and the judging panel, with several people in the image wearing outfits that mainly consisted of one or more of the UK's Union Jack flag colors of red, white, and blue. Put simply, this online content appeared to be as much about nation-branding as it was about celebrating the platinum jubilee—not to suggest that either has ever existed independently of the other. The tone of such promotional material was a blend of whimsical (signified by the music that accompanied a video on it) and earnestly patriotic and celebratory (indicated by the semiotic power of implicit and explicit depictions of the Union Jack).

When analyzing what the marketing of the platinum jubilee pudding competition might reveal about dimensions of nation-branding, it is helpful to reflect on the different ways that the UK has been branded throughout the decades. Writing about Britain's (and more widely, the UK's) international image from the late 1990s onward, Dinnie (2008, 3) states, "'Cool Britannia' replaced 'Rule Britannia', although it is important to note that it was the media and not the government who attached the 'Cool Britannia' label to the rebranding of Britain that was attempted in the late 1990s." Dinnie (2008, 3), also describes criticism of attempts to (re)brand Britain at that time: "The rebranding of Britain campaign could be viewed as a salutary lesson for those engaged in nation-branding campaigns in the United Kingdom and elsewhere. Media reaction was almost hysterically hostile, and the campaign died before it could gain any momentum. The potential benefits of a nation-branding strategy did not appear to be communicated effectively to target audiences. There seemed to be insufficient integration of all the stakeholders in the nation-brand, and the perception arose of an exaggerated emphasis on the modern and cutting edge to the detriment of the traditional and established."

The branding activities that surrounded the platinum jubilee pudding competition may be more "Rule Britannia" than "Cool Britannia" in tone. However, and particularly due to digital culture, the promotion of the platinum jubilee pudding involved a playfulness that is perhaps demonstrative of how nation-branding efforts have increasingly drawn on the informality and interactivity associated with social media, while still pushing the message that people in Britain have a moral duty to support and celebrate the monarchy. Examples of this in action include the digital presence of several British embassies that posted emoji-peppered tweets encouraging people to share photographs of their attempts at making the winning pudding. The platinum jubilee pudding competition and its unabashed celebration of the British monarchy contrasts with nation-branding efforts that have been criticized for appearing to be unpatriotic.

Since "God Save the King/Queen" was first performed in 1975 to express UK patriotism, there have been many changes to how the British monarchy and the nation that it "rules" over are celebrated and globally positioned. Then again, as many of the messages that surrounded the platinum jubilee pudding competition suggest, when it comes to UK nation-branding, tradition often triumphs. Still, "while it does not take the shape of a formal and structured polling of people's political positions, digital remix culture can communicate, and perhaps forecast, facets of Britain's changing socio-political landscape" (Sobande 2019c, 155)—including republican calls for the dismantling of the monarchy, as expressed via social media comments, hashtags, memes, and long-form critical commentaries that surrounded the platinum jubilee.

Much has moved on since scholar Jennifer Lees-Marshment's (2004, 3) incisive assertion that developments "helped by the advance of technology, are producing more interactive media in radio and television that increase the participation of consumers" across various political and public spaces. Analysis of the role of digital remix culture in nation-branding is in its relative infancy in comparison to research regarding the use of different types of media in such efforts to brand nations. Yet if digital remix culture continues to expand at the rapid rate that it has since the turn of the twenty-first century, it will play even more of a foundational role in the future of nation-branding and critiques of nation-brands.

Digital culture contributes to influential discussions, debates, and denouncements regarding politics and the actions and attitudes of nations. Another example of this, which chapter 1 introduced, is how brands—individuals and institutions—turned to social media to share content and commentary on July 4, 2022, in the US, days after the overturning of *Roe v. Wade*. The date of July 4th (also known as American Independence Day, which obfuscates the violences of settler colonialism) is a federal holiday in the US, intended to commemorate the Declaration of Independence of 1776. Due to the date's significance regarding the history of the US, July 4th presents a prime opportunity for forms of nation-branding and is also responded to in ways that challenge US nationalism, settler colonialism, and imperialistic patriotism.

Accordingly, in 2022 I studied how brands commemorated or denounced so-called Independence Day. Informed by the work of Daniels (2021) on "nice white ladies," I paid attention to the social media posts of celebrities such as Katy Perry, Kim Kardashian, and Jessica Chastain. When examining such content on July 4th, I also turned to the scholarship of Alison Phipps (2020, 5), which defines mainstream feminism as "mostly Anglo-American public feminism. This includes media feminism (and some forms of social media feminism) or what media scholar Sarah Banet-Weiser has called 'popular feminism'".

Although July 4th is far from being associated with feminism, the date's proximity to the overturning of *Roe v. Wade* in 2022 resulted in much digital discourse that foregrounded (white) feminist perspectives on the state of the US and, by extension, its nation-brand. Some social media posts that criticized calls to celebrate July 4th are indicative of how politics, nations, branding, celebrity culture, and activism coalesce in ways that yield commentary on a national "holiday," which becomes a discursive space within which people push (against) the values of a nation-brand. Writing for Buzzfeed News, Ellen Durney (2022) comments on which celebrities said the 4th of July should be canceled due to a "shortage of independence" for women after *Roe v. Wade* was overturned. As Durney (2022) notes, "since the ruling, many public figures have denounced the decision [to overturn *Roe v. Wade*]. And over the past few days, as millions of Americans came together to celebrate Independence Day, celebrities have used their platforms to put reproductive rights at the forefront, highlighting that people across the nation have been stripped of their freedom."

Indeed, in 2022 many US celebrities used their digital presence to denounce both July 4th and the overturning of *Roe v. Wade*. However, much media coverage of this focused on the social media posts of white women, which is unsurprising given that, as Daniels (2021, 1) highlights, the protection of "nice white ladies" is "fundamental to American culture." But the protection of Other(ed) women certainly is not. Daniels's account of gendered and affective dimensions of structural whiteness in the US includes reflections on what it means to challenge "the safe emptiness of whiteness, and to detox from the poison of ladyhood" (1). My conceptualizing of white sincerity and the spectacle that digitally mediated expressions of it can spark is influenced by the work of Prins (2022) on whiteness and famous white women, Daniels's (2021) critical account of "nice white ladies," and the work of Phipps (2020, 6) on how "white and privileged women dominate mainstream feminism. These demographics shape the movement's politics, but are perhaps partially hidden by monikers such as 'neoliberal feminism', 'popular feminism' and the rest."

White sincerity, which in this specific case can be regarded as an affective component of mainstream feminism, appeared to be on display on the 4th of July. It was present in, or implied by, the earnest tone of the posts of famous white women who seemed to perceive the overturning of *Roe v. Wade* as the ultimate American sin and so were suddenly compelled to frame "American Independence Day" as immoral. The research of Prins (2022, 105) outlines how the popularized archetype of "the woke white woman articulates a more politically conscious self embedded in trajectories of self-education and ongoing personal growth," which are trajectories that often play out on social media. Prins argues that "the neoliberal emphasis on self-improvement allows the woke white woman to reassume an older moral position. She can lead by example" (105). In dialogue with Prins's work, in addition to Lentin's (2020) critical analysis of the ways that "white comfort" is implicated in contemporary ideas about racism, I regard white sincerity and its public reception as being entangled in dynamics between celebrity self-brands and nation-branding, as well as dynamics between wokeness and a gendered whiteness.

Press preoccupation with the July 4th comments of white women who are celebrities, such as Katy Perry and Jessica Chastain, reflects the social capital and currency of white sincerity—specifically, sincerity that is perceived as being embodied and expressed by famous white women, whose potentially unpatriotic social media posts are unlikely to be punitively treated as a threat by the nation-state. Previously, my work on white sincerity has focused on examples of white celebrities who have spoken out against racism. But by critically considering white sincerity in the context of how famous white women have spoken out against the overturning of *Roe v. Wade*, it is possible to grasp some of the granular details of how gender politics are enmeshed with how perceived expressions of white sincerity are received. Even though Black, Indigenous, and people of color (BIPOC) have been denouncing the 4th of July "holiday" for a very long time, it is the social media posts of famous white women that the media were fascinated with in 2022. Headlines such as "All The Celebrities Who Have 'Cancelled' 4 July Celebrations Amid Roe v Wade: From Kim Kardashian to Katy Perry" (Habbouchi 2022) are illustrative of how the narratives of those perceived to be "nice white ladies" (Daniels 2021) often dominate public discussion and debate related to issues such as reproductive rights and the broader oppressive actions of nations.

Much media coverage of the online words of these famous white women also exemplifies how the self-brands of celebrities are formed and interpreted in ways connected to the extent to which they appear to praise, or push against, the values of the nation-brand that they are most associated with. It may be cynical to conjecture that some of the content that denounced July 4th was part of celebrities' efforts to strategically, yet merely momentarily, distance their own image from that of the US nation-brand. But it would also be naïve to presume that such content is simply nothing other than a reflection of the views of the women who posted it.

Previously, I have explored "how the perspectives of white celebrities receive visibility, praise, and critique amid mediated discourse on BLM and social injustice" (Sobande 2022b, 130). That analysis involved scrutiny of how "famous people have been attempting to strike a balance between using their platforms to amplify messages about structural antiblackness and using their platforms in ways intended to preserve their own public image. The reality is that many celebrities may be more concerned about brand reputational risk than the racial injustices that they choose or do not choose to speak up about" (Sobande 2022b, 133). That the words of famous white women have been centered amid much mediated discourse on both July 4th and the overturning of *Roe v. Wade* reflects how "white celebrities' efforts to call out and critique whiteness and [as in this case, other] social injustices can in fact have the effect of reinscribing the dominant and marketable status of whiteness" (133)— including the power and praise imbued in the position of the "nice white lady" (Daniels 2021) who is perceived as sincere.

Even if celebrities commenting on July 4th and the SCOTUS decision were not doing so in ways that were strategically aligned with their work to manage and market their self-brands, the press attention and platforming that they received because of their social media posts suggest that there was a public relations dimension inevitably at play. Some of the online words of celebrities such as Katy Perry and Jessica Chastain may, at least on the surface, appear to challenge elements of nation-branding (e.g., criticizing celebrations of July 4th) by highlighting structural oppression that nations typically seek to obscure. Nevertheless, these celebrities' words may also constitute self-branding practices and may result in media attention, and even praise, because of their aesthetic and attitudinal palatability, which may be consistent with that of mainstream and popular (white) feminism (Banet-Weiser 2018; Phipps 2020).

America's embrace of "nice white ladies" (Daniels 2021) means that these digitally mediated dynamics under analysis are shaped by matters at the intersections of gender and "the dominance of whiteness, which bolsters the market logic that underlies celebrity culture" (Sobande 2022b, 132). It remains the case that "white celebrities and their self-brands can stand to gain something from attempting to denounce the type of social hierarchies that to some extent make their celebrity status possible" (132). The rapid development of digital culture and its connection to various marketing and branding activities in recent years have been entangled with online conversations and content related to racism, anti-racism, and racial justice work. Conscious of all these power relations connected to issues of gender, race, and capitalism, I now expand on my analysis by focusing on the business of activism, antagonism, and aging, in chapter 3.

3 The Business of Activism, Antagonism, and Aging

CGI (aka virtual) influencers, TV shows such as *Succession*, and the When We Were Young (WWWY) music festival in Las Vegas are just a few of many media and marketing examples that illuminate elements of the business of activism, antagonism, and aging. Focusing on these topics, chapter 3 examines the dynamic between social justice, (self-)brands, moral judgments, online optics, and the marketing of nostalgic experiences associated with certain ages/stages of life. It expands on chapter 2's discussion of the politics of morality and the marketplace, to consider how influencer culture is implicated in ideas about intersectionality and activism and to examine the ways that social and political movements align themselves with, or denounce, forms of influencer culture. Focusing on key examples (e.g., the racial and social justice framing of CGI influencers, the idolatry and inconsistencies associated with influencers, and tensions between influencer culture and BLM), I reflect on what the relationship between influencer culture and social justice reveals about branding practices *and* activist approaches.

As illuminated in the pivotal edited collection *Commodity Activism: Cultural Resistance in Neoliberal Times*, "abiding axes oppression and inequity—race, gender, class, and so on—interact with consumer culture to reinvent grassroots identifications as well as tactical strategies for resistance and reimagination" (Mukherjee and Banet-Weiser 2012, 5). The relationship between consumer culture and activism is complicated. In the decade since *Commodity Activism* was published, this dynamic has been impacted by the rise of influencer culture (Lekakis 2022; Sobande, Kanai, and Zeng 2022; Yesiloglu and Costello 2020)—a by-product of celebrity culture and the ascent of many social media and content-sharing sites. In addition, the relationship between consumer culture and ideas about inequity and activism has been shaped by "the marketing industry's recent embrace of intersectionality," which reflects an ongoing "shift in the commercialization of identity politics and difference for the purposes of capital accumulation" (Rosa-Salas and Sobande 2022, 180). This chapter explores these matters while picking up on chapter 2's points regarding the role of disharmony in the marketplace.

Drawing on the work of Hall (2013), I also discuss the circuit of so-called culture wars, which involves critiquing the loaded ways that this notion functions in the marketplace and in society more widely (Richmond and Charnley 2022). Following on from that, I turn my attention to six TV shows (*Industry, Partner Track, Severance, Succession, The Bold Type, You*) that depict branding and corporate culture issues or are marketed in a way that highlights such issues, including the pressure on businesses to cultivate a favorable digital presence that draws on fan-related online content. My analysis of pop culture depictions of corporate culture involves discussion of the controlling anxieties of brands (e.g., fictional brands depicted in shows and real brands behind the creation of them) and how they connect to the ongoing corporatization of digital remix culture. That is, I consider how brands attempt to control the relatively uncontrollable terrain of social media commentaries about them, including by making use of meme culture and the do-it-yourself (DIY) spirit of various content creation trends and styles that were once typically more associated with the work of fans than of brands.

Focusing on the framing of the distinctly Scottish and patriarchal character of Logan Roy (powerfully played by Brian Cox, who is also from Scotland) in HBO's *Succession*, I continue my consideration of how notions of nations are embroiled in pop culture (e.g., how a Scotsman in the American business world is depicted on-screen and how specters of Scottishness are portrayed) (Sobande 2023b). Then I analyze a range of pop culture examples, including the brand voice of Netflix's *You* on Twitter and how it is constructed in a way that blends the feel of fandom with brand strategy. Finally, informed by my experience of attending the emo and alternative music festival When We Were Young (WWWY) in Las Vegas, I reflect on the relationship between Big Tech and the nostalgic remixing of the emo music subculture and sense of youth that it is associated with. My analysis of this is informed by the perspective that "'alternative' and 'independent' don't designate something outside mainstream culture; rather, they are styles, in fact *the* dominant styles, within the mainstream" (Fisher [2014] 2022, 9). Therefore, a festival such as WWWY should be understood as being part of mainstream consumer culture rather than existing in opposition to it.

These analyses of the entanglements of business, activism, antagonism, and aging are shaped by the fact that "marketing's role in a capitalist economy is to craft and communicate messages that promote the cultural practices and ideologies of consumption" (Rosa-Salas and Sobande 2022, 178). Such messages are sometimes aided by brands alluding to activist symbols and sentiments without contributing to activism themselves or by brands embracing disharmony in the marketplace and making expressions of antagonism part of their brand image. In other cases, brands benefit from nurturing a sense of nostalgia that is associated with aging and reminiscing about years gone by. Chapter 3 is grounded in a focus on all of this, including examination of what the notion of activism means at a point in time when brands have been grasping at it with haste and with the use of the tools of digital culture.

SOCIAL JUSTICE SELF-BRANDS, "INTERSECTIONAL" OPTICS, AND VIRTUAL INFLUENCERS

"Profit is not a dirty word," claimed Liz Truss, the former secretary of state for foreign, commonwealth and development affairs of the UK, who went on to serve the shortest term (forty-nine days) of any prime minister in the nation's history. In August 2022, while campaigning to become prime minister, Truss declared that "the fact . . . [profit has] become a dirty word in our society is a massive problem" (Demianyk 2022). This statement was uttered during a surging heat wave that may be attributed to the damaging impacts of industrialization and the greedy profit making that it aids. Attempting to paint Big Business in a positive light is typical of the Conservative Party that Truss is part of, so there is nothing novel about such attempts to praise profit making and claim that business is being bashed. However, the defensive statements of politicians such as Truss signal the powerful presence of critiques of capitalism, which such people are eager to dismiss. But it is not only politicians who are desperate to alter perceptions of profit making. Many brands are invested in the public perceiving profit making as "good," even self-brands such as celebrities and influencers.

Attempts to polish the image of profit making or present it as being valuable for various sociopolitical reasons can involve brands invoking representations and rhetoric related to activism. This includes business and brand activity that occurs as part of the ongoing marketization of intersectionality, which entails commercial entities emptying the term *intersectionality* of its original focus on the effects of interconnected structural oppression such as racism and sexism and the legal system's inadequate recognition of these. As Rosa-Salas and I argue (2022, 181), "Marketing's use of intersectionality is positioned by industry professionals and journalists as a new way for brand marketers to approach consumer segmentation in a globalizing marketplace; rather than turn singular classifications into market segments, as has been done by brands in decades past, intersectionality as market segmentation strategy proposes that marketing reflect more complex conceptions of identity to make more people feel included in consumer culture. Intersectionality surfaces as a concept centered on consumer preference, not political mobilization."

Thus intersectionality, as framed by many market actors and commercial entities such as brands, sometimes simply functions in ways that are intended to appeal to consumers by encouraging them to like, follow, and spend money—under the guise that this engagement and consumption amounts to structural changes aligned with the underpinnings of intersectionality (e.g., efforts to address both systemic racism and sexism). Marketized notions of intersectionality can be a foil for meaningful efforts to tackle oppression. As affirmed by critical legal scholar Harris (2021), "Racial subjugation is not a special application of capitalist processes, but rather central to how capitalism operates." One of the numerous limitations of marketized ideas about intersectionality is that issues of inequality become framed via the self-preserving lens of the marketplace, which avoids critiquing the racial capitalist foundations upon which the marketplace and its many brands rest.

As Harris (2021, ix) articulates, "Race is everywhere in law. But it appears in legal doctrine through a 'recognition' paradigm that assumes that the problem of white supremacy is exclusion." Similarly, mobilizations of intersectionality in the marketplace, and in some scholarly accounts of it, prioritize modes of recognition, representation, and inclusion in the marketplace at the expense of critically accounting for the history and impact of racial capitalism, which renders the marketplace inherently oppressive. Recent work that stems from critical studies of race in the marketplace has elucidated such dynamics between race and capitalism (Crockett 2022; Johnson et al.

2019) and has highlighted that "advertising research generally overlooks such historical dimensions while investigating representations or testing 'race' in advertising" (Thomas, Johnson, and Grier 2023). Informed by such scholarship, I expand on my reflections regarding racial capitalism throughout the subsequent sections.

Sure, social and political struggles can play out, and *have* played out, in marketplace contexts—from boycotts and picket lines to investigative reporting and legal action against brands (Klein 2000; Littler 2008; Mukherjee and Banet-Weiser 2012). However, when intersectionality, and social justice more generally, is leveraged as a marketing tool, it is important to be frank about the extent to which such activity is often commerce oriented as opposed to being evidence of activism or different forms of social action. This point is particularly vital to make when recognizing the history of how the ideas, experiences, and struggles of Black people have been commodified and treated as a means for brands—*including individuals*—to platform themselves and cultivate capital. Given the gendered *and* racial dimensions of capitalism (Harris 2021), the marketization of intersectionality might be regarded as merely another example of how concepts and work intended to address the oppression faced by Black women and other women of color are repackaged as a marketing device and a way for brands to attempt to appeal to such demographics, but simply as potential consumers with purchasing power.

It is not uncommon to encounter the terms *intersectionality* and *intersectional* in the online biographies or content captions of various influencers, including individuals who might be identified as feminist and/or environmentalist content creators. Inclusion of the word intersectionality in the context of influencer culture is neither inherently "good" nor inherently "bad." Rather, it reflects the fact that social, political, and commercial machinations collide in many ways in the marketplace, including as part of how influencers position themselves or are positioned by others. There are online lists about "intersectional influencers" (Bååth 2022; Schwingle 2021; Weinstein 2022), some of which may be interpreted as simplistically using intersectional as a proxy for "not white." In some such contexts, the notion of intersectionality can become both amorphous and akin to marketing jargon, such as by predominantly functioning as an arbitrary description of different people and categories of influencer culture and by being used in the service of market-oriented goals that are untethered from a concern with the intersecting nature of forms of structural oppression (e.g., ableism, sexism, racism, misogyny, and capitalism).

Scholarly work on influencer culture covers a wide range of themes and questions. These include, but are far from being limited to, studies of work and labor experiences (Brown 2022, Duffy 2015, 2017; Duffy and Hund 2015; Duffy and Jefferson 2017; Glatt 2022; Hund 2023), "political and ideological influencers" (Lewis 2020, 201), marketing and promotional culture (Lekakis 2022; Yesiloglu and Costello 2020), inequality (Bishop 2018; Brown 2022; Glatt and Banet-Weiser 2021; Sobande 2018, 2020), body image (Sharp and Gerrard 2022), de-influencing (Mardon, Cocker, and Daunt 2023), the rise of YouTubers (Abidin 2021; Stokel-Walker 2019) and TikTok (Rauchberg 2022; Stokel-Walker 2021), the commodification of blackness and CGI influencers (Sobande 2021a, 2021b), and the experiences of families (contentiously, including babies and children) who are influencers (Abidin 2015, 2017).

A lot has changed between the early 2000s, when ideas about influencer culture were emerging; the 2010s, when "in 2016, YouTube acknowledged the most influential Black content creators by inviting them to Los Angeles to take part in a conference—YouTube Black [#YouTubeBlack]" (Sobande 2018, 270); and today's established influencer industry, which is also sometimes referred to by using words other than *influencer culture* (e.g., *creator culture*). While I am ambivalent about the societal interchangeable use of such terms, it is worth noting what a preference for focusing on creating as opposed to influencing might suggest. Specifically, a focus on advertising, marketing, and branding techniques may be strategically decentered when referring to *creators*, a term that sometimes simply signals forms of influence by another name but might more palatably connote making and producing rather than persuading and pushing. Then again, although the influencer industry involves much profit making and many commercial practices, influencer culture is not just about business and branding.

Social justice, influencer culture, and their connections and disconnections have been the focus of insightful writing and research. But some of this scholarship seems to center on the question of whether influencers can be activists and vice versa. This is a question that I have previously considered, and one that will no doubt continue to be the source of many debates and discussions. However, my current approach to analyzing this topic is based on the view that there are undoubtedly relationships between aspects of influencer culture and activism, and while such relationships may be far from harmonious, this does not mean that influencer culture and activism are always completely disparate domains. After all, the cult of personality has played a part in activist work for decades, and although influencer culture may be part of a distinctly twenty-first-century vocabulary, this does not mean that the activities it describes are entirely new. As the author of *Cultish* argues, "The twenty-first century has produced a climate of sociopolitical unrest and mistrust of long-established institutions, like church, government, Big Pharma, and big business. It's the perfect societal recipe for making new and unconventional groups—everything from Reddit incels to woo-woo wellness influencers—who promise to provide answers that the conventional ones couldn't supply seem freshly appealing" (Montell 2021, 21). It is in this climate that the positioning of influencer culture in proximity to activism has ascended, and it is in this climate that the business of antagonism has also flourished.

Recognizing the existence of relationships between influencer culture and activism is not the same as suggesting that such terms are interchangeable. I do not believe that influencer culture and activism exist on an innately interconnected continuum, but I do believe that market logics and elements of the celebrification of social justice issues affect both. In view of that, I share here my thoughts on the notion of "social justice self-brands" and examine various dimensions of influencer culture and activism, while cautioning against compulsions to portray influencer culture as less commerce oriented than it typically is. Before discussing this in more detail, it seems pertinent to acknowledge that although influencer culture does not solely consist of the work, public image, and online content of white people, much media, political, and academic discussion of influencer culture in the UK and the US tends to focus on their perspectives and experiences (particularly those of white women)—as influencers themselves, as researchers of influencer culture, and sometimes as both. Thus, there is scope to interpret elements of influencer culture, including media, political, and scholarly reporting on it, as being entangled with the power dynamics that Daniels (2021) breaks down in *Nice White Ladies*.

On a similar topic, focusing on "good girls and woke white women: *Miss Americana* and the performance of popular white Womanhood," the celebrity studies scholarship of Prins (2022, 105) argues, "'Woke white womanhood' offers individualised political resistance to its audiences as the outcome of personal growth—facilitated through ageing—and gendered autonomy. The question remains whether celebrities like [Taylor] Swift, invested in neoliberal success stories and deeply embedded in the power relations that structure current inequalities, will be able to move audiences, and perhaps white women specifically, from the symbolic to the substantial."

Relatedly, my collaborative work with scholars Kanai and Zeng argues that in the context of a digital culture that promotes the idea that social media is the prime site of political action, various notions of wokeness emerge as "a response to both the increasing but uneven pressures and rewards of *being recognized* as 'woke', heightened by the rhythms and infrastructures of social media" (Sobande, Kanai, and Zeng 2022, 8). We argue that such rhythms result in expectations that people make their "self visible in particular ways to audiences, and to be attributed with enlightened progressive values as a personal and/or brand identity. The ambivalent status of 'wokeness' is thus evident if we reflect on the conflicting ways in which the actions of people may be simultaneously praised and policed for allegedly being 'woke'" (8).

When rooted in an understanding of notions of wokeness and digital culture being experienced in this way, the contemporary relationship between social justice and self-brands becomes clearer. The influencer industry includes expressions of "woke white womanhood" (Prins 2022) and subsequently both praise and criticism of white women who are perceived as such, including individuals who identify or are identified as "intersectional" feminists. Schisms between praise and criticism of the positioning of such self-brands reflects tensions between commodified conceptualizations of wokeness, social justice, and intersectionality and contrasting positions that are explicitly critical of racial capitalism and may by extension be critical of influencer culture. As the saying goes, actions speak louder than words. Hence, the rise in intersectional as a descriptor of elements of influencer culture (e.g., a self-descriptor of influencers on social media or a term used to describe them in media pieces) should not be mistaken for evidence of activism and may merely reflect the marketization of terms and ideas with roots in the work of Black people, particularly Black women.

The work of sociologist and gender studies scholar Alison Phipps (2020) provides a crucial analysis of mainstream (white) feminism, which is a critical account that can aid analysis of the relationship between social justice and self-brands, including the centering of white womanhood amid some of these media and marketing practices. Phipps (2020, 8) contends, "Racial capitalism does not just create inequality based on categories such as class, race, gender, disability, age and nation, it *relies* on it. To maintain a stratified system, to ensure that the economically privileged can monopolise resources, some people must be relegated to marginalised economic and reproductive roles. Others must be placed outside the system completely—stripped of their humanity, to be dispossessed and eventually done away with."

What role might influencer culture play in some of the structural processes that Phipps outlines? If influencer culture might involve embracing capitalism—that is, by nature, *racial* and *gendered* capitalism—who and what are being defended and protected as part of certain efforts to legitimize the work of influencers and the image of the overall industry that they are part of?

I would not describe myself as anti–influencer industry and anti–creator culture. Instead, I am skeptical of the extent to which these digital domains have the potential to challenge, rather than reinforce, systemic forms of oppression. As has been analyzed and emphasized in significant research on the oppressive nature of algorithms (Noble 2018) and "algorithmic injustice" (Birhane 2021), digital platforms and online spaces can reflect and reinforce power regimes and inequalities. This includes what media studies and internet culture scholar Jess Sage Rauchberg (2020) terms "algorithmic ableism." Drawing on the innovative work of Noble (2018) in *Algorithms of Oppression: How Search Engines Reinforce Racism*, Rauchberg (2022) has highlighted nuances in "Queer, Trans, and Disabled Creator Responses to Algorithmic Oppression on TikTok." As Rauchberg (2022, 197) explains, "An account may be public and have thousands of followers, but once it is shadowbanned, the algorithm hides the user profile and content from the public." The process of shadowbanning particularly impacts people from structurally oppressed demographics, including content creators who are affected by the intersections of ableism, colorism, fatphobia, homophobia, misogyny, racism, and transphobia. Hence Rauchberg's poignant provocation, "Representation or Erasure?" (197).

Informed by the work of both Noble (2018) and Rauchberg (2022), I am wary of how terms such as *intersectional* might be used in the influencer industry to aid commerce that thrives on structural inequality (e.g., the profit making of people who are not impacted by shadowbanning and accordant forms of oppression), as opposed to challenging it. Further still, I am mindful of the potential for some influencers (e.g., middle-class white women) to commercially benefit from the structural struggles faced by others (e.g., working-class Black women). Hence, I am critical of how some media and scholarly framings of the influencer industry and content creation in the UK and the US appear to be based on perceptions of capitalism *and* morality that may be tied to a distinctly classed and gendered whiteness, which fails to meaningfully address the forms of oppression that both Noble (2018) and Rauchberg (2022) name and analyze.

Sometimes influencer culture and certain defenses of it appear in ways that suggest the industry is mainly the domain of women who might be perceived as "nice white ladies" (Daniels 2021), who are consistently among those who profit most from the industry, and who at times are positioned as beyond reproach and are deemed in need of protection. Some efforts to advance influencer culture's image seem steeped in the #GirlBoss qualities of mainstream (white) feminism, which takes the experiences of middle-class white women and universalizes them in ways that uphold oppressive and self-serving respectability politics that are tethered to whiteness. Hence, as my collaborative research with David Hesmondhalgh and Anamik Saha (Sobande, Hesmondhalgh, and Saha 2023) highlights, Black, and Asian people working in the UK's creative and cultural industries can face raced, classed, and gendered expectations of digital presence, "professionalism," and "respectability" online, which contrast with encouragement and praise of the online outspokenness and perceived "quirkiness" of white middle-class peers in the industry.

Influencer culture is far from solely being the domain of white women, but it is often the experiences of white women that are foregrounded in public, political, and scholarly discourse on the industry in the UK and the US. Additionally, such women are more likely to generate capital from their work than are Black women and other women of color, who are affected by the intersections of racism, sexism, misogyny, classism, ableism, and other forms of oppression. As the work of Glatt and Banet-Weiser (2021) rightly asserts, the world of content creators is far from being a meritocracy; therefore, it is important to remain critical of the ways that the influencer industry is entangled with structural inequalities and forms of oppression. For these reasons, when writing critically about influencer culture, I do so in response to how the influencer industry may predominantly involve the reinforcement of gendered and racial capitalism, including under the guise of "empowerment" and "entrepreneurialism" that essentially benefit those who are least marginalized.

Writing for *Novara Media*, Anna Cafolla (2022) argues that "in the influencer vacuum, protest is a placard reposted to a temporary Instagram story, community organising is a *very exciting* brand partnership to be revealed across a series of vlogs, calls to action are platitudes about *working smarter and not harder* so you can live the influencer lifestyle too." Cafolla is one of many people who have questioned the motives of influencers who appear to create and post content about issues of inequality and injustice. While Cafolla's words concern the actions of human influencers, others have studied and critiqued the development of virtual influencers—sometimes also referred to as CGI and/or artificial intelligence (AI) influencers (Hund 2023; Jackson 2018; Miyake 2022; Sobande 2021a, 2021b). Although in comparison to the wider influencer industry, the virtual influencer space is germinal, such influencers have attracted the attention of many Big Brands, including in Big Tech.

In an article for the *Nation*, "Branding Fake Justice for Generation Z," Emmeline Clein (2019) discusses how virtual influencers can "offer a balm to corporate boards anxious that their influencers won't behave. Not only are they exempt from the logistical difficulties of employing humans (like labor laws); they resolve the inherent issue with political consciousness for material promotion." Focusing on one of the most high-profile and successful CGI influencers—Miquela (aka @lilmiquela, who currently has 2.8 million Instagram followers)—Clein (2019) wrote: "The specific social justice causes with which Miquela chooses to accessorize are revealing. While her Instagram bio until recently read Black Lives Matter—and now shouts out nonprofits combating youth incarceration and the persecution of

LGBTQ people—Miquela has been notably silent on issues of income inequality, a necessary hole in a leftism that wears Prada and Proenza."

Miquela, who in an interview for the *Zach Sang Show* (2019) self-describes as having been "created by a lab called Cain Intelligence . . . programmed to believe that I was a 19-year old half Brazilian, half Spanish girl," is now far from being a new virtual influencer. But a 2021 video on her YouTube channel, titled "I'm Miquela, a Real-Life Robot Mess," reflects the fact that the influencer appears to have been reintroduced, or maybe even rebranded, at different points in recent years. Such content may be demonstrative of what Emily Hund (2023, 115) points out in *The Influencer Industry: The Quest for Authenticity on Social Media*: "Indeed, the case of Lil Miquela showed that a nonhuman influencer's seeming lack of 'authenticity' would not necessarily be a problem. After the unveiling of some of social media's hidden industrial orchestrations, the key to conveying authenticity seemed to be strategic deployment of *honesty*: if something is sponsored, disclose it; if someone or something is not 'real,' have fun with it."

Perhaps unsurprisingly, during the COVID-19 pandemic the virtual/CGI/AI influencer industry seemed to expand, as is alluded to in Miquela's YouTube video, which features the influencer casually saying:

> You're probably asking yourself "how is this robot talking to me right now?" Did y'all hear about the robot invasion of 2020? I mean, I've been around for a minute, but I feel like last year was on a whole other level.

The YouTube video that is featured on Miquela's well-followed channel (currently at 280,000 subscribers) is five minutes and twenty-two seconds long and covers different aspects of Miquela's public image. Miquela comments on a variety of topics, including the impact of the COVID-19 crisis, which is framed as having resulted in the influencer spending much less time with her "hot boyfriends," "hot girlfriends," and "hot *them* friends." Miquela states that "like the rest of the world I spent way too much time on TikTok" and then goes on to detail how during that time she "explored some of the weirder circumstances of who created me and why." One of several key themes in the video is that of "belonging" and feeling connected to people, as well as Miquela's plans to "just spread love, joy and community." But another marketable dimension of the CGI influencer's digital rendering is her racialization—specifically, her *mixedness.*

"Mixed" (also referred to as "biracial," "multiethnic," and "multiracial") identities have often been exoticized and intentionally framed as symbolizing racial harmony and supposedly progressive racial politics in the context of consumer culture in the UK and the US (Harrison, Thomas, and Cross 2017; Sobande 2019b). So it is no coincidence that the most prominent virtual influencers include those that are constructed as "mixed," and that this is communicated in the form of statements that are attributed to them in addition to their aesthetic appearance, which often maintains a proximity to whiteness.

In "The Mixed-Race Fantasy behind Kawaii Aesthetics," interdisciplinary scholar Erica Kanesaka (2023) explains that "the term given to this mixture of Japanese and Western aesthetics is 無国籍, *mukokuseki,* meaning 'without a nationality.' It is a common aspect of kawaii. By combining racial and cultural elements, kawaii characters are thought to be able to float freely across national borders." Virtual influencers such as Miquela perhaps function in a similar way—floating across and between different parameters and perceptions of racial, ethnic, national, and cultural identity. Undoubtedly the construction of the supposedly "half Brazilian, half Spanish" identity of Miquela is different to the ways that Japanese and Western aesthetics combine in the examples discussed by Kanesaka. However, both reflect Western consumer culture's interest in, and fetishization of, racial and cultural mixedness, particularly when such mixedness still foregrounds whiteness and is interpreted as amounting to cute commodities and marketable representations.

Arguably, the virtual influencer sphere and the influencer industry more broadly reflect the gendered and racial nature of capitalism. Some of such influencer activity can also be interpreted as
evidencing the pervasiveness of what visual culture scholar Nicholas
Mirzoeff terms "white sight": structural looking and power relations
based on the combined impact of histories of racism, settler colonialism, and white supremacy, yielding "a hierarchy, at once racial-
izing and patriarchal, which is then projected onto external reality"
(2023, 5). Such projections onto reality might include examples
of CGI influencers who are racialized, gendered, exoticized, and
fetishized in ways that reflect both the patriarchal nature and whiteness of the marketplace—including "the powerful sensation of being
the spectator, not the show" (Mirzoeff 2023, 9). When I refer to *sight*
and accompanying terms such as *gaze* and *watch* in my book, I am
not simply describing visual experiences. Rather, I am describing
structural forms of observing that can include, but are never limited
to, visual modes of doing so.

In the UK and the US, while the human influencer industry is
particularly associated with the digital presence of white women, the
world of virtual influencers seems to foreground CGI of Black and
"mixed-race" women. This is suggestive of the reality that racism,
sexism, misogyny, and capitalism coalesce in ways that result in the
different and specific forms of exoticization, fetishization, objectification, and oppression faced by Black and "mixed" women, whose
embodiment appears to proprietorially be treated as fodder for the
creation of virtual influencers. It is also important to acknowledge
differences between such forms of oppression, including the fact
that light-skinned Black and "mixed" women do not face the vitriol
and violences of colorism that are directed at dark-skinned Black
and "mixed" women.

In the age of the notion of "social justice sells," for brands in
search of a so-called intersectional image, the prospect of partnering
with virtual influencers may appeal. The reasons for this include the
potential for brands to position themselves in proximity to Black and

"mixed" women, without having to meaningfully engage with, work with, credit, and support such real women. The opaqueness that surrounds the origins of some virtual influencers and the details of who profits from their production, and how, means that the virtual influencer world is ripe with the potential to be portrayed as diverse, inclusive, and equitable while masking and reinforcing oppressive power, gender, and racial regimes. Regardless, virtual influencers continue to be a marketable means for brands to attempt to participate in the business of activism—to commercially benefit from being perceived as supportive of social justice movements such as those that virtual influencers espouse.

Commenting on a profile of Miquela that featured in *V Magazine*, Clein (2019) asserts that "the easy blending of promotion and principle" that is evident in much media and framing of Miquela "reduces social justice to a predilection used to reveal personality in a celebrity profile, as flimsy as personal style. This is perfect for huge corporations, which would like the status quo of capitalism maintained, but definitely don't mind a few Instagram posts about diversity." Following on from the scholarship and work of Lauren Michele Jackson (2018), as my prior research acknowledges, the virtual/CGI/ AI influencer industry also includes several high-profile influencers who are clearly racialized as Black (Sobande 2021a), including the characters Shudu and Koffi, who are dark-skinned and are often depicted as visibly glistening in ways that add to the spectacle that surrounds them. Their caricatured existence may be interpreted as exemplifying how blackness and Black people have been objectified and treated as commodifiable muses in the ongoing context of "imperialist, white supremacist, capitalist, patriarchy" (hooks 1984).

Previously, I wrote that "CGI influencers mirror their human counterparts, with well-followed social media profiles, high-definition selfies, and an awareness of trending topics. And like human influencers, they appear in different body types, ages, genders and ethnicities. A closer look at the diversity among CGI influencers— and who is responsible for it—raises questions about colonialism, cultural appropriation, and exploitation" (Sobande 2021a). Since then, scholars such as Esperanza Miyake have produced powerful work on the digital orientalism that is involved in parts of the world of virtual influencers. Miyake (2022, 1) "provides a critical examination of Japanese raciality and gender within the context of virtuality, (im)materiality and digital consumption." Such research "problematises the ways in which 'Western' popular media texts present Japanese virtuality to consumers" (1).

There are many different structural and watchful gazes that seem to guide the direction of the virtual (aka CGI/AI) influencer industry, as I have experienced when receiving antagonistic and defensive messages after publishing critiques of it. However, it is the gaze of colonialism and whiteness that tends to loom large, resulting in exoticized and caricatured constructions of influencers that are often intended to resemble Black people or racially ambiguous individuals, but which may manifest in ways that mainly stem from the whims of "white sight" (Mirzoeff 2023). "On its surface, influencer culture presents itself as poreless, pacifying, and most pertinently, apolitical" (Cafolla 2022), but beneath the veneer of neutrality is the persistent pulse of politics and power dynamics, such as the commodification of blackness and the marketing of what might be perceived as a malleable "mixed" aesthetic. While some brands seem to be enamored of the industry of uncanny and computer-generated creations, others are instead continuing their interest in real humans who are influencers, and who face pressures to share their perspective on a wide range of social and political issues.

THE IDOLATRY AND INCONSISTENCIES OF INFLUENCER CULTURE

When asked about their thoughts on influencers, the media, marketing, and business experts whom I interviewed shared detailed examples of how influencer culture and adjacent public spheres have changed in recent years. On the topic of influencers who post content and comments on social and political issues, writer and journalist Aaron said, "It's a combination of the political, the societal and the technological elements that have all come together to create this perfect storm, in the sense of this idea that you always have to have a point of view on something." Elaborating on his thoughts on this topic, Aaron remarked:

> The kind of influencer accountability thing is an interesting one, because there are these weird dynamics that go on. Like, invariably, if a major issue comes about, there's this idea that because it's a major issue it can attract idols, and so you'll always have a person that feels the need to then come out and comment on it, because they know that, by doing so, they, I guess, get an advantage on this stuff. They plant their flag and sort of say, I am owning this topic, I know this area, this is my . . . [a]gain, another weird, loaded phrase, that you can't really use any more, *my social justice* issue, or something like that. And then, because one person does it, there's an expectation, particularly in influencer culture, of this idea that if you're not participating, then you are somehow complicit.

The idea that if you are not saying or doing something about a specific issue of social injustice, you are complicit in it (e.g., "silence is violence") (Kwittken 2022) has gained traction in certain activist and community organizing spaces in addition to marketplace contexts such as influencer culture. However, the former focuses on collective action that involves being accountable to communities that the action is intended to support and serve (e.g., Black communities), while the latter tends to focus on public relations issues and the management of reputational risk. Some of what Aaron shared on the topic of influencer culture, including his use of "idols" and "plant their flag," made me think of the cultish qualities of aspects of influencer culture and some of the territorial ways that influencers establish a niche for themselves. Tropes infused with moral panic have followed influencer culture since it emerged, so I am conscious of the risk of reinforcing tired stereotypes such as that of the YouTuber whose content is passively consumed by a sheep-like audience. Still, it is also important that people name and critique aspects of influencer culture that appear to be more cult-like than casual.

In *Cultish: The Language of Fanaticism*, Montell (2021, 12) contends that "our speech in regular life—at work, in Spin class, on Instagram—is evidence of our varying degrees of 'cult' membership." Distinguishing between *cultishness* and actual cults, Montell (14) affirms that "the motives behind culty-sounding language are not always crooked. Sometimes they're quite healthy, like to boost solidarity or to rally people around a humanitarian mission." In agreement with Montell, I regard influencer culture as involving various cultish tendencies. Such tendencies are evidenced by influencers who speak authoritatively on a wide range of social and political topics that they are far from being informed about, possibly influencing the views and actions of a large and often loyal following. These cultish tendencies include influencers' use of subtle yet hard-sell marketing techniques that would not be out of place in the context of some cults.

As Montell (2021, 15) notes, "wherever there are fanatically worshipped leaders and belief-bound cliques, some level of psychological pressure is at play. This could be as quotidian as your average case of FOMO, or as treacherous as being coerced to commit violent crimes." My focus on the idolatry and inconsistencies that are part of influencer culture involves considering how these matters relate to the marketing of social justice and the strategic blurring of boundaries between activism and advertising. Consequently, I reflect on examples of influencers who have been praised but who have also been positioned as a character to be critiqued, not coveted.

Sarah, a freelance journalist in the UK whom I interviewed, spoke in detail about the development of influencer culture and the ways that brands have enlisted the help of influencers. In addition to being a journalist, Sarah has worked "in music and event PR, so quite often that was working with big alcohol brands on creating festivals, sort of touchstone points for consumers to go and engage with the brand but done in the cool/youth focused way. . . . [S]o I've kind of seen both sides, of working with Big Brands and now being a journalist." Before discussing the intricacies of influencer culture, Sarah shared her thoughts on how the concept of CSR has developed over the last decade:

> In the mid-2000s there definitely wasn't as much of a push for corporate social responsibility and stuff. I think that's definitely something that has evolved over the past 20 years or so to perhaps becoming. . . . I'm sure there are big departments now for each Big Brand, that their role will be to investigate that. The reason it all just comes down to that, I think it's a load of bollocks, is because we live in a capitalist society. Brands are selling us something, that's their job, and I think to encase it in something other than that is just disingenuous really. But I'm very cynical about it, as you may be able to hear. What I do think is quite good is that, for all social media's ills, it works because people call them out on it.

As Sarah's perspective highlights, in the present day there is much criticism of the concept that brands can be activists or entities with a socially conscious focus and with concerns other than selling us something. In addition, there are individuals whose work explicitly takes the form of political and ideological influencing (Lewis 2020), and there are societal critiques regarding the potential for brands to engage influencers to distract from their own history of harmful actions that have been protested. So while in 2023 there continue to be connections between ideas about and experiences of consumer culture and social action, there are also numerous disconnections and distortions, which the influencer industry is implicated in.

Having written for a variety of publications (e.g., *Guardian*, *Vulture*), Sarah's work of more than thirteen years spans a range of topics. Recently, the main areas of journalism that Sarah has focused on "are entertainment, celebrity, culture, in particular tv," so she shared her expert opinion on elements of this industry activity. Reflecting on their perceived powers of persuasion, as well as some of the potentially problematic actions of influencers, Sarah highlighted recent media discourse on Molly-Mae Hague, a 23-year-old woman who was a contestant on the UK reality TV show *Love Island* in 2019 and went on to become the creative director of fast fashion retailer PrettyLittleThing, before leaving the role to focus on motherhood. Sarah said:

> [I]t just seems like . . . [influencers are] kind of pawns that have been caught up in this whole thing. Like Molly-Mae being Creative Director of PrettyLittleThing and it's the staff that aren't paid a living wage and she's posting all this really "tone-deaf" stuff. Well, firstly, she's on podcasts, like "everyone has got the same amount of hours in the day" [in a high-pitched, jolly voice], and then posting content that shows her hard at graft, like "what kind of canapes are we going to have at our launch event? It's just so difficult," and not thinking about the women in pretty much a sweatbox in Leicester, their fingers red raw from trying to run off all this fast fashion stuff. The lure of the money is there for influencers, and when you're that young, you're not clued in on things and you won't question, what is fast fashion and why is it so cheap, and, how often do you think people wear these before they throw them in the bin?

As Sarah alluded to, Molly-Mae has been criticized for her work at PrettyLittleThing, a retailer that anti-fast fashion activists have protested. Additionally, the influencer has been criticized in response to comments she made during an interview for the podcast *The Diary of a CEO* (hosted by Steven Bartlett), in which Molly-Mae implied that everyone has an equal opportunity to be successful in the business world (e.g., the same number of hours in a day to succeed and make money).

The issues named here have resulted in contentions being made about influencer culture and its connections to the damaging impacts of fast fashion as well as procapitalist notions of productivity and classist concepts of supposed meritocracy. For these reasons and more, Molly-Mae has been responded to in ways that include very critical media and public framings of her, as well as framings that veer

toward the rhetoric and representations of idolatry. Thus the inconsistencies of influencer culture include fluctuating and fickle perceptions of individual influencers who are simultaneously revered and
reviled. Moreover, as the powerful title of Symeon Brown's (2022)
book captures, such inconsistencies are also evident in the ways that
some influencers attempt to *Get Rich or Lie Trying*.

The fast fashion industry has rightly been criticized since long
before Molly-Mae became an established influencer. In *Consumer
Activism: Promotional Culture and Resistance*, Eleftheria J. Lekakis (2022, 2) highlights some of the many issues that are part of
this industry, including the pressures faced by people working in
Bangladesh during the COVID-19 pandemic: "In Bangladesh, the
garment industry was exempt from the national lock-down. Workers
in fast fashion supply chains were the inevitable and unsung 'heroes'
of consumption under COVID-19. In spring 2020, even years after
the Rana Plaza disaster, UK fast fashion retailers severed their
orders from the Bangladeshi garment industry, leaving over a million workers without pay or job security. Ongoing campaigns from
organizations such as Fashion Revolution, Clean Clothes, and
Labour behind the Label have been raising attention to the haz-
ardous and precarious conditions under which garment workers
(mostly women) have been operating during the pandemic."

Other critiques of the fast fashion industry include those that the
words of a survey respondent highlight, and which stem from the
perception that Big Brands are watching (and *poaching*) the work of
Black creatives and designers: "Fashion Nova & Shein—I don't like
them simply because they are fast fashion brands that offer nothing
new to the fashion industry. Also, they tend to simply copy trends
that are popular or steal from Black designers." This perspective,
which was also voiced by other survey respondents, echoes the scholarship of Tounsel (2022, 6): "Mainstream brands and mass media
companies have consistently sought to acknowledge Black women's
possession of a distinct magic or power when it suits their profit
agendas," such as by observing, praising, and using but *not* crediting

and paying for the creative fashion designs of Black women. Related critiques articulated in survey responses are a reminder of the gendered *and* racial nature of capitalism, which bolsters the entwined worlds of fast fashion and influencer culture—where white middle-class women can become the face of a brand that might depend on the exploitation of other women (e.g., the creative, design, and/or production work of Black and Asian women). As indicated by a viral and much critiqued TikTok video of a white and American influencer (Dani DMC) praising and touring alleged Shein factory premises in China, the image of both influencer culture and fast fashion is impacted by racial, gender, and global politics and power regimes.

To some people, influencers such as Molly-Mae and Dani DMC are perceived as legitimizing harmful and exploitative practices that are part of the fast fashion industry and its culture of competition and rapid production and consumption. As Littler's (2008, 1) work on ethics and consumption affirms, "social exploitation in the production of goods has become a heightened media issue: as the speed and availability of technologies increase, we can see and learn more about how those very technologies were produced using exploited labour, and about how clothing available on the high street was produced halfway around the world by children in sweatshops."

The development of digital technology and the speed at which it operates has also enabled the impact of critique of industry activity, such as online critique of the work of fast fashion brands and those who are their ambassadors. This point was made by another survey respondent, who shared the following comments in response to the question, "What do you think will impact the future of advertising, branding, and marketing approaches?":

> The overlap of politics and values to marketing feels like it's increasing. Companies used to be able to hide behind their board with anonymous CEOs but now people are brands and the reputational risk of misalignment is huge. Everything you post online and that is in public record doesn't go away, I think people will become even more

judgmental and hold public figures at a higher standard which impacts organizations, who they select for brand representation.
    —African American woman, US (36–45 years old)

As that remark hints at, the dominance of self-brands in contemporary marketing means that critique of brands often involves directly criticizing individuals who are perceived as being the brand, or at least representing it. As an industry that is premised on the idea that people can be brands, the influencer culture sphere is especially susceptible to the sort of critiques described in this survey response. In a *Refinery29* piece, "Molly-Mae Exposes the Problems at the Heart of Influencer Culture," Sadhbh O'Sullivan (2022) states that "meritocracy in every arena—particularly the influencer economy— propounds the idea that anyone can reach the top but there can only ever be a few at the top of the pyramid. The law of averages dictates that most who try won't make it. But for you to keep trying and to keep buying into the whole economy you have to believe that it's possible." As O'Sullivan's comments point out, the influencer industry is premised on contradictory and commerce-oriented logics that very few people benefit from, regardless of how hard they might try to. The need to buy into such logic can be interpreted as another cultish component of influencer culture.

Highlighting the flippant nature of Molly-Mae's statement that "we all have the same 24 hours in a day," O'Sullivan (2022) writes, "It's disingenuous to argue that a 22-year-old who works two jobs to cover rent and spends her little spare time doing all the cooking, cleaning and maybe socialising has the same amount of free time to invest in her future as an influencer on a seven-figure contract." Elsewhere, in a *Dazed* article titled "Molly-Mae, Influencer Culture, and the Myth That Hard Work Reaps Rewards," Diyora Shadijanova (2022) describes the influencer's appearance on *The Diary of a CEO* as representing how "the paradox of Instagram girlboss grind culture, offering mantras and productivity tips to an audience of which some are certainly struggling to pay their bills, was getting a much-needed rinsing."

Still, Shadijanova (2022) points out that to position Molly-Mae as hypocritical because of the views she expressed on the podcast is misguided. Put differently, if influencer culture is a product of gendered and racial capitalism, why would people expect some influencers to challenge the very structures and unequal material conditions that arguably make their work and celebrity possible? To expect influencers such as Molly-Mae to espouse socialist tendencies or become bastions of certain social justice messages is to promote a perception of influencer culture that dilutes the extent of its commercial orientation. As a number of survey respondents stated:

> I think that the constantly increasing exposure to advertising in our lives will have a polarising effect—people who find identity through their consumer choices will get more and more emotionally invested in advertising (both positively and negatively), and those who get "burnt out" and tired of this will engage even less with brands. Most people I know use browser extensions to reduce the amount of advertising they are exposed to on the internet, and the "influencer marketing" that social media users are exposed to has become so pervasive that it basically never feels genuine.
> —white nonbinary person, UK (18–25 years old)

> Social media platforms like TikTok are changing the world of advertising. The use of influencers on YouTube and Instagram will play an increasingly important role in the next few decades as the new generation of digital natives grows up.
> —British Chinese woman, UK (18–25 years old)

As these survey responses emphasize, influencer culture plays a central role in current marketing and advertising processes. By extension, it can play a crucial part in the preservation of the values and logic of the marketplace and the racial capitalist system that spawned it. These activities include the promotion of myths of meritocracy, such as the nationalistic American dream ethos (and variations of it), which implies that if you work hard enough, *no matter who you are*, you will get to enjoy the fruits of your labor.

Returning to the topic of the idolatry of influencer culture, Sarah, whose journalistic work covers digital trends, commented:

> I kind of thought, during the pandemic, that people might have tired of influencers. Again, there's the whole mental health issue as a side of that, portraying a perfect life, which is unattainable, that people aren't being honest about, "I've actually had surgery on my body," or "my dad's a millionaire and he pays for my lavish lifestyle," and so that's been an interesting turnabout. And then influencers can become mouthpieces for these companies as well. Again, by being offered money, they can parrot whatever they want on social media to their huge followers. And so that can be difficult because, whether they like it or not, they are inspiring a younger generation, and a lot of people put them up on pedestals and want to follow them, and so that can be really problematic.

Like Aaron's comments, which included reference to "idols," Sarah's remarks are a reminder of how influencer culture can be implicated in cultish practices that are particularly aimed at a young audience. Every person I interviewed for this book spoke of the increased societal expectation that influencers comment on social and political issues, and many survey responses referred to this too. Specifically, people discussed debates and disagreements about the potential for influencers to be activists.

Writing for the *Guardian*, Rachel Connolly (2022) states, "Just like their bland aesthetic, social media stars' low-risk, high-gain activism has become a core part of how they attract attention." Following momentous BLM and racial justice organizing in 2020 (Taylor 2021), viral visuals, videos, hashtags, and statements associated with anti-racism were (re)posted by influencers and incorporated into brands' marketing campaigns. Such content included the posting of black squares, which flooded social media timelines.

The flurry of posts of black squares in June 2020 originated from the work of two Black women, Jamila Thomas and Brianna Agyemang, who established the #TheShowMustBePaused mission to address the (music industry's) exploitation and oppression of Black people. This involved Thomas and Agyemang asking people to pause their usual social media activity and to opt to post a black square, which could amplify their message to the music industry and beyond. As Cedric G. Johnson (2022 xi) describes the attempts of corporations to participate in such online activity, "Corporate anti-racism is the perfect egress from these labor conflicts. Black Lives Matter to the front office, as long as they don't demand a living wage, personal protective equipment and quality health care." The corporate anti-racism of brands can bolster racial capitalism rather than rebuking it and thus maintains systems of structural oppression, including, but not limited to, racism and classism.

Often without attributing the idea to Thomas and Agyemang, online users began to post black squares to signal their acknowledgment and critique of racism in general. In "The Triumph of Black Lives Matter and Neoliberal Redemption," Johnson (2022) notes that during the period of time that has been dubbed Blackout Tuesday, corporate brands engaged in gestural anti-racism—superficial gestures to express their disapproval of racism despite their contradictory track records of issues such as undermining labor unionizing and the work of Black labor activists. Also, in "Black Squares for Black Lives? Performative Allyship as Credibility Maintenance for Social Media Influencers on Instagram," Mariah L. Wellman (2022, 2) affirms that "users' feeds were full of black squares for hours, and if one selected the hashtag, it became very difficult to find the necessary information about protests, supplies folks needed, and links to non-profits collecting donations." Wellman (1) argues that "for many influencers, the posting of black squares was performative allyship utilized strategically to build and maintain credibility with followers. Influencers were unable to genuinely merge their existing brand image with the Black Lives Matter movement long term, resulting in the memeification of social justice activism and no substantial progress toward diversity, equity, and inclusion within the wellness creator industry on Instagram."

The question of whether BLM has become a brand itself continues to be discussed in society. Regardless of the answer to this question, as Wellman (2022) explains, influencers sometimes make use of aesthetics and genres of content that are associated with activist and grassroots organizing efforts, including in ways that can trivialize the issues that community organizers are trying to address. When accounting for this, it is helpful to acknowledge that the challenges of digital remix culture include the fact that "despite the intended message of the content put together by a person, such a message can be diluted, decontextualised and recontextualised. This can involve individuals with oppositional motives skewing and (re)working the content's meaning" (Sobande 2019c, 157). Such challenges of digital remix culture can result in online efforts to tackle social injustices becoming a digital trend that essentially platforms individuals and brands rather than mobilizing collective action.

The commercial undercurrents of social media mean that platforms such as Twitter may be more likely to engender idolatry than they are to aid community organizing, particularly in recent years, during which time Elon Musk acquired Twitter and became the chief executive officer, appointing Linda Yaccarino as CEO in June 2023. Musk has spoken candidly about believing that the media is "racist against whites" (Oremus 2023) and has nonsensically been critical of an allegedly "woke mind virus" (Goldsmith 2022). While the effects of Twitter's change of leadership are yet to fully be realized, it is already apparent that the platform has shifted in ways that aid right-wing ideologies (Warzel 2022), which its algorithm has been identified as being biased toward in the past, too (Milmo 2021). Therefore, were the black squares posts of 2020 to occur now, it is worth considering the extent to which they would or would not have gained the same degree of visibility on Twitter. Then again, as extensive Black feminist work points out, forms of racist, misogynistic, sexist, and right-wing organizing and abuse have existed on Twitter long before now (Hampton 2019). The intentions of people who posted black squares in 2020 have been analyzed in detail, so my interest in this lies elsewhere. I am interested in what this example of the overlapping spheres of social media and social justice suggests about societal norms concerning contemporary activism and advocacy, including expectations of online visibility and its immediacy. In collaboration with Kanai and Zeng, previously I have considered "the nuances of how digital cultures of hypervisibility are connected to discourses of 'wokeness', including related interests (desires to be seen as 'woke' and speaking up) and actors involved (from celebrities, influencers to everyday social media users)" (Sobande, Kanai, and Zeng 2022, 9). On that topic, during Amanda's interview she discussed such pressures to speak out about societal issues online. Drawing on her seventeen years of expertise as a journalist, Amanda said:

> In terms of influencers, there is a pressure nowadays for an element of seriousness around Instagram. Because social media has been bashed so much in terms of it being not real, in terms of mental health issues and all that kind of stuff, I think there has been a shift where there has been a pressure for people to be more vocal, to campaign more for different things and give their opinion. I do think influencers are commenting more on social issues and social injustices, and I do think it's a positive thing in terms of conversations around things. I think nowadays, even when you think about social media and you think about influencers, why do we follow people, it's because we're interested in what they do, we maybe feel like we align with them in many ways, or we aspire to be like that.

There are numerous examples of the role of digital technology in how people, including influencers, attempt to raise awareness of social injustice and specific forms of oppression such as anti-Black violence. But does drawing attention to such matters constitute activism and contribute to structural change, or are there times when it mainly aids the online visibility, and even the capital, of people who post content about these matters? The answer to this question is complicated and depends on additional questions, such as these: Who is posting about these issues? How are they posting about them? What is the intention behind such posts? How are they responded to? While strategic forms of visibility can be crucial to the efforts of community organizers and social movements, the visibility of their efforts, documented by others (e.g., coverage of them on social media and in mainstream media), should not be assumed as evidence of substantial and sustained support of such work. Furthermore, racial and gender power dynamics—and the persistence of "white sight" (Mirzoeff 2023) in the world of Big Tech and beyond—can underpin how such visibility unfolds.

Research published in "Through a White Lens: Black Victimhood, Visibility, and Whiteness in the Black Lives Matter Movement on TikTok" (Krutrök and Åkerlund 2022, 1) indicates that within this landscape of digital content, many of the most liked videos are the work of "white content creators who, in their videos, seemed to be addressing an imagined white audience." Krutrök and Åkerlund (14) highlight that "while there were exceptions that promoted the perspectives of marginalised communities, and while the white narratives were consistently supportive of the movement, they also work to displace focus on racial (in)justice away from those directly affected by it, that is, away from Black people's own experiences of police brutality." Such content created and/or shared by white people, including online influencers, may (un)intentionally reinforce the power of "white sight" (Mirzoeff 2023)—structural looking and oppressive relations that involve forms of spectatorship, surveying, and surveillance that are bolstered by whiteness and an accordant sense of entitlement to watch and document Black and other people of color. There can be a fine line between white people bearing witness to racial injustices and their spectacularizing such harm and violence in ways that simply yield viral content rather than bolstering efforts to tackle racism and white supremacy.

The concept of white sincerity and its marketability is again relevant here—particularly given that Krutrök and Åkerlund (2022, 11) note that some of the most liked videos about BLM that they studied were made by white content creators, whose potential iconicity and idolatry may be influenced by a capacity to benefit and accumulate capital from online expressions of white sincerity and the assumption of whiteness as credential (Ray 2019). The marketability of white sincerity, I argue, is a by-product of "white sight," which "does not see everything there is to see but projects a white reality" (Mirzoeff 2023, 1). As the compelling work of Mirzoeff (1) outlines: "Other-than-white people, needless to say, see and experience lived realities. The visual politics and practices of whiteness nonetheless seek to create a time and space such that people identifying as white can act as if their reality is all there is." Thus, white perspectives of antiblackness, racism, and efforts to address them are sometimes foregrounded online in ways that paternalistically perpetuate "white sight" and "white reality"—even as part of discourse that, on its surface, is sincere and is intended to be supportive of Black people and other people of color.

As Krutrök and Åkerlund (2022) point out, such white content creators seem "to predominantly address an imagined white audience, pleading with them to inform themselves on the issue of racial inequality." This may reflect the reality that for brands (including influencers), being "associated with inclusivity and minorities is also important for appealing to the 'general market' or white consumers" (Banks 2022, 7). In other words, even if a brand's target audience is (predominantly) white, it may navigate expectations that it be seen to say something about issues of racism. Accordingly, the work of influencers that becomes associated with social justice issues must be understood in a way that is attuned to the marketability of perceived white sincerity, including "woke white womanhood" (Prins 2022) and its imagined and intended audiences.

Previously I have spent time wrestling "with what it means to witness white celebrities accruing social capital, clout, or at least, media attention and praise, when they are claiming to push against white supremacy and decentre whiteness and inequalities through their words and work" (Sobande 2022b, 131). However, when doing so, I have seldom focused strongly on the content and media framing of individuals whose fame appears to be a direct result of speaking out about such matters. In the future, will the world of celebrity and influencer culture include more white individuals who are famous—first and foremost—for what they appear to say and do to address racism and white supremacy? How might the cultish qualities of influencer culture and its embrace of idolatry be implicated in this? To return to Aaron's words, in some cases it seems as though influencers appear to "plant their flag and sort of say, I am owning this topic, I know this area, this is . . . *my social justice* issue." Thus, perhaps the future of influencer culture will be directed by the continued marketization of matters of social justice and even a race to become a "first mover" known for "speaking out."

BLACK LIVES MATTER, THE WHITENESS OF CONSUMER CULTURE, AND "BRANDING ACTIVISM"

As extensive research has made clear, digital technology, online platforms, and hashtags are often used as part of effective activist and social movement approaches, including those rooted in racial justice politics and led by Black women (Bailey, 2021; Jackson, Bailey, and Foucault Welles 2020). The 2020 Google Trends report reiterates the fact that many people are turning to the internet as part of how they try to learn more about notions of activism, allyship, and, specifically, *anti-racism*. According to Google Trends, that year there was a significant spike in searches about "anti-racism," the phrase "how to be an ally" was searched more than "how to be an influencer," "Black Lives Matter" was searched five times more than the year before, and "how to change the world" was searched twice as much as "how to go back to normal." Other similar searches that were highlighted in the Google Trends 2020 summary include "How to donate to Black Lives Matter?" and "How to help Black Lives Matter." In addition, searches for "black-owned" and "where to buy Black" doubled that year, signaling some of the ways in which consumer activities are linked to contemporary ideas about racial justice (Banks 2022; Thomas, Johnson, and Grier 2023).

The COVID-19 crisis that has been ongoing since 2020 undeniably has resulted in many societal changes, including in relation to experiences of work and collective organizing. However, as Táíwò (2022, 1) notes, even though the pandemic resulted in "lockdowns" and the closure of various public and commercial sites, "it did not stop police murders around the globe."[1] Despite the ongoing efforts of governments to prohibit protests during the COVID-19 pandemic, around the world many people took to the streets to speak out about the murder of Black people and the forms of everyday violence that they face. As Táíwò (3) explains, such "global solidarity undoubtedly owes itself to the steadfast international organizing work of Black Lives Matter [BLM] chapters, the umbrella Movement for Black Lives, and a number of other organizations around the world working in partnership and solidarity with them."

While it can feel flippant to move from discussion of BLM to the actions of brands such as retailers, the reality is that much media and public discourse about Black and racial justice activism is understood and framed through the prism of consumer and pop culture. The ripple effects of recent Black and racial justice activism include a so-called racial reckoning in the marketing industry, which attempted to acknowledge BLM but in a way that ultimately brought attention to brands and their marketers (Thomas, Johnson, and Grier 2023), yielding a swell of "corporate punditry" (Johnson 2022). Put simply, BLM's efforts to address racism and violence inflicted on Black

---

1. Aligned with critical perspectives on the term *lockdown*, I contend that use of the term in reference to the coronavirus (COVID-19) crisis can involve false equivalences being made between incarceration and experiences of quarantining and isolation during the pandemic.

Figure 6. "BLACK LIVES MATTER" sign on a brick wall, Washington, D.C., 2022. Photo by author.

Figure 7. "STRIKE FOR BLACK LIVES" sticker on back of street sign, Washington, D.C., 2022. Photo by author.

people was responded to by brands in ways that involved platforming themselves. Some of these brand reactions to BLM were constitutive of what Táíwò (2022, 4) describes as "two strategic trends," which involve "the elites' tactic of performing symbolic identity politics to pacify protestors without enacting material reform; and their efforts to rebrand (not replace) existing institutions, also using elements of identity politics." In some cases, brands appeared to use words such as *racism*, *equality*, and *inclusion* interchangeably—while avoiding specifically referring to Black people, white supremacy, or antiblackness—demonstrating Sam's perspective that many brands are softening social justice to DEI initiatives that are palatable to the gendered and racial capitalism at the core of the marketplace and its "mass" (aka white) market (Rosa-Salas 2019).

The scholarship of Banks (2022) and Tounsel (2022) yields insights related to the commodification of issues of injustice facing Black people. Specifically, "[by] developing the concept of diversity capital, *Black Culture, Inc.* shows how cultural practices related to African Americans and other racial and ethnic minorities are a resource for establishing and maintaining racial images at the organizational level" (Banks 2022, 2–3). As the work of Banks (2022) underscores, in the US many corporations engage in sponsorship and philanthropic practices that specifically focus on the Black cultural sector, including in ways that complicate the questions of who benefits most in such situations and how they benefit. Focusing on the topic of Black women and Black womanhood, Tounsel (2022, 3) outlines how corporations "offer their target audience media citizenship, a conditional form of agency bound to the image economy." Tounsel affirms that "the better we understand affirmative visibility and how it becomes commodified, the better our chance as Black women, of reclaiming the authority to decide when and how we intend to be seen" (3). Both Banks (2022) and Tounsel (2022) help readers take seriously the politics of representation, without uncritically celebrating or reductively dismissing the impacts of media and the marketplace on the lives of Black people.

The following comments of Sam from his interview seem to echo some of the sentiments of Banks (2022) and Tounsel (2022). Drawing on his expertise in the advertising industry, Sam said:

> Of course, it's really key that consumers see themselves in advertising, but it isn't necessarily . . . it can sometimes be a bit like, we're going to add some diverse casting to a commercial and, even though you might have diverse talent on-screen, it may still be shot and produced by a whole, white, middle-class male creative team, for example. To consumers it's signaling, "look this brand is more inclusive, more modern, more with today's times," but the reality is what is that business *actually* doing beyond that?

Writing for *Forbes*, Kian Bakhtiari (2022) reports that "consumers and employees won't hesitate to call brands out for performative activism. Young people can now research and investigate words against actions. A quick Google search can reveal the disparity between your marketing communications and internal leadership team." In the related words of Sam, who reflected on his experience as an advertising director:

> To me, woke-washing means when advertisers, or brands, use social justice movements to help sell their goods and services. To drive profitability for their campaigns by foregrounding social justice movements, by trying to cast their commercials in a more diverse way, effectively kind of piggy-backing off the work and activism of various social justice movements, be it Black Lives Matter, or here, in North America, a lot of work around Indigenous Lives Matter, and all that sort of stuff.

Sam's perspective focuses on the statements of corporations in the retail, media, and entertainment sectors, but in the North American higher education sector, which has become more marketized in recent decades (Klein 2000), universities also make statements on issues of racism and histories of settler colonialism. These include land acknowledgment statements, which university institutions make as part of meager gestures to acknowledge the histories and violent ongoing oppression of Indigenous people. Whether by uttering the statement at the opening of an event or encouraging staff to include it in email signatures, various North American universities have taken up the practice of communicating land acknowledgment statements while still ultimately operating in oppressive ways. Therefore, such statements might be interpreted as yet another example of how organizations attempt to comment on issues of injustice, colonialism, and racism while essentially excusing and maintaining the oppressive status quo.

Like Sam, during her interview Sarah shared thoughts on the hollow statements and superficial attempts of brands that want to appear to be allies and supporters of social movements. She spoke about the rise in comedians and influencers mocking this trend:

> If someone comes into a boardroom one day and says, "we're going to get behind Black Lives Matter," or "we're going to celebrate Pride Month," it's very rarely done in a way that's authentic, or good, or credible, or that actually holds weight. . . . There's a comedian called Meg Salter and she kind of encapsulates it all. She does all these little Instagram comedy videos, and I think it's something like, "corporations every Pride Day," or "celebrating LGBT+ stuff," and it's like [said in a jolly, high-pitched voice] "hi gay, would you like to come to our shop, we've got money off, we're going to give you some money off for some candles, if you want to do gay stuff with them, or you just want to use them." That's what comes across, and it makes me happy that people are smart enough, and wise enough, that that kind of got turned into a meme. . . . [P]eople see through it.

Speaking as an expert on the beauty, wellness, and lifestyle industry, Amanda shared a perspective that resonates with Sam's and Sarah's:

> From what I see it's [brand responses to BLM] been more superficial and it's things like hiring Black people, people of color in junior roles, not hiring Black people in senior roles or people of color in senior roles, but just being able to have a colorful face on your team picture or things like that. . . . So, it feels like the bare minimum has been done.

As the research of Judy Foster Davis (2018, 134) emphasizes, "extant literature indicates a relationship between racism, marketing and social hierarchies which manifest with regard to marketing representations of people of colour and racialised groups; discriminatory practices in the marketplace and the roles of marketing professionals of colour." Thus, even during times when brands attempt to comment on and engage with public discourse on racism, antiblackness, and white supremacy, this sometimes occurs in ways that demonstrate the pervasive power of whiteness and brands' intentions to appeal to or retain interest from a "mass" (aka white) market (Rosa-Salas 2019).

A slew of documentaries released in 2022 have probed how brands have attempted to address or avoid issues regarding diversity, inequality, discrimination, and structural oppression. Netflix's *White Hot: The Rise & Fall of Abercrombie & Fitch* documents the experiences of employees who successfully pursued legal action in response to their treatment by the company (Fashion Law 2022). The blurb for *White Hot* explains: "All the cool kids were wearing it. This documentary explores A&F's pop culture reign in the late '90s and early 2000s and how it thrived on exclusion." In the *Guardian* article "'Discrimination Was Their Brand': How Abercrombie & Fitch Fell Out of Fashion," Adrian Horton (2022a) describes Abercrombie & Fitch as being "a brand that was 'white hot, not only in a financial sense, during a period of cultural ubiquity at the turn of the millennium, but also one that promoted, internally and externally, an exclusively white vision of beauty and style.'" In previous decades, scholars such as Dwight McBride (2005, 1) examined what the brand "has successfully packaged and marketed—a rarified form of elite whiteness that depends on the racist thinking and logic of its consumers for its very success."

The deluge of 2022 documentaries about the oppressive actions of brands includes Hulu's *Victoria's Secret: Angels and Demons* documentary series, which also sheds light on exclusionary and predatory brand practices while highlighting the capital attached to notions of Englishness and its iconicity. In episode 1, viewers learn how the brand's identity was constructed by its founder (Roy Raymond), who invoked ideas associated with England's nation-brand by naming his brand "after the Victorian era in England, wanting to evoke the refinement of this period in his lingerie" (Hanbury and Cain 2023). Providing more details concerning the rationale behind the brand's name and alluding to its association with colonial Britain, in a *Slate* article Naomi Barr (2013) states that "Raymond imagined a Victorian boudoir, replete with dark wood, oriental rugs, and silk drapery. He chose the name 'Victoria' to evoke the propriety and respectability associated with the Victorian era; outwardly refined, Victoria's 'secrets' were hidden beneath." Exemplifying how the image of monarchy is connected to the image of nations and eras, Fabry (2015) writes that Victoria Secret's store image "was meant to impart the sense of class and dignity associated with the Victorian era, and the Queen for which it's named. They chose 'Victoria' to emphasize the historic association, and 'Secret' to double up on the sense of intimacy for shoppers."

One of the themes that cuts across both the Netflix and Hulu documentaries is that of whiteness—from the title of *White Hot* to most of the models and people involved in Victoria's Secret. Critical research on culture "underlines the crucial role of the *symbolic* domain at the very heart of social life" (Hall 2013, xix), including the symbolic qualities of brands that become associated with an "elite"— essentially, *white* and wealthy—social status. Since the heydays of brands such as Abercrombie & Fitch and Victoria's Secret—both of which appeared to take pride in their exclusivity—discussion of industry diversity (or a lack of it) has expanded. "'Diversity' is the prevailing concept of difference embraced by corporate marketing today, and one that affirms that difference must come with a business case to underscore its value to a firm" (Rosa-Salas and Sobande 2022, 180). Hence, the actions of various brands following the galvanization of BLM in 2020 may illustrate how commercial imperatives (e.g., the need to manage brand reputational risk) are sometimes framed as moral imperatives, or at least are undertaken in ways that mask aspects of "the business case" for diversity.

In a blog for The Marketing Society, Becks Collins (2020) discusses the fact that "many brands are now making Black Lives Matter statements, but a rare few are actually contributing to change." According to Collins, "more and more brands are realising that silence is unacceptable, that anti-racist statements must be made." Still, it is not only brands that have been critiqued regarding their response—or lack thereof—to structural racism and the interconnected forms of oppression that impact Black people. Aspects of the actions of those involved in the BLM movement have raised questions about the relationship between activism and business, including the relationship between Black social movements and influencer culture.

Barbara Ransby's (2018) significant book, *Making All Black Lives Matter: Reimagining Freedom in the Twenty-First Century*, details the development and impact of BLM, including components of it that have become celebritized. On this topic, Ransby observes that some individuals who have been involved in or associated with BLM activity have become brands themselves. As Ransby (102) puts it, "With hundreds of thousands of followers on Twitter, a high-profile presence at major protests, and numerous media appearances, for which he nearly always wears his signature blue Patagonia vest, [DeRay] McKesson has become his own brand." Ransby (23) deftly points out: "There are more Black millionaires and billionaires, CEOs, and highly paid celebrities than ever before. Still, Black poverty and suffering remain dire. And there is simultaneously greater economic disparity within Black America than ever before. Instead of a trickle down of resources from wealthy Black people to the Black poor, the growth of a more visible, albeit small, Black political and economic elite has obscured the suffering below." The Black political and economic elite in question, some may argue, includes aspects of, or individuals involved in, the BLM movement, whose class politics has been critiqued, and which is a movement that some have deemed to be "more of a sentiment than a fully formed political force" (Johnson 2022, ix).

In spring 2022, BLM faced criticism following reports that funds had been used to purchase a $6 million property in California. Questions about the use of BLM funds have mounted over the years since the political and social movement was first established in 2012. Therefore, critiques of this property purchase may be the culmination of long-standing "tensions over money" (Ransby 2018, 96) and critical claims that "the liberal character of the hashtag [#BlackLivesMatter] should be more apparent now than ever" (Johnson 2022, ix). Writing for *New York Magazine*, Sean Campbell (2022) describes the property in question as being "far from a box, with more than 6,500 square feet, more than half a dozen bedrooms and bathrooms, several fireplaces, a soundstage, a pool and bungalow, and parking for more than 20 cars, according to real-estate listings." The purchase may be viewed as an indication that aspects of, or some individuals involved in, the movement are connected to a corporate anti-racism that benefits from capitalism rather than seeking to disrupt it.

Headlines in other publications reporting on BLM's California property purchase featured words such as "luxury," "mansion" (Kilander and Buncombe 2022), "secretly" (Campbell 2022), "buying binge" (Vincent 2021), and "skeptical" (Chang, Fuller, and Fox 2022)—signaling public concern regarding BLM's potential hoarding of wealth in ways that are at odds with racial justice, anti-capitalist, and reparative work. Between the comments of social media users and the provocations of the press, there was a clear collection of criticism of what appeared to be a disconnect between the professed Marxist values of aspects of BLM and the spending of millions of dollars on a property. BLM's "positions on class and capitalism which have been a subject of internal discussion and debate" (Ransby 2018, 117) continue to proliferate. Indeed, BLM spending has been the source of a whirlwind of media pieces at various points in time. But there are many other examples of debate and discussion about the perceived business of activism, and moments when the work of social justice movements appears to be more akin to that of brands than that of grassroots organizers.

One of the six people I interviewed for this book was Alessandro, who had worked in the retail sector for a decade in the UK, including on consumer rights. On the topic of activism, branding, and their distinct differences, Alessandro said the following:

> I'd just like to see there not be such a reliance on brands being the pushers of social rights, issues, and such. The other thing that I'd like to happen is that brands are less relied on, that they're not the thing driving the conversation. That they're not the thing, with their massive PR machines, being, "here's the issue, please follow this issue, please tackle this issue by buying our stuff." No, I don't want that, I want people to be able to go out there, protest, and be like, you're all doing an absolute horrendous job, so we're going to protest this issue, we're going to do what we need to do, and we aren't going to just buy your stuff because you think that's the way we want to deal with this.

Activism and branding differ in many ways, including the commonly commercial oriented outlook of the former and the contrasting liberationist and community organizing roots of much of the latter. Although there are a lot of differences between activism and branding, both have a history of using representations and rhetoric in an influential and potentially persuasive manner. The power of communication is often an anchor of activist work, as well as bolstering branding strategies, but that should not be confused for activism amounting to branding or branding being activism. Then again, there are times when a social movement develops in ways that can result in it being regarded as a brand of some sort or being accused of selling out—so the dynamic between activism and branding is complex and is not always completely diametric.

Depictions and discourses associated with activism have featured in brands' marketing material long before the twenty-first century, but the way that brands have positioned themselves in proximity to activism has altered with the ascent of social media and the spectrum of stardom that has been generated by the digital presence of people who have come to be known as influencers. During his interview, when discussing his experience of the retail sector and what the future of branding and activism might involve, Alessandro scoffed, then said:

> My thing is that this idea that you can buy into activism, that that's your way of being an activist, to me is just absolute garbage. Like I get that, in this consumer society, that's maybe the only way it seems that you can change things, but I just think that's completely ridden with so many issues and ethical questions. It's like you're buying a product to then go online and say, "I bought this product, that means I'm being an activist and I'm protesting against such and such."

The business of activism is certainly not something that is specific to the twenty-first century; however, social media and online content-sharing sites such as YouTube have contributed to both the visibility and veneer of this activity and corresponding accusations in the present day.

In the case of BLM's purchase of the property in California, among the examples of BLM-related online content that were highlighted as potential red flags was an online video that seemed to have been shot in spring 2021. As Campbell (2022) notes, in the video "three leaders of the Black Lives Matter movement—Patrisse Cullors, Alicia Garza, and Melina Abdullah—sat around a table on the patio of an expensive house in Southern California. The women were recording a YouTube video to mark the first anniversary of George Floyd's murder, and they discussed their racial-justice work and the difficulties they had faced over the year." The video's backdrop is the property that would go on to be a source of much public scrutiny. It's luxury lifestyle aesthetic undoubtedly contributed to criticism of BLM's purchase of the property—highlighting that the culture of online visibility that typifies the twenty-first century can be both a help and a hindrance to activists and the movements that they are part of.

Articles such as Campbell's (2022) suggest that the BLM property purchase was shrouded in relative secrecy, or at least (un)intentional ambiguity, which "creates the impression that money donated to the cause of racial justice has been spent in ways that benefit the leaders of Black Lives Matter personally." Shortly after the storm of media coverage of the property purchase, a statement appeared on the BLM website (blacklivesmatter.com), titled "We Want to Talk to You about the Creator's House in California." Dated May 13, 2022, the statement describes the California property as having "served multiple functions for all of us and our movement over the past 18 months." Pushing back against the notion that people are justified in their questioning of such property ownership, the statement implies that such questioning reflects a racist double standard rather than recognition of what the movement's leaders deem to be "smart, diversified investment decisions so we can control and define our own destinies."

Framing the purchase of the property in various ways, the BLM statement refers to headlines that it argues "grossly mischaracterize the Foundation's intended use of a property that has been set to support our Creator's Fellowship." The statement also suggests that "this property serves as an opportunity for us as Black people to own our land interest free and unencumbered by any white corporate establishment" (Black Lives Matter 2022). However, what the statement does not explicitly address are critiques that the purchase might reflect the possibility of BLM being implicated in Black capitalism. Although this section of the book focuses on BLM, the whiteness of consumer culture, and the branding of "activism," it is important for me to clearly state that the structural whiteness that underpins much of consumer culture and the racial capitalist system that it is part of does not negate the existence and harms of Black capitalist ideologies. After all, as has been argued, "most Americans have now rejected the worst instances of police abuse, but not the institution of policing, nor the consumer society it serves" (Johnson 2022, xii).

While I disagree with Johnson's (2022, x) characterization of the BLM sentiment as simply being "essentially a militant expression of racial liberalism," I do agree that some social movements, including, potentially, some elements of, or individuals involved in, BLM, are implicated in the neoliberal project in ways that may ultimately reinforce rather than rupture it. But that does not mean that the meaningful work of BLM as a whole movement should be dismissed.

In its statement on the purchased property in California, BLM describes it as being "known as the Creator's House." Acknowledging the potential for the house to be used as part of the work of influencers, the statement includes these words: "Through the Creator's Fellowship and House, we are celebrating and uplifting Black creatives, dancers, filmmakers, culinary artists, musicians, storytellers, narrative artists, digital influencers—you name it!" From the use of phrases such as "diversified investment decisions" and "creative industries" to expressions such as "movement work" and "Black liberation," throughout BLM's statement about the Californian property are many signs of how the worlds of activism and business overlap or bump up against each other.

As Ransby (2018, 117) states, "some have argued that Black business and Black capitalism should be part of a strategy for Black liberation," but it seems "that the majority consensus within BLMM/M4BL circles builds on Cedric Robinson's assessment of racial capitalism as one of the foundations of Black social and economic oppression." When accounting for the fact that the work of Black artists and creatives is often obstructed and oppressed in predominantly white societies, I have argued that the arts need to "work to redistribute resources and power more equitably, including to ensure the autonomy, freedom of expression, and support of Black artists who may otherwise face pursuing their creative practice in predominantly unfunded ways, or having to (re)frame their work so that it's deemed 'legible' or 'palatable' to funders that seldom reflect them" (Sobande 2023a, 22). However, it is also imperative to acknowledge that Black art is not inherently activist in nature, nor should it have to be. Additionally, the work of Black artists and creatives, including those that BLM might support, can meld into the world of marketing and branding, complicating claims about the extent to which Black art, Black activism, and Black capitalism (dis)connect.

As marketers—including those who may also identify as artists or creatives—continue to attempt to contribute to or comment on public discourse about social injustice, it is likely that there will continue to be many examples of marketing mistaken for, or misrepresented as, activism. Such problems are not the outcome of the influence of social media in society, but social media is certainly implicated in how these processes play out, including trending topics on activism. I am not claiming that the BLM house in question will exclusively be a space that aids marketing activity. Instead, I am recognizing that the work of Black creatives, artists, and others whom the house may be partly intended to support may include forms of marketing *and* activism—leaving questions about how the two are distinguished from each other, and by whom.

Not all societal critiques of BLM are intended to be antagonistic or are just bad faith claims articulated by people with completely different social and political values, but there are certainly some that appear to involve an intention to provoke BLM and perhaps to gain public visibility and even *marketing opportunities* in the process of doing so. As I stated earlier, the term *culture wars*, to me, collapses the complexities of the experiences and perspectives that it is often intended to describe. However, regardless of my view that culture wars is relatively redundant, it has remained a buzzword in recent years and as such cannot simply be discarded as part of a critical account of the relationship between marketing, branding, and social justice. For this reason, and from a point of view that is critical of the concept of culture wars, I move on to a deeper discussion of the business of antagonism and how it might connect to Hall's (2013) widely cited concept of "the circuit of culture."

THE CIRCUIT OF SO-CALLED CULTURE WARS

The discerning work of scholar and activist Stuart Hall is expansive and defies disciplinary boundaries. Hall's (2013) many scholarly contributions include the concept of "the circuit of culture," which outlines the interconnectedness of forms of representation, identity, production, consumption, and regulation, but without overstating the ways that each informs the others. The concept of the circuit of culture was developed long before current discourse on the so-called culture wars. However, Hall's (2013) theory of "the circuit of culture" can contribute to critical understanding of how the term *culture wars* seems to function in the present day. Pairing Hall's (2013) theorizing of the circuit of culture with Towns's (2022) account of Black media philosophy yields an analytical lens that is attuned to how meaning-making in society is an iterative and infinitely ongoing process that is shaped by power relations and the impacts of the histories of racism and colonialism. Further still, shaped by Clark's (2020) influential work on "cancel culture," I acknowledge the way that culture wars and adjacent expressions such as cancel culture have been used to dismiss the accountability practices of Black people, including in digital spaces.

In the insightful article "Drag Them: A Brief Etymology of So-Called 'Cancel Culture,'" Clark (2020, 91) explains: "In their attempt to separate Black discursive accountability praxes—calling out, reading, and canceling—from their origins in the creative spaces occupied by the oppressed, and reposition them as a threat to their real and aspirational peers, elite public figures fall victim to their own worst fears: a realization that the social capital they've worked so hard for is hyperinflated currency in the attention economy." As Clark's (2021) work emphasizes, the concept of cancel culture often functions in ways that are essentially intended to belittle and block the accountability practices of Black people. Similarly, culture wars is often used as part of statements that recast powerful elites as victims of critique and harmed by being in the proverbial line of fire.

In addition to some of the similar ways that these terms are wielded, another quality that the concepts of cancel culture and culture wars share is their explicit reference to *culture*. But how is culture defined? Contrary to what is sometimes implied by authoritatively expressed claims about supposed culture wars, the concept of culture is a complicated one, and there are many different perceptions of what even constitutes culture. Hall (2013, xvii) writes that "to put it simply, culture is about 'shared meanings'. Now, language is the privileged medium in which we 'make sense' of things, in which meaning is produced and exchanged. Meanings can only be shared through our common access to language," and such language includes the many different signs, symbols, and representations that make up present-day visual and digital culture—including the logos and overall identities of brands that draw on cultural practices. Such contemporary cultural practices include how words take on new or altered meanings in ways affected by how they move around and between different digital and political contexts. One such example is the warping of notions of wokeness and the right-wing fiction of "woke mind virus," which has at least partly been propelled by elements of digital culture, such as the right-wing algorithmic bias of certain platforms.

Digital spaces are key sites of the (re)production, sharing, and consumption of culture. Drawing on Hall's (2013) reference to consumption and "the circuit of culture," my use of the term *consumption* is intended to encompass some of the power relations involved in the forms of commodification of race that hooks (1992) wrote about, such as the elite capture of identity politics that Táíwò (2022) has theorized. Unlike concepts such as that of the "cultural dope" (Garfinkel 1967), which is associated with the uncritical and unreflective reception of media and consumer culture representations, *consumption* can be used to critically refer to the intentional, extractive, and acquisitive ways that people engage with, and feed off, aspects of culture.

In an essay in *Los Angeles Review of Books*, "Cultural Dopes," G. D. Dess (2022) attests that "we're living in an era of cultural dopes," going on to describe a cultural dope as "someone like me or you, a consumer of culture or a 'creative content provider' (through social media aren't we all these days) who produces, or consumes, the preexisting cultural artifacts of the dominant political economy while functioning under the illusion that what they are creating or consuming—a TV series, a song, a novel, etc.—is 'new.'" Particularly as the concept of the cultural dope sometimes has the effect of projecting a passivity onto people that can obfuscate their agency and intentionality, I turn instead to the imperfect notion of consumption, while recognizing its limitations, and the brief yet generative theory of "the circuit of culture" (Hall 2013). Consumption too can be used in ways that portray people as passive consumers. However, the term can also critically connote vampiric elements of engagement with cultural practices and products, such as the exoticizing and fetishizing process of the white mainstream "eating the Other" (hooks 1984), as is symbolized by the framing of various Black and "mixed-race" virtual influencers.

When reflecting on critical concepts of both consumption and culture in relation to recent media and political claims about culture wars, it is clear that beyond the surface of such statements lurk struggles over meaning-making, including conflicting accounts of the origins and implications of words such as woke. A case in point is how woke was weaponized as part of the campaign activities of several Conservative Party members who stood to be considered for the role of prime minister of the UK in the summer of 2022. At that time, the media reported on how Rishi Sunak had vowed "to tackle 'woke nonsense' and 'left-wing agitators'" (Wingate 2022) when trying to convince the Conservative Party (*not* the British public) to elect him. Media coverage of the race to become prime minister also documented that the supposed "'Ben & Jerry's tendencies' of woke businesses" (Warrington, Hannah, and Bottaro 2022) were attacked by Kemi Badenoch, another Conservative member of parliament. In particular, the coverage of Badenoch having equated Ben & Jerry's with wokeness points to how the marketing of politics—including the marketing of Badenoch herself—is caught up with the wider *politics of marketing* (e.g., how brands come to be known as upholding or denouncing certain political perspectives).

By 2023 the weaponization of the term woke included the efforts of Florida governor Ron DeSantis to push his Stop-Woke (Wrongs to Our Kids and Employees) Act, which prohibits educational institutions and business from teaching students and employees anything that would cause anyone to "feel guilt, anguish or any form of psychological distress, due to their race, color, sex or national origin" (Mudde 2023). The ridiculous way that the word woke was flung around as part of the work of DeSantis and as part of how Conservative Party members competed to become prime minister in 2022 seemed to provide evidence of what a survey respondent had described in previous months:

> I'm familiar with the term "woke" so I assume this links to the perceived shift of brands pandering to what some people consider to be "woke" ideologies. To me, the whole idea of "wokeness" is a bit dumb and often raised by more conservative (and often, but not always, members of older generations) where they don't like the idea of change even when their ideologies are harmful/racist etc. I am a younger and more left-leaning person though, and generally think it's ["woke"] a case of just not being an arsehole.
>
> —White British person (gender undisclosed), UK (26–35 years old)

The research interview with Sam offers yet another take on what woke and woke-washing can mean:

> Woke-washing, as like a critique, I'm sure exists in some environments, but I don't hear it so much in my day-to-day working. I hear a lot about DEI, the need for DEI, and all of that sort of stuff, but I don't necessarily hear the term "woke-washing." I do think, however, at least in the industry press, there has begun to be a critical analysis/critical engagement with how the politics of social justice and the realities of business kind of intersect. I do think, in some examples, there is more of an active engagement of how problematic the act of woke-washing can be. Whilst the term "woke-washing" isn't used,

I also think that a lot of the types of engagement/conversations speak to woke-washing.

The differences between the perspective of Sam, the survey respondent, and the Conservative Party members are striking. Such conflicting perceptions of what words such as woke mean reflect that societal culture involves "the production and exchange of meanings— the 'giving and taking of meaning'—between the members of a society or group" (Hall 2013, xviii). When taking seriously such words on culture's constitutive parts, terms such as culture wars may be regarded as an expression that simply stands in the place of referring to age-old societal disagreements and political disputes over the meanings of different terms, texts, and the language systems that they are part of. I do not stake this claim to dismiss the very *real* and very *violent* reality of wars around the world. Instead, I do so to draw attention to how expressions such as culture wars and some uses of woke function as a distorting rhetorical device that frames long-standing disagreements, divisions, and forms of discrimination as "new"—including to stoke tensions and reinforce structural oppression such as racism, sexism, and classism. On that note, it is helpful to remember that despite claims that the concept of culture wars is a by-product of the twenty-first century, it is a well-established concept that has been examined as part of studies in earlier decades, including Thomas Frank's (1998, 1) analysis of "commerce and counterculture," which makes the claim that "for as long as America is torn by culture wars, the 1960s will remain the historical terrain of conflict."

Although culture wars is sometimes used in reference to the contrasting perspectives of people from distinctly different cultures, at times it is applied to the conflicting perspectives of people with ostensibly similar cultural backgrounds and/or cultural values. What the vague concept of culture wars rarely explicitly articulates is exactly *whose* and *what cultures* are being referred to or are viewed as being "at war." The distinction between *inter*cultural (or cross-cultural) and *intra*cultural conflict often goes unnamed. Consequently, the concept of culture wars not only results in hyperbolic accounts of disagreements; it is also used in ways that conflate intracultural disagreements and disunity with those of its intercultural or cross-cultural equivalent. Put plainly, contrary to the image of opposing factions from different cultures that may be invoked by the words culture wars, the label is often simplistically applied to examples of acrimony and antagonism between people who sometimes have more in common culturally than they, and perhaps society, may care to admit.

Here, it is helpful to revisit the concept of "white sincerity." As I have argued with Kanai and Zeng (2022), "racial justice campaigns that appear to convey a sense of 'white sincerity' are interpreted in ways which include scepticism and sometimes, derision, by other white people across the political spectrum." Certain media and political institutions continue to be quick to bandy about terms such as culture wars when commenting on disagreements between white people with diverging political perspectives, or people with different racial identities but who both have a cultural background connected to nations and investments in the state. But the questions remain: How is culture being defined in such a context (including in ways connected to or disconnected from race, ethnicity, and nationality), and how might the term culture war conveniently obfuscate elements of shared cultures? I pose these provocations with the work of Hall (2013, xix) in mind: "This focus on 'shared meanings' may sometimes make culture sound too unitary and too cognitive. In any culture, there is always a great diversity of meanings about any topic, and more than one way of interpreting or representing it. Also, culture is about feelings, attachments, and emotions as well as concepts and ideas."

The concept of culture wars sometimes seems to emerge from an imaginary that frames two or more distinct cultures as sparring with one another, and which positions such cultures as being both unitary (e.g., everyone of one culture thinks the same) and oppositional (e.g., different cultures relate to each other in inherently oppositional ways). However, conflict within cultures is commonplace, precisely because cultures are not homogenous, and differences between political perspectives do not always indicate distinct differences between cultural connections. The use of the term culture wars can contribute to the spectacularization of debates, disagreements, and discrimination in a way that belies the fact that there is nothing new about much of such dynamics, beyond the viral visibility of antagonism that is propelled by contemporary digital culture.

So far, my book has mostly moved between analysis of research interviews, survey responses, the media and marketing of brands, and archived material related to the history of advertising in the UK and the US. An in-depth analysis of power dynamics between branding, activism, and digital practices that does not feature analysis of pop culture portrayals of such matters would feel incomplete. Therefore the final section of this penultimate chapter is dedicated to discussing six TV shows that spotlight corporate culture and the strategies of fictional brands that closely resemble those of many real ones or that have been marketed in ways that relate to how brands tap into different dimensions of digital culture. By analyzing features of the plots and positioning of *Industry, Partner Track, Severance, Succession, The Bold Type*, and *You*, I discuss how the world of branding and corporate culture is portrayed on TV and what the marketing of such shows might suggest about the relationship between branding, activism, digital culture, and pop culture. Finally, at the end of the section I focus on the marketing of, and my attendance at, the When We Were Young (WWWY) festival in Las Vegas in 2022, which involves reflecting on how ideas about and experiences of aging, branding, Big Tech, nostalgia, and "alternative" music cultures merge.

BRANDS AND CORPORATE CULTURE IN POP CULTURE

The domain of digital remix culture was once mainly associated with DIY practices and processes, which involved people on the internet remixing existing media and material to produce "new" and referential content connected to a range of cultural references—from the art of fandom communities to the memes of political dissenters. I have argued that some such "digital content production processes can draw attention to issues and experiences that are pertinent to those who are most marginalised and are rarely represented and supported in British politics and public life. Still, it can be these same processes that are used to perpetuate the societal oppression of such individuals, in the form of vitriolic online abuse and which extends to offline threats and violence" (Sobande 2019c, 159). Beyond this, it is crucial to recognize that what was once deemed a form of DIY digital remix culture has now been corporatized in ways that prompt questions about the potential power of content that was originally regarded as user-generated and fan-led but has now become part of strategic brand approaches. Additionally, analyzing pop culture portrayals of brands' engagement with digital remix culture can aid understandings of the contemporary connections between these various consumer-culture-oriented entities and phenomena.

Take for example, *Succession*. The award-winning dark comedy from HBO follows the lives of the dysfunctional and wealthy Roy family, owners of a global media and entertainment conglomerate named Waystar Royco. The show centers on the dynamics between different family members, particularly the characters Logan Roy (masterfully played by Brian Cox)—the mercurial and domineering patriarch of the family, who is of Scottish ancestry—and Kendall Roy (enigmatically played by Jeremy Strong), who seems to want nothing more than his father's (Logan's) validation, even when warring with him and trying to take over the family business. Over the course of *Succession*'s four powerful seasons, the audience witnesses characters expressing concern about how they and the brand(s) that they represent are discussed on social media. Season 3 of *Succession* picks up from Kendall's shocking betrayal of his father at the end of season 2, when Kendall publicly spoke out against Logan's corruption and enabling of abuse.

In episode 1 of season 3, Kendall is depicted frantically trying to track how he is being discussed on social media following his public denunciation of his father, which could even result in Logan facing a prison sentence for the corruption he is accused of. When summoning the help of those who essentially form Kendall's entourage at this point, he declares, "I might need you to take my cultural temperature . . . slide the socio-political thermometer up the nation's ass and get a reading." This brief line perfectly encapsulates how Big Brands are watching you (*watching them*)—both the fictional self-brand of Kendall Roy, who is hell bent on succeeding his father to claim his business and frequently monitors Twitter coverage of him and his family, and the brand of *Succession* (and by extension, HBO), which seems to have its finger on the pulse of digital culture and how online backlash (e.g., the creation of mocking memes) plays out.

The phrase "cultural temperature" can be linked to the notion of "social intelligence," which relates to forms of gathering, monitoring, and attempting to moderate, or even manipulate, public conversations and commentaries about brands. As Turow (2012, 142–43) argues, "Social intelligence becomes grist for advertising agencies that create their clients' commercial messages." In the case of *Succession*, mining social media becomes a way for its protagonists' entourages to sense-check their (un)popularity (aka discern social intelligence), with a view to trying to manage self-brands (e.g., Kendall's public image). Responding to Kendall's request for a reading of his cultural temperature, his aloof and goofball cousin Greg (brought to life by Nicholas Braun) earnestly but nervously says, "Nice memes. Good memeage and so on." Although this is a comedic scene in *Succession*, the decision to focus on how Kendall was being "memed" signals the significance of dimensions of digital remix culture in the overall image and mitigation of backlash against public figures and the brands that they embody. In that same season, viewers see Kendall and his friends play a drunken game of "Good Tweet, Bad Tweet," during which they read out positive and negative comments about him on Twitter—again demonstrating that (self-)

brands are invested in tracking, and trying to change, their cultural temperature on social media.

Returning once more to the topic of nation-branding, it is useful to consider the example of *Succession*, which is shaped by the show's depiction in season 2 of Dundee (where Brian Cox is from)—a Scottish city that was my home for years. The representation of Dundee in *Succession* (episode 8 of season 2) offers a glimpse into this unique Scottish city's recent history. This includes contemporary symbols of its perceived economic development—or what might be regarded as its gentrification and unequal distribution of wealth across the city. One such example is the Victoria & Albert (V&A) Dundee building (where, in *Succession*, during a celebration of 50 years of Logan running Waystar Royco, Kendall raps for his father, in front of a cringing audience), which is part of a broader brand (V&A) that is inextricably linked to the interconnected brands of the British monarchy and the UK.

Throughout the episode of *Succession* that is set in Dundee, there are allusions to distinct disparities between the material conditions faced by different people in the city (e.g., those who are working class and those who are wealthy). There are also hints at the fact that Logan Roy is experiencing both nostalgia and discomfort at returning to his hometown (e.g., when he declares "the water used to taste sensational . . . it's changed"). The portrayal of Dundee plays a key role in the development of the tempestuous character Logan Roy, including in the construction of his image as somewhat of an outsider, even when at "home" in the American world of business that he has thrived in or when at "home" in his hometown of Dundee.

In the fourth and final season of *Succession*, in the episode prior to the death of Logan, his character is depicted once more commenting that "everything tastes different." In a dimly lit restaurant, following an eerily lonesome walk tailed by his bodyguard (Colin), Logan is depicted speaking to him over dinner, during which he refers to Colin as his "best pal," before sharing his thoughts on life. In a simultaneously perturbed and resigned manner, Logan repeatedly asks, "What are people?" before coldly answering his own question with the words "economic units." Expanding on his explanation, Logan describes "a person" as having "values and aims," while also stating that "it operates in a market . . . marriage market, job market, money market, market for ideas etc." In a melancholic line that appears to foreshadow his demise, Logan hypothesizes, "Nothing tastes like it used to, does it? Nothing is the same as it was." Although Logan does not mention Dundee, the lines are a nod to his reflections in the Dundee episode ("the water used to taste sensational . . . it's changed"), reiterating the character's sense of in-betweenness—not quite here (not quite the stoic business tycoon of the present), not quite there (not quite the young boy that he once was in Dundee), and not quite living but not quite dead.

In a sense, the cyclical nature of Logan's repeated reflections on taste and the passing of time highlight that despite his view that people are mere markets and his image as an indestructible force to be reckoned with, his own mortality is inescapable. Consequently, audiences may be reminded that even brands deemed to be "taste-makers" cannot completely control changes in the tastes and pal-ettes of everyone—that is, they cannot control the inevitable passing of time and changes that it catalyzes. Logan's lonesome days before his demise, and his employees' focus on how his death will impact the stock market moments after he dies, is a stark reminder of the extent to which the world of Big Business reduces people to dispos-able units of value.

Caught between the competitiveness and opulence of New York corporate culture and a very different and humble start in life in Scotland, Logan is best understood as a product of these contrasting yet connected environments, reflecting how the images of different nations and the regions within them creep into pop culture portrayals of fictional brands, their corporate cultures, and the people who lead them (Sobande 2023b). To me, Dundee is just as much a character in *Succession* as the self-destructive Logan family members. The unas-suming city—which in real life is sometimes derogatorily referred to as "Scumdee"—is an anchor in the character arc of Logan Roy and a reminder that the Roy family's roots are shaped by specters of Scotland. *Succession* has a Shakespearean quality to it in terms of how tragedy and familial conflict transpire, but it is also unmistakably a contemporary commentary on the ruthless world of business, particularly global media and entertainment brands. Thus, the show's portrayal of the Roy family includes depictions of their navigation of different ideas about morality and mortality, including expectations that are imposed on, and dismissed by, their shared brand.

Succession's portrayal and exploration of the relationship between morality, activism, and the marketplace includes lines uttered by the character Kendall, who speaks about "an alternative corporate manifesto" and claims that if we "detoxify our brand we can go supersonic." Sometimes expressed through his use of terms associated with digital discourse on social justice, Kendall's character develops in ways that reflect corporate culture's engagement with, and reframing of, issues of inequality and injustice. By the third season of *Succession*, Kendall has begun to establish his image as a man in the business world who, on occasion, speaks out against issues of misogyny and the harassment, assault, and abuse of women—leading to a fictional tweet that is read in the show and that implies that he is one of the "allies." But as Erin Gee (2021) notes in an article for *Harper's Bazaar*, Kendall's character might be perceived as embodying a "performative faux feminism" that is ultimately palatable to the world of business, even if he presents some pushback directed at specific brands, such as Waystar Royco.

Depending on a person's perception of the conflicted character of Kendall, they may regard his character's arc as reflecting shifts in the corporate world based on a recognition of the fact that marketized notions of social justice can sell but can also result in much criticism. As Gee (2021) states, "the thing about Kendall is that he believes that he is a good person who does the right things for the right reasons," but he is also a person who appears to be committed to the corporate world, insofar as he benefits from it. In that sense, even though Kendall comes to be known for his criticism of the corruption that his family's business has participated in, like many brands his actions speak louder than his words; they suggest that despite becoming versed in the language of justice, Kendall may be far from invested in the downfall of the entire corporate world.

Netflix's show *Partner Track* also portrays many of the ways that the worlds of business, branding, social media, and social justice spar. In a storyline that focuses on the character Tyler Robinson (played with conviction by Bradley Gibson), viewers witness the fallout that ensues after Tyler—a Black gay man pursuing a partner role at his law firm—is targeted by a white heterosexual man whom he works with, after Tyler challenges his racism. After turning down a $500,000 nondisclosure agreement (NDA) from his employer, who seems desperate to orchestrate his departure, Tyler turns to social media to stream a video of himself speaking out about the experience. This plot, including its portrayal of the different perspectives of Tyler's (mostly) white colleagues, offers a depiction of brands and their corporate culture that captures the controlling anxieties of businesses—their concerns about reputational risk, resulting in brands grasping for ways to obstruct employees from publicly discussing them.

The popular genre of TV shows set in corporate culture settings also includes Apple's *Severance*. The thriller, which is fronted by Adam Scott as the character Mark S, explores themes such as control, power, and surveillance in the workplace, following the day-to-day lives of employees at the fictional company Lumon Industries, where they agree to be part of a "severance" program that results in their nonwork memories being separated from their memories of and at work. Such forms of control include Lumon Industries using the language and logic of NDA policies to refuse to provide employees with answers to certain questions. This creepy and corporate workplace setting is one within which expressions of emotion appear to be absent and handshakes are only available upon request. In short, *Severance* explores an extreme manifestation of the ways that Big Brands are watching you (and, in this case, trying to control you).

The business at the center of *Severance* (Lumon Industries) seeks to create the illusion of choice and agency among employees who are ultimately, mostly, under their control. This is alluded to in the trailer for season 1, which opens with Mark saying, in a slightly hypnotic sounding voice, "Every time that you find yourself here, it's because you chose to come back." The trailer also features Mark referring to having made the decision "of his own free accord to undergo the procedure known as 'severance.'" Other words uttered by Mark during the eerie trailer include "consent" and "I make these statements freely." Unsurprisingly, the motivations of Lumon Industries in *Severance* are nefarious and based on unbridled self-interest, including a desire to exercise control and authority over employees in a way that is intended to prevent them from publicly discussing their employer.

On the topic of businesses' efforts to control employees, during his interview Aaron discussed some of his own experiences of dealing with an employer that appeared to be monitoring, and sometimes attempting to coercively manage, his use of social media. Accounting for the impact of the COVID-19 crisis and reflecting on how employers attempt to discourage employees from using their personal social media accounts on their own terms, Aaron said:

> As workplace communication has changed from physical conversations in person to digital stuff, there's always the risk of there is a paper trail, and that things can leak out. Social media is like a public forum of discussion and so there might be an attempt to try and gain more ownership over how people act on there, but I don't. . . . [I]t's like you can't restrict someone's speech on these things. There is a boundary there, and I don't think a public social media platform can necessarily be owned by an organization that you work for.

As the actions of Tyler in *Partner Track* make clear, and just as Aaron described, despite their desire to control the social media presence and online posts of employees, many employers struggle to do so. Another example of this is depicted in the US TV drama *The Bold Type*.

Based on the experiences of women working in the magazine industry in New York, *The Bold Type* particularly focuses on the theme of feminism. This is indicated by the character Jane Sloan (convincingly played by Katie Stevens), a journalist writing about her experience of being a "failed feminist." The show follows the lives, loves, and losses of three best friends working at a women's magazine named *Scarlet*. The character Kat Edison (which Aisha Dee plays with charisma) is the magazine's social media director for much of her time at *Scarlet*. As a "biracial" woman who eventually realizes that she is also bisexual, Kat is sometimes treated in a tokenized way at her workplace, as well as being tokenized by external brands, who try to partner with her to boost their image as supposedly "intersectional." At one point this results in the character Kat creating social media content to explicitly critique a brand that she was meant to be promoting, following the revelation that they had sought her out to do damage control, ahead of their support of racist organizations being exposed.

It is not just the character Kat on *The Bold Type* that reveals much about the portrayal of brands and their corporate culture in pop culture. Toward the end of the show, Aisha Dee publicly spoke out about *The Bold Type*'s diversity problem behind the scenes. Reporting on this in a piece for *Vanity Fair*, Christopher Rosen (2020) writes: "As several legacy publications find themselves caught in a broader cultural reckoning, it seems only fitting that a television series about a fake media brand would follow suit. On Wednesday night, Aisha Dee—who stars on *The Bold Type*, the Freeform series about the fictional *Scarlet* magazine—called for the show to address its lack of diversity behind the scenes, and questioned a recent plot arc that found her character falling for a conservative woman."

The portrayal of Kat Edison and Aisha Dee's public critique of *The Bold Type*'s issues concerning diversity exemplify the fact that, even within brands that appear to be relatively inclusive and progressive, there are often still issues related to (in)equality and diversity, some of which is eventually exposed online (e.g., in the form of social media posts or mainstream media coverage of cast members). The depiction of fictional brands and their corporate culture on TV is never just about responding to audience demand for certain types of shows. Rather, such media depictions and discourses, and the casts' discussion of them and the production process that makes them possible, can be a window into parts of the world and workings of Big Brands. No matter the differences between the genres, styles, and marketing of shows such as *Partner Track*, *Severance*, *Succession*, and *The Bold Type*, in one way or another they all—to borrow the words of Kendall Roy—take and respond to the "cultural temperature . . . the socio-political thermometer." In turn, such TV shows offer audiences reflections as well as fictional representations of Big Brands.

In an article for the *Guardian*, Adrian Horton (2022b) discusses "why some of the best TV focused on work in 2022." Horton observed that "if there is one uniting theme of workplace television in 2022, it's that none of the characters in any of these shows would consider work-life balance to be a practical or relevant concept." It is no coincidence that there has been a surge in such shows recently. We are still at a point in time marked by an ongoing pandemic that has catalyzed significant shifts in terms of people's experiences of work and labor (Horgan 2022; Sobande and Klein 2022; Sobande 2022a). For some people, work/personal life boundaries were eroded by a sudden shift to remote working, combined with employers' expectations that employees be visible to them during all video calls and available to do work at any time, even when at home. Some TV shows, including *Industry*, featured plots and depictions that capture elements of people's experiences of work during the COVID-19 crisis.

Shown on HBO in the US and on BBC in the UK, *Industry* follows a group of graduates who are in competition with each other for permanent positions at a London-based investment bank, Pierpoint & Co. The young employees find themselves dealing with a predatory corporate culture in which, in season 1, one of them dies, seemingly because of the overwork that they endure. The overlap between the themes of shows such as *Succession* and *Industry* is poignantly captured by a scene in season 2 of *Industry* in which one character is depicted commenting that another looks like they have dressed as Kendall Roy. *Industry's* exploration of corporate culture's response to the COVID-19 crisis includes its portrayal of the protagonist Harper Stern (captivatingly played by Myha'la Herrold), who in season 2 struggles with readjusting to working in the office, and on whose mental health remote working has taken a toll in the previous months.

My personal and professional interest in *Industry* not only relates to its exploration of the world of financial services Big Brands and the cravings of corporate cultures. Rather, my interest in *Industry* is also shaped by the fact that parts of it are shot around the building that happens to be my own place of work—a building that is the location of the School of Journalism, Media and Culture (Cardiff University) and a law firm, but that has also been portrayed as the premises of Pierpoint & Co. Thus, while analyzing depictions of brand activity and corporate culture in *Industry*, I also found myself thinking about how real-life workplace buildings are remediated and (re)presented in pop culture. Of course, Pierpoint & Co is a fictional brand. But as someone who works in one of the same buildings that *Industry's* lead character Harper Stern is portrayed as working around, I found that elements of the show particularly resonated with me—such as when witnessing Harper (who is also a Black woman) navigate a predominantly white industry during the ongoing COVID-19 crisis, experiencing pressures to perform, produce, and be visibly present. However, unlike the character Harper, I have never worked in the world of financial investments. Someone who does understand that world, though, is Inaya.

As discussed in chapter 2, when interviewed Inaya spoke to me about the increasing demand for ESG investments. Inaya shared her experience of working for an employer that provides such investment opportunities, while making clear that as a business they are not taking a stand on any specific moral matters. Inaya's employers regard their provision of ESG investment routes as being based on a commercial imperative—there is demand for such investments, and such demand is informed by their clients' interest in mitigating the prospect of their investment decisions being deemed by others as unethical. Interestingly, the topic of ESG investments came up in season 2 of *Industry*, around a year after I interviewed Inaya. In episode 3 of that season, the audience is shown one character speaking about their interest in stakes from an "ESG perspective," which they articulate as being "contingent on broadening access so we can service lower income households." The stakes in question concern health-care-related business activity. Elsewhere in that same episode there is discussion of "social impact funds" and "moral investment," which reminded me of Inaya's perspective that the future of the financial services sector will have to contend with increased demand for ESG investments.

Beyond the pop culture context of *Industry* and on-screen portrayals of corporate verbiage, discourse on ESG investments is being picked apart by various news and media publications that have been covering pushback against such types of investments. In a piece for the *New York Times*, "How Environmentally Conscious Investing Became a Target of Conservatives," David Gelles states, "Now, Republicans around the country say Wall Street has taken a sharp left turn, attacking what they term 'woke capitalism' and dragging businesses, their onetime allies, into the culture wars." There are numerous other articles on this topic, which highlight that the backlash against supposed wokeness and woke capitalism dovetails with Conservative and Republican criticisms of ESG investments.

Headlines and commentaries on these topics also bring the concept of culture wars into the discussion, which is yet another example of how terms and ideas (e.g., wokeness) associated with specific activist, social justice, and socially conscious positions are antagonistically contorted, weaponized, and used as synonyms for "left," "liberal," and "progressive." As Gelles (2023) notes, "in recent months, conservatives have increasingly attacked the practice [of ESG investing], arguing that it promotes liberal priorities ranging from renewable energy to the Black Lives Matter movement." Indeed, as the *Financial Times* reports, "Anti-ESG sentiment has 'gained momentum' across the US" (Temple-West and Masters 2023). Perhaps similar sentiments will follow in the UK, where fearmongering about "wokeness" and "conservative propagations of 'identity politics'—a political smear that has been monopolized by the right, but also has form on the centre and left" (Richmond and Charnley 2022, 1) have impacted discourse on activism, politics, and the marketplace.

Industry's portrayal of discussions about ESG investing appears to hint at the limitations of the supposedly socially conscious nature of such investments. Moments after the season 2 scene that shows a character articulating their "ESG perspective," another character brings the discussion to a close by abruptly ushering everyone on to a recreational shooting activity, saying, "Let's go see about them birds before they start to unionize." That reference to labor unionizing, following a grilling on the ESG potentials of the investing opportunity being proposed, is a reminder of the undeniably capitalist foundations upon which financial investing, *including ESG*, depends. Despite the label ESG being intended to refer to investments that are typically regarded as environmentally and socially conscious in some way, it may simply be one that corporations can leverage to frame some investments as "less harmful" than others, while aiding commercial activity that continues to prop up an inherently oppressive system.

TV shows such as *Industry, Partner Track, Severance, Succession*, and *The Bold Type* bring different issues of the worlds of Big Brands to the small screen—from how businesses try to commodify social justice, to their attempts to control and oppress their employees. While media representations that feature in these shows shed light on some of the ways that Big Brands are watching you (and watching each other), the marketing of TV shows can also reveal much about the relationship between brands, digital culture, and different issues related to identity, iconicity, intertextuality, and injustice. Thus, the last TV show that I focus on in this book is Netflix's *You*.

Since its 2018 release, *You* has generated much controversy. Based on Caroline Kepnes's novel of the same name, Netflix's show follows the life of Joe Goldberg (powerfully played by Penn Badgley). Joe is a young(ish) white man who initially appears to be a lonesome but endearing lover of literature. However, as the plot of *You* transpires, Joe turns out to be an obsessive and calculating serial killer who stalks women. By the time that viewers arrive at season 4, Joe has become a husband and father, before faking his own murder to conceal his murderous tracks and moving to London, child-free, where he continues stalking women. In the opening of season 4, various statements made by Joe include, "As a problematic man appropriating the words of a queer poet once said: the heart wants what it wants." This line perhaps best captures the character's conviction that he is one of the few "good" guys and is even an ally of those who are marginalized (Sobande 2023c).

Critiques of *You* have included many articles on the show's potential to romanticize abuse, misogyny, and stalking. Following season 1, young actor Millie Bobby Brown (of Netflix's *Stranger Things*) was accused of defending the character Joe Goldberg after she tweeted, "He's not creepy, he's in love with her and it's okay" (Reilly 2019). As indicated by such accusations and some of the polarizing responses to them, *You* has divided opinions, particularly due to its focus on a protagonist who perceives himself as a misunderstood romantic but is in fact a serial killer who stalks women. Although *You* has prompted many commentaries and critiques in response to its portrayal of Joe and its plot, which centers on him and his inner monologues, there seems to have been less critical discussion and analysis of the marketing of the show and the construction of its brand voice and overall persona on Twitter.

The official Twitter account for Netflix's *You* has posted a fascinating range of content and comments that reflect the phenomenon described in "When Brands Become Stans" (Sligh and Abidin 2022), while also pointing to how such an approach to branding and marketing involves simultaneously foregrounding and denouncing a fictional character in a TV show—in this case Joe Goldberg, who is reviled while also being the face featured in playful memes and Twitter posts that seem to meander between attempts to express sincerity and to embrace silliness. Undoubtedly, sincerity and silliness can exist at once, but what I am pointing out in relation to the official Twitter account for *You* is that content sometimes oscillates between discouraging fan-type reactions to the character Joe, while including representations of him in fun and humorous posts that have a fanlike feel. There is friction between what seems to be Netflix's push against the notion that the show romanticizes and glamorizes Joe (e.g., posts discouraging admiration of Joe but not of the esteemed actor Penn Badgley) and its use of content that treats the character as a text from which to invoke humor, banter, and commentaries on topics such as sex, relationships, and Valentine's Day.

In addition to featuring light-hearted posts that promote the actor Penn Badgley while dismissing support of Joe but using images of him to promote the show, the *You* Twitter account makes use of intertextual content that harks back to Badgley's character Dan Humphrey in the iconic 2000s/2010s show *Gossip Girl* (also based on books). In a tweet on February 25, 2023, Netflix's *You* Twitter account posted a brief video of Joe saying, "I'M A WRITER," accompanied by the caption "xoxo, joe goldberg." The video clip features parts of season 4 of *You*, which focuses on a plot that involves Joe criticizing and sneering at the vapid world of wealth inhabited by people whom he befriends while posing as a professor in London. The tweeted caption that accompanies the video on *You*'s Twitter account is presumably a nod to the *Gossip Girl* finale revelation that Badgley's character, Dan, was the anonymous online gossiper who signed messages with "xoxo, gossip girl," and who had created chaos in the cliquey world of teens at a fictional New York private school, which he was critical of while also being part of. Thus, *You*'s intertextual tweet on February 25 is made possible by the iconicity of both *Gossip Girl* and *You*, the respected celebrity of Badgley, and similarities and differences between the fictional characters Dan

Humphrey and Joe Goldberg—both of whom are writers who are critical of those deemed to be elite in society, both of whom keep secrets from everyone in their lives, both of whom seem to obsess over women, but only one of whom is a serial killer and stalker.

In their insightful "When Brands Become Stans," scholars Casta Sligh and Crystal Abidin (2022) examine "brand personification on social media at a niche angle." Focusing on Netflix original series Instagram accounts, they explain how each of three of such accounts "co-ops fan practices and enacts its own specific fannish persona." From the Instagram accounts that they analyzed, they outline different personas that are enacted across such social media spaces: "the emotional fan," "the fannish friend," and "the legitimated fan" (Sligh and Abidin 2022). The brand voice and persona established through *You*'s Twitter account appears to draw on elements of "the emotional fan," which is defined as involving a voicing style that "performs relating to the series" and "displays emotional investment in story and characters." Specifically, *You*'s Twitter account includes content that relates to the series and different emotional responses to the characters and plots that are part of it, including strong reactions to plot twists and the fate that might lie ahead for returning and new characters in the fifth and final season of the show.

Although *You*'s Twitter account draws on fan-type digital practices, including memes and GIFs that refer to multiple shows that share the same actor, its constant reiteration of the distinct differences between the actor Penn Badgley and the character Joe Goldberg reflects the brand's awareness of the problematic nature of being perceived as aiding a fan following of its protagonist. Hence, the fan-like qualities of *You*'s Twitter account may be tempered by strategic marketing decisions that are intended to protect a brand's image from criticism and disrepute (e.g., by praising Penn Badgley but not Joe Goldberg). That said, the content featured on the account includes posts that seem to embrace a degree of ambiguity in terms of the voice of the brand. Namely, while some Twitter posts are made in a voice that is demarcated as not being that of the character Joe, others seem to take on his persona, resulting in an overall brand voice that is neither entirely detached from, nor attached to, that of the show's protagonist.

For example, in a tweet on Valentine's Day (February 14, 2023), the Twitter account posted an image of Joe featuring the text "My To-Do List: YOU," accompanied by the tweet caption "send this to someone you promise you'll never harm or obsessively follow [wrapped heart emoji] [via @NetflixUK]." However, in a different post on the same date, *You*'s Twitter account created a thread that was described with the following explanation: "joe's the princess in his story and these are his frogs. First up on why they didn't make it [according to joe]: beckalicious." The remaining posts in that thread are expressed from the point of view of Joe, which despite the disclaimer in the opening post of the thread veers more toward a brand voice that sees the benefit of inhabiting the persona of Joe, even if infrequently.

The idea that there is no such thing as bad press is not one that the Netflix *You* brand seems to align with. However, as *You*'s Twitter account still features humorous content that pokes fun at the character Joe (e.g., describing him as "smiling on the outside, reading you to filth on the inside"), the brand does not seem to be committed to rebuking Joe at the expense of creating engaging content that is more comical than it is earnest and more casual than corporate. Therefore, while Netflix's *You* brand may seek to avoid antagonism and acrimony by reaffirming that Joe is not someone to be admired, it also appears to fly close to the sun by making jokes about Joe that some people may view as trivializing the reality of being stalked. Overall, *You*'s Twitter account is an intriguing case study that demonstrates some of the ways that the branding and marketing of TV shows involves the creation and posting of content that draws on the styles and sentiments of fan-like digital experiences, while painting an image of the show that involves the management and narrativization of aspects of it that might be regarded as problematic or even immoral (e.g., by denouncing the actions of Joe, despite constantly using depictions of him in light-hearted social media content).

It is not only the marketing of TV shows that can blend forms of pop culture, fandom, digital culture, and the work of corporate brands. Music festivals and their promotion can be supported by such activity too. Although there may be people who ardently dismiss claims that festivals can constitute brands, there are numerous examples of iconic festivals that are clearly commercial in nature and have become established brands of their own (Klein 2020). Woodstock is an example. Initially, the music festival appeared to be the antithesis of corporate culture and was presented as being much more about the pursuit of peace than the maximization of profit. However, as is depicted in the Netflix documentary series *Trainwreck: Woodstock '99*, by the late 1990s the festival had descended into a state of chaos that was perhaps more capitalist oriented than geared toward changing the world for the better. Destruction had replaced generative dissent, community had been eclipsed by capitalism, and festival freebies from corporate sponsors had taken the place of a counterculture of collective care. However, as Joseph Heath and Andrew Potter (2006) argue in *The Rebel Sell: How the Counterculture Became Consumer Culture*, expressions of counterculture activity sometimes have the effect of reinvigorating capitalism rather than disrupting it.

The '99 Woodstock festival's eclectic lineup included a who's who of nu-metal at the cusp of the second millennium, as well as a range of iconic musicians and performers that included James Brown. Originally developed as a festival of peace, music, and art in the summer of 1969, Woodstock became known as a gathering that was grounded in countercultural sentiments and bohemian sensibilities (Lang 2010). The festival was long regarded as upholding a communal ethos of care and certain social and political values. These included a concern with protecting the environment and protesting wars; think more flower power than the harassing chants such as "show us your tits" that were part of Woodstock '99. Among the many issues with Woodstock '99 was that it seemed to be the site of much misogyny, as indicated by numerous reports of sexual harassment, sexual assault, and rape (Morgan 2022). A festival that was once celebrated for the sense of social consciousness that appeared to be at its core came to be known as a space where misogyny went unaddressed and where women were assaulted.

Trainwreck: Woodstock '99 documents many aspects of the festival that year, including the carnage that was on display in the form of the vast amount of waste that the festival produced. In the Netflix documentary, shots of piles of plastic rubbish and footage of trash flying through the air while being flung at performers remind viewers that Woodstock '99 was a mess: *literally*. Perhaps the commodification of the festival's ethos (Saunier 2021) is best described using the words of Metallica's guitarist Kirk Hammett, who in a 1999 interview about the festival stated, "Peace plus love equals capitalism." No matter what words are used to encompass the troublesome reality that was Woodstock '99, when viewing recorded footage of the festival and testimonies from those who were in attendance, the undeniably unsafe nature of it is apparent. From the unsettling sight of cascading festival infrastructure to disturbing depictions of women being harassed, *Trainwreck: Woodstock '99* chronicles some of what happened at the festival that would mark the last of Woodstock.

When Woodstock '99 took place, social media as we know it had barely been conceived. While watching the documentary, I thought about what Twitter or TikTok commentary about the festival might have been like at the time, if such social media platforms had existed then. Fast forward from 1999 to 2022, and the music festival landscape includes When We Were Young (WWWY), marketed as a feel-good festival that takes emo fans down memory lane. An abbreviation of emotional hardcore, *emo* is a type of music and overall scene that stems from post-punk and adjacent genres (Fathallah 2020) and is linked to a sense of youthful angst and yearning, the embrace of emotion-laden lyrics, an acerbic attitude, and a sartorial style once typified by skinny black jeans and a thick side-fringe hairstyle. Although emo is strongly tied to an age and stage in life that is particularly associated with high school and teenage heartbreaks between the 1990s and 2010s, it has maintained the attention and

Figure 8. Advertisement for When We Were Young Festival, Las Vegas, 2022.
Photo by author.

loyalty of many followers whose time at high school is now a dis-
tant memory. Put differently, emo may not be old news, but both it
and many of its fans have aged, including since their days on iconic
websites such as AbsolutePunk.net (Doherty 2023; Fathallah 2020;
Greenwald 2003; Markarian 2019; Ozzi 2021; Payne 2023). Cue the
arrival of WWWY, which, following on from its first incarnation as
a festival in 2017 (Gaca 2017), seemed to reestablish itself in 2022,
first and foremost on Twitter and social media platforms.

While the 2022 festival's website was relatively sparse for many
months after it was announced in a tweet, the WWWY Twitter
account appeared to be contrastingly active in terms of its curation
and frequency of posts. WWWY seemed to burst onto the music
scene at a point in time when the music festival industry was just
beginning to reestablish itself after grinding to a halt during the

Figure 9. When We Were Young Festival entrance, Las Vegas, Nevada, 2022. Photo by author.

ongoing COVID-19 crisis in 2020 and 2021. The WWWY brand image has heavily drawn on aesthetics, phrases, and trends associated with 2000s and 2010s emo digital culture and online communities that were based on the DIY sharing of demos, the coding and customizing of lo-fi websites, and playing with dark color palettes that were often accented by punk-rock pops of neon and gunmetal silver. As I reflected on in a piece for *Paste*, "Despite the imaginative ways that people were creating emo music and online communities in the early 2000s, most media corporations at that time did not pay serious attention to the emo world—and some that did just fed moral panic" (Sobande 2022c). By 2022, emo was far from being a music-based subculture that sparks fear mongering, and although it continues to be associated with an "alternative" style, it is arguably the most mainstream and embraced by mass media that it has ever been. This partly reflects the business of aging and the pull of nostalgia in consumer culture (Sobande 2022d).

Festivals such as WWWY do not simply cater to a demand for a gathering based around emo music. Rather, they provide a nostalgic experience that is marketed via rose-tinted messages and memes about emo's era years ago and, by extension, memories of experiences of youth from yesteryear. As an emo fan, in October 2022 I found myself queuing for day one of a three-day festival that featured some of my favorite bands from my early teens. My initial excitement would be temporarily dampened by the cancellation of day one—due to dangerously high winds—moments before the WWWY festival was to be opened. While the decision to cancel day one seemed to be the safest decision to make (and I got to attend day two), it was communicated in a chaotically last-minute and casual way, which reflects some of the risks involved in brands trying to cultivate a relatable, fan-like, and casual brand voice on social media.

To me, "WWWY's tweet on the cancellation and the backlash that followed was a reminder that Big Tech shapes online and offline aspects of emo music festivals—from crisis communications to event partners" (Sobande 2022c). While the branding of the festival may have successfully drawn on the spirit and aesthetics of DIY digital culture, the fan-type brand voice that WWWY had developed seemed to come up short when delivering news about the logistics of the festival, in a manner that seemed flippant rather than funny, unprofessional rather than cute, and cold rather than cool. WWWY's engagement with digital technology as part of the branding, marketing, and delivery of the festival included the use of a festival app—the announcement of which fell flat and was criticized for reasons that included alleged issues with functionality and concerns about how people's data might be stored and used by Big Brands.

As the communication studies of Joseph Turow (2021, 12) outline, "The spiral of personalization is the guiding spirit behind the new marketing order. Marketers believe that in order to remain

Figure 10. Netflix Horrorscope entrance at When We Were Young Festival, Las Vegas, Nevada, 2022. Photo by author.

competitive, they must gather as much data as possible about current and prospective customers and send them individualized messages and product offerings."

Mindful of this, critiques of WWWY's app that articulate concerns about their collection and use of data might reflect a broader critical sentiment in response to the dominance of brand datafication and personalization processes. The music festival's app functions included being able to link Facebook to view friends' festival schedules. The app could also highlight top Spotify tracks by acts performing at WWWY. If a person granted permission for the WWWY app to access their Spotify account data, tracks from there could become linked to the festival app. While such elements of the app may have provided a novelty of some sort, they also reflect the presence of Big Tech in the commercialized emo scene, where the DIY ethos that once seeded emo may have been usurped by datafication processes and the strategies of brands seeking to cash in on the business of the marketable nostalgia of aging genres and their fans. "Case in point, the #NetflixandChills 'Horrorscope' pop-up where people could receive tarot readings and scan a QR code to see their 'aura,' assuming they consent to potentially being photographed and filmed" (Sobande 2022c), which was highlighted in a framed statement in the branded onsite experience area.

No doubt I support there being more emo music festivals, and I am under no illusions about the fact that brands and corporate culture have coupled with music scenes for decades (Klein 2020). What I am critical of, though, and curious about, is the ways that nostalgic ideas about youth, aging, and the bands that soundtracked experiences of it become opportunities for brands to capture consumer data, push Big Tech products and services, and frame music genres and their history in revisionist ways that commodify the community that can be part of music festivals and their origins. Whether it is portrayals of businesses in TV shows or the actions of Big Tech brands that capitalize on nostalgia for music and youth, there is a well-established and ever-expanding list of examples of the mixing of branding, corporate culture, digital culture, and pop culture. More than that, the business of activism, antagonism, and aging is alive and kicking and includes advertising, marketing, and commercial activities that respond to recent discourse on activism, stir up or seek to squash antagonism, and tap into demand for events that remind people of yesteryear.

4   Forecasting the Future of Morality in the Marketplace

- Who is the judge of what is and is not moral in the marketplace, and beyond it?
- What criteria are used as part of moral judgments in/of the marketplace?
- Can the marketplace ever be moral?

Answers to these questions depend on many factors, including the extent to which the ideological foundations of the marketplace—often, *capitalism*—are societally deemed inherently immoral. If I were to directly answer such questions, I would no doubt respond to them with more: How are *judge* and *judgment* being defined? Where is the marketplace in question? Moral by whose and what standards? Accordingly, my book does not provide tidy answers to the listed provocations. Instead, it critically deals with the ways that discourses of morality and adjacent concepts such as judgment, sanctimony, culture wars, and wokeness are discursive sites of struggle, filled with many different and conflicting perspectives of "right" and "wrong," "normal" and "abnormal," and "moral" and "immoral."

Indeed, at the center of my book is a critical focus on morality in the marketplace, from the perspectives of industry professionals to the views of people regarded as "consumers" whom marketers target. But such a focus on morality also involves taking a close look at how ideas about identity and social justice are discussed, depicted, and debated in market settings, and how digital culture is at the crux of much of this. In this concluding chapter, I reflect on what the future of morality in the marketplace might hold, discussing the relationship between marketing and moral arbiters and considering the ways that brands are vying to be moral vanguards in the digital age. Before considering what the future of morality in the marketplace might hold, I turn to extant work on the marketplace of morality (MOM) (Dunfee 1998), which particularly focuses on "the individual level" (Dunfee 1998, 129) of marketplace experiences.

PAST THE MARKETPLACE OF MORALITY

Outlining the concept of the MOM as being "a place where individuals act under the influence of their moral desire," Thomas W. Dunfee (1998, 127) reflects on how commercial entities—*firms*—tap into this: "Firms respond by social cause marketing and other devices which encourage customers to align their social preferences with those represented by the firm." Dunfee articulates differences between the moral desires of individuals but also conceptualizes the MOM in a way that involves discussion of the "principles of universal morality" (127)—a phrase that warrants more critical attention due to its potential to frame certain moral positions as "universal," without unpacking the power relations that result in them being perceived and pushed as such.

While I recognize that various moral positions have been regarded, by some, as "universal," my account of morality in the marketplace involves more of a focus on the constructed and contested nature of different stances related to morality (Sedgman 2023), rather than on a framing of morality that positions it as being a matter of individual choice and different "universal" perspectives. Consequently, I turn my attention to the power dynamics imbued in both morality in the marketplace and scholarly theorizations of it. Unlike Dunfee's (1998, 127) work on the notion of the MOM, which is described "as a place where individuals act under the influence of their moral impulse," my work more strongly focuses on how brands act in response to expectations and perceptions of *their* moral position—including expectations and perceptions expressed by consumers, employees, and other stakeholders. I contend that the focus on individual agency and sovereignty in some prior studies of the marketplace and morality (e.g., Dunfee 1998) has been at the expense of a sufficient account of structural inequities between the capacity for people to express agency and sovereignty in ways that will be respected as opposed to dismissed, and even pathologized and criminalized.

The impact and presence of the COVID-19 pandemic are ongoing in the marketplace and beyond it. Despite claims of so-called crisis fatigue, people continue to be moved to act in resistance to crises, such as the climate crisis, the cost-of-living crisis (capitalism), and the crisis of societally condoned anti-blackness. Related forms of activism, community organizing, and protest include modes of direct action and unionizing in the marketplace, which institutions often respond to obstructively and punitively. Relatedly, Dunfee grounds the theorization of the MOM in the "foundational assumption" that "all competent human beings are sovereign in their personal right to make judgments and commitments concerning their own interests" (1998, 128). But this assumption overlooks the fact that such perceived personal sovereignty and rights are contingent on myriad structural factors that are affected by forms of state-sanctioned oppression (e.g., governmental efforts to prohibit and police protests) and ongoing histories of ableism, classism, colonialism, racism, and xenophobia. As a result, the concept of "competent human" that Dunfee refers to is a loaded one that obscures how, throughout history, Black, disabled, Indigenous, and working-class people have often been treated as incompetent and even subhuman. Put briefly, personal sovereignty and rights are not accessible to all people, and the concept of "competency" that these notions are often anchored in can have the effect of foreclosing the sovereignty and rights of many oppressed people. Indeed, as Dunfee (1998, 133) acknowledges, "we do not act purely as autonomous individuals disconnected from others. Instead, people act within the contexts of groups, communities and organizations," and as I argue, such contexts include geocultural and sociopolitical environments that constrain the personal (including bodily) sovereignty and rights of some people (e.g., the overturning of *Roe v. Wade*) while seeking to protect those of others. Therefore, throughout my book morality is discussed in ways that make clear that there are distinct disparities between how the moral positions of some demographics are (dis)respected and responded to (e.g., in the context of racial capitalism, the role of "moral arbiter" is typically wedded to whiteness).

In contrast with Dunfee (1998, 129), who argues that the MOM can "reflect a society's overall position on issues such as affirmative action, gender equality and environmental preservation," I see the marketplace as a space where prevailing positions on moral matters (e.g., the positions that brands adopt and amplify) might simply be the most marketable messaging on morality, rather than reflecting the stance of a perceived societal majority. Sometimes the messages of morality adopted or dismissed by brands simply signal their segmentation strategies, including their attempts to appeal to certain groups of people. What is or becomes most marketable may at times correlate with which moral positions are most upheld in society, but it may be misguided to affirm that the moral stances that gain most traction in the marketplace signify an overall societal position. The marketplace is not an equal playing field and is not accessible to all people who are part of a society—that is, it is important to stay alert to how power dynamics impact which moral matters the marketplace (and scholarship on it) become preoccupied with and which matters remain sidelined. On that note, there is a continuing need for more critical work that moves past the concept of the MOM and delves into the details of who and what plays the role of "moral arbiter" in this market-oriented world. My hope is that this book is part of the work that takes up this challenge.

MARKETING AND MORAL ARBITERS

My emphasis on morality *in* the marketplace (as opposed to the marketplace *of* morality) is intended to mark a different focus that takes seriously the relationship between morality and the marketplace *and* the relationship between academia and the preservation of the marketplace's image as moral (or at least *moral enough*). Institutions and individuals who are intent on becoming moral arbiters, or who already assume such a position, include commercial brands, social enterprise entities, and academic disciplines. I recognize that in my effort to critically contribute to ongoing work and words on morality in the marketplace, I risk the prospect of merely framing myself as yet another self-professed arbiter on these matters. As Phipps (2020, 1) notes, "Knowledge is always partial, and we learn through dialogue with one another." So my hope is that my book's analysis of morality in the marketplace is understood as continuing to contribute to, open up, and expand on conversations and work on these topics, rather than relaying reductive ideas about advertising and activism that betray their uncomfortable intermingling or that rely on tired and oppositional binaries of "moral" (or purportedly woke) and "immoral" (or allegedly anti-woke) brands.

For the aforementioned reasons, the notion of brands' moral impositions, outlined in my work, and accompanying concepts such as white sincerity can be interpreted as ideas that I hope will be built upon, rather than blithely agreed with or assumed as being closed off from further development. In contrast with how a brand's perceived "purpose" is often deemed to be part of its signature brand identity, the concept of brands' moral impositions contributes to a more critical grasp of the gradations of how structural power dynamics, pressures, and interactions between brands shape those brands and the public positions that they take on moral matters. Related to the throwaway nature of how some brands signal their supposed stance on issues of injustice and inequality, my theorizing of brands' moral impositions involves proposing the concept of "brands' disposable duties." Such disposable duties relate to the ephemeral expectations and actions of brands that connect to significant moments and events in society that called them to speak up or act out, *but* only for a short period of digitally documented time.

In the decades since Dunfee (1998) wrote "The Marketplace of Morality," the marketplace—both literally and conceptually—has changed. Among key changes is the increased emphasis on surveillance and internet technologies (Cottom 2020; Noble 2018); the personalization of consumer experiences (Turow 2008); and the cultivation of a brand's digital presence, personality, and voice, via social media (Sligh and Abidin 2022) (e.g., TV shows such as *You* promoted via a Netflix Twitter account). When Dunfee (1998) conceptualized the MOM, hashtags such as #GoWokeGoBroke—used to criticize brands perceived as woke (i.e., left/liberal)—were yet to be imagined. Although social media was not entirely absent in the 1990s, the microblogging platform Twitter was yet to enter the arena, and influencer culture was in an embryonic form that might be unrecognizable to many people today. Thus, both the marketplace and morality that Dunfee (1998) wrote about were untethered to various present-day norms, including the dominance of digital culture in today's world of marketing and moral judgments, where businesses such as Tony's Chocolonely are discussed as an example of "the risks of being a woke brand" (Irving 2021).

Littler (2008) provides crucial insights into the dynamics between ethics and consumption, which relate to the relationship between morality and the marketplace. However, as happens with the passing of time, a lot has changed since Littler's (2008, 2) fruitful work affirmed that "consumer protest and ethical consumption have received much mainstream press attention in recent years, but academic discussion about it has until recently been noticeably limited." Taking heed of Littler's (2008, 2) assertion that "we need a more expansive vocabulary and to open up new approaches of enquiry in order to understand the areas' many contradictions, strengths and weaknesses," I have conceptualized brands' moral impositions.

Perceived stakeholders in the same brand (e.g., employees, investors, brand partners, brand parent companies) may hold and communicate moral positions that conflict with those that are attributed to the overall brand. Therefore, as my book details, I view component parts of moral impositions that shape brand actions as including, but not being limited to, the following:

- When, how, and why brands communicate and contest moral positions, as well as associated social and political perspectives.

- Impression and reputation management techniques that market and/or mask messages about morality, identity, politics, and society.

- Power dynamics, profit-making activities, people, and processes that are part of the relationship between branding, morality, identity, and politics.

- When, how, and why brand stakeholders communicate and contest moral positions (both internally *and* externally), as well as associated social and political perspectives.

Morality is not passive, nor is it pure, but it is *political*. I acknowledge the imposing nature of morality (e.g., how individuals and institutions are coerced or compelled to express and uphold certain moral positions), rather than framing morality as merely choice based (e.g., an individual and/or brand simply deciding to take a stand). Morality is a matter of both structural manifestations and interpersonal interactions and behaviors. Brands' negotiation of moral impositions can result in responses that range from carefully constructed long-term strategies to knee-jerk reactions that do not entail more than a one-off comment or gesture. In other cases, brands may seek to be regarded as "authentic" by cultivating a voice and a communication style that seem to be based on candor, not claims to "care."

Whether it is the efforts of brands, scholars, politicians, or other public figures and firms, at any given time there is much work occurring as part of attempts to (re)establish certain individuals and institutions as "moral arbiters"—authorities on who and what is or is not moral. When it is a brand that is working in ways intended to position them as an authority on matters of morality and associated issues of (in)justice, such attempts can involve trying to paper over internal cracks and disagreements. As I have highlighted, the idea that any firm (or brand) can portray a coherent image of itself as taking a unified stance on moral, social, and political issues is fundamentally fragile. Although a brand may typically be discussed as though it is a single entity, it is best understood as an overall image that is carefully constructed and strategically (re)presents the work of a multitude of people (and often, across different places), including employees whose moral positions may drastically differ from each other's. Accordingly, while much research on brands, morality, and social justice has focused on the public position and stance professed by brands, future research could benefit from paying more attention to the internal politics of brands and the processes involved in determining whose and what moral positions become known as those of the brand itself.

BEYOND WOKENESS AS AN "AMERICAN IMPORT"

Since the days of social cause marketing in the 1990s, digital developments have moved the needle in terms of the relationship between the marketplace and morality. I am not suggesting that social cause marketing is dead, although its pulse does seem dulled. Instead, I am articulating clear changes to the marketplace and societal terrains that such marketing is a part of in the first quarter of the twenty-first century. Not only has the social media and digital culture of recent decades provided people with more channels through which to critique brands, it has also impacted the ways that morality and social justice more generally are discussed and derided. A case in point is the different ways that the word *woke* and derivatives of it have been taken up in various parts of the world. For example, the 2023 edition of the French dictionary *Larousse* includes the addition of "Le wokisme" (Connexion 2023), reflecting the culmination of digital and global media discourse on wokeness, much of which has often obscured the term's origins and meanings in Black American culture, community organizing, and history.

At the time that I am writing this, a Google "news" search of "wokisme" yields pages of headlines that point to the term's common fearmongering use as a metonym for left/liberal/Black politics and a derogatory way to dismiss the concerns, rights, and lives of structurally marginalized groups of people. Referred to as having played a part in the 2022 French presidential election, wokeness and cancel culture continue to be particularly popularizing in the context of American (and eventually global) digital culture and have since been decontextualized and recontextualized in ways that serve the political agendas of individuals and institutions around the world.

While some critics of notions of woke(ness) or wokisme attempt to disregard the terms as nothing more than American imports, the fact that they have traveled far and wide in ways that are shaped by contemporary political and public discourse reflects much more than alleged American hegemony. Further still, claims that such terms are simply American imports often specifically dismiss the significance, insights, and impact of *Black* American people, culture, and history, including Black Twitter—which propelled much contemporary discussion of BLM, racial justice work, and many different facets of the lives of Black people.

Undoubtedly, ideas about morality and social justice differ around the world, but people outside of America who dismiss the notion of woke(ness) as irrelevant to where they are, may obfuscate the transnational nature of forms of liberationist organizing and Black consciousness-raising, in addition to denying the global nature of structural oppression. Woke is far from being the first word to travel beyond where it originated from and is certainly not the only expression with roots in the US that has made its way to places such as the UK and France. Hence derision of the term reflects much more than criticism of the US allegedly encroaching on the cultural and political environments of elsewhere.

I argue that many dismissive redefinitions and denouncements of woke(ness) are a by-product of racial capitalism—symbolic of the pervasiveness of antiblackness and the marketability of so-called political positions that are predicated on the ongoing oppression of Black people, including by proprietarily and dismissively weaponizing the word woke(ness). Thus, rather than merely being an example of matters of morality in the marketplace, contemporary discourse and debates about wokeness across media and market settings often signal the state of a range of interconnected power relations between people and places, steeped in ongoing histories of capitalism, colonialism, racism, and antiblackness, that shape who and what is deemed as an authority/arbiter, including on the matter itself.

VYING TO BE THE VANGUARD IN THE DIGITAL (AND VIRTUAL INFLUENCER) AGE

As art critic John Berger (1972) poignantly notes in the pivotal book *Ways of Seeing*, "publicity turns consumption into a substitute for democracy," and consumption is also sometimes flippantly framed as activism and a form of resistance. Examples of this include the commodification and marketization of rhetoric and representations that

were once associated with collective struggles, community organizing, and activism—the chants of protesters somehow become the slogan of a brand, and a hashtag created to bring attention to issues of
oppression seemingly becomes a launchpad from which products can
be highlighted. Such examples are indicative of a pervasive capitalist
system that has yielded conditions under which "what we are dealing
with now is not the incorporation of materials that previously seemed
to possess subversive potentials, but instead, their *precorporation*:
the pre-emptive formatting and shaping of desires, aspirations and
hopes by capitalist culture" (Fisher [2014] 2022, 9).

One of the defining characteristics of contemporary consumer culture is its relative embrace of the pretense of "brand activism" and,
in some cases, the nebulous concept of "caring capitalism." Arguably,
attempting to occupy both the position of moral authority/arbiter and
ally/activist, some brands have turned to digital culture as a resource
to be mined for trending hashtags and topics to tap into, or in the
case of brands such as Lush (e.g., its statement on becoming "anti-
social"), actively position themselves as turning away from. In other
words, the ways that brands are vying to be vanguards in the digital age include negotiating ideas about visibility, morality, and social
justice through their engagement with, and disengagement from,
social media. In light of contentious changes to Twitter in the months
since its purchase by Elon Musk, the site may become one that many
brands (continue to) disassociate themselves from and even disavow.

Advertising, the Uneasy Persuasion (Schudson 1984, 209) offers
insights that are still resonant today: "Understanding advertising
entails understanding the difference between personal and printed
or broadcast communication; the differences entailed in the 'decon-
textualization' of thought and feeling that systems of mass communication make possible." Such efforts to understand advertising now
also include trying to understand the difference between various
forms of digital communication, such as those between the affordances of a range of social media and content-sharing platforms (e.g.,
Instagram, TikTok, Twitter, YouTube). As the work of Noble (2018, 6)

illuminates, "Marketing and advertising have directly shaped the ways that marginalized people have come to be represented by digital records such as search results or social network activities." As such, the ways that brands are vying to be vanguards in an always crowded marketplace include drawing on digital tools and platforms, including online trends popularized by Black people, to establish a brand personality, voice, and overall image, which remains coherent while flexibly responding to various moral (im)positions.

During the years that I was writing this book (2019–23), although many brands continued to watch what real people say and do online, they also became enthralled with the marketing possibilities presented by virtual, CGI, and AI models and influencers. So in 2023 Levi's (Levi Strauss & Co.) announced that the American clothing company would "test AI-generated clothing models to 'increase diversity'" (Weatherbed 2023). Writing for the *San Francisco Chronicle*, Justin Phillips (2023) states, "Levi Strauss' decision to use AI-generated models to improve representation raises thorny questions about whether companies are more interested in selling diversity than achieving it." Elsewhere, in the *Guardian*, Levi's plans are described as amounting to "computer-generated inclusivity" (Demopoulos 2023). In another response to the news, reporter Brianna Holt (2023) writes about the concerns of real Black models and other people in the modeling industry: "In a bid to improve inclusivity by representing customers of every size and skin tone, the use of AI–generated models doesn't only impact models, but also members of the production crew, who will lose jobs."

As Holt (2023) notes, in response to the backlash that followed its initial 2023 announcement about using AI models, Levi's updated its press release: "We do not see this pilot as a means to advance diversity or as a substitute for the real action that must be taken to deliver on our diversity, equity and inclusion goals and it should not have been portrayed as such." The March 28, 2023, "Editor's Note" by Levi Strauss & Co. (2023) also includes statements about its alleged commitment to "creating a workplace, a business and a marketplace where people from all backgrounds feel confident that they will be seen, their voices will be heard and their contributions welcomed. This involves making sure our employees and our consumers can see themselves in how we share our products with the market, which has also manifested in a commitment to support multicultural creatives behind and in front of the camera. It's not just the right thing to do—it's a business imperative."

Acknowledging that "there is understandable sensitivity around AI-related technologies" (Levi Strauss & Co. 2023), Levi's has attempted to reassure consumers by stating "We are not scaling back our plans for live photo shoots, the use of live models, or our commitment to working with diverse models. Authentic storytelling has always been part of how we've connected with our fans, and human models and collaborators are core to that experience."

As Levi's words signal, there can be porous parameters between marketplace matters related to morality (e.g., positions on diversity and inequality) and those related to a "business imperative." The brand's invocation of concepts such as authenticity and diversity in response to the backlash that it faced reflects ongoing criticism about the inauthenticity and potentially oppressive and fetishizing effects of Black and "mixed" virtual/CGI/AI models and influencers. The mounting nature of such criticism in recent years has led to brands presumptuously contacting me to ask how they can create virtual/CGI/AI models and influencers in a way that circumvents backlash—questions that highlight brands' insistence that these models/influencers could help them to appear "diverse" (enough).

As this example indicates, the ways that brands are vying to be vanguards in the digital age include doubling down on tokenizing, turning to virtual/CGI/AI Black and "mixed" models rather than hiring real people in those roles. The future of morality in the marketplace may be shaped by brands' increasing use of virtual/CGI/AI models and influencers, such as their use of them as spokespeople, in ways that may ultimately make a mockery of the very issues of injustice that such computer-aided creations sometimes claim to seek to combat. Currently, there is much panic—moral and otherwise—about the existence of what is referred to as "generative AI." Despite critiques consistently being articulated across public spheres, there has been a relatively steady growth of the virtual/CGI/AI model and influencer industry—perhaps, in part, reflecting that the marketplace predominantly disregards public concerns about the objectification, tokenization, and fetishization of Black people.

It is not only the virtual/CGI/AI model and influencer industry that highlights how brands, as part of a longer history of doing so, attempt to capitalize on the image, aesthetics, and culture of Black people. Examining other forms of this, my recent collaborative work with scholar Emma-Lee Amponsah focuses on related questions as part of a study of "demands, displays, and dreams of 'Black joy' during times of crisis." "By analysing adverts, media narratives, and elements of the overall landscape of public (re)presentations of Black people, we critically consider[ed] how 'Black joy' became *'Black Joy*TM'—a way for brands to market themselves by tapping into the racial, national, and capitalist politics of emotion, advertising, and media" (Sobande and Amponsah forthcoming). Focusing on a broader range of examples of such power relations and forms of (re)presentation in the marketplace, my book highlights dimensions of the digital, gender, racial, and capitalist politics of transient brand impulses to make moral, social, and political claims in a manner that constitutes "single-use social justice"—a mere commodified shadow of social justice (e.g., "corporate anti-capitalism—[see Fisher (2014) 2022] and "gestural anti-racism" [see Johnson 2022]), which lacks substance and may be molded by "white sincerity" (e.g., the marketability of the perceived sincerity of individuals and institutions racialized as white).

Focusing on the structural nature and oppressive effects of such iterations of whiteness, future research could benefit from further exploring the dynamics between "white sincerity" (Sobande et al. 2022), "white sight" (Mirzoeff 2023), "white comfort" (Lentin 2020), the "general"/"mass" (aka white) market (Rosa-Salas 2019), "whiteness as credential" (Ray 2019), and notions of moral authority and ethics in the scholarly areas of business, media, and marketing studies. Then again, there remains a risk of reinforcing whiteness by foregrounding it, even if critically, in analyses of the marketplace and the many power regimes that it is a part of. Focusing on some of these issues, the following paragraphs dive deeper into the ways that brands are vying to be moral vanguards in the digital age and contemplate what the future of such efforts may entail.

In a future that may continue to be referred to as a time of "permacrisis," brands may end up vying to be regarded as a vanguard in their sector or industry by heavily nodding to nostalgia for supposedly comforting times before now. While allegedly "values-based" consumerism is continuing to expand, so too is criticism of the concept that brands, and capitalism, can ever be "caring." There is a demand for "no-frills" brand communication approaches that involve brands communicating in a way that appears to be frank and departs from a focus on visibility to a "less is more" strategy. Think not quite silence, but a move away from amplifying. Corporate verbiage is certainly not going anywhere. But some of the marketized buzzwords from recent years that brands have sought to benefit from (e.g., commodified concepts of "intersectionality," "wokeness," "allyship," "activism," "social justice") will be replaced by other terms of the moment or may even be denounced by brands who once referred to and praised such concepts while they also reframed their meanings. Even the term *permacrisis* may undergo permutations by corporate entities that stand to gain from normalizing ongoing crises, signaling that "there is no punctual moment of disaster; the world doesn't end with a bang, it winks out, unravels, gradually falls apart" (Fisher [2014] 2022, 2).

Undoubtedly the world of Big Brands will continue to be competitive, but some brands may distance themselves from a culture of comparison that underpins the marketplace, or at least feign a lack of interest in it, to construct an image of themselves as being more invested in the collective "good" of the world than outpacing competitors. Again, there is a potential for perceived forms of "white sincerity" and, I believe, "white comfort" (Lentin 2020), to function in ways that aid the advertising and marketing of brands, including corporations that a "mass" market audience (Rosa-Salas 2019) interprets as taking seriously a range of moral matters and issues of injustice.

My use of the concept of white sincerity is intended to capture how structural power regimes and oppression (e.g., colonialism, racial capitalism, and whiteness) contribute to perceptions of who and what constitutes sincerity and the value that is or is not ascribed to perceived expressions of it. This means that rather than being a term that relates to the relationship between race, racialization, and emotion, I use white sincerity to describe systemic dynamics between colonialism, racial capitalism, whiteness, value systems, and constructions and perceptions of sincerity, as opposed to focusing on more amorphous concepts such as authenticity.

Amid a time of much turmoil—from the ongoing COVID-19 crisis to the concerns of climate justice—many brands are clawing at the whimsy and irreverence nostalgically associated with the 1990s and early 2000s to cultivate a marketable sense of comfort (Sobande 2022a) and, sometimes, to avoid explicitly recognizing the problems and perils of the present day. Of course escapist ideas and the suspension of disbelief have long been part of advertising and marketing approaches, and of life in general, but the tenor of some contemporary examples suggests an implicit, if not explicit, denial of the crises of current times. Whether done with a marketing style that is meant to be imbued with sincerity or humor, brands will be, and have been, reaching into the vault of 1990s and 2000s media and consumer culture, including to convey a lack of interest in the all-consuming digital culture that so far has come to define the twenty-first century. The explosion of the pop culture reboot (e.g., TV shows and films that rehash well-worn iconic predecessors) is one of many examples signaling that aspects of today's marketplace are anchored in clinging to past times.

Of course, brands have treated nostalgia as a marketing tool for decades (Klein 2020), so there is limited novelty found in such an approach. But given the sense of global uncertainty that is specific to the first quarter of the twenty-first century, more brands are, and will be, opting to moor their messaging and marketing in nostalgia for the (relatively recent) past, rather than in marketing fantasies of the future. How brands choose to portray the past—including who and what are depicted as being part of it, and how they are framed—may reveal revisionist accounts of the 1990s and 2000s (including experiences of digital culture then) and may tell us much about how matters of morality and issues of injustice are portrayed as past or present-day problems.

When analyzing and discussing morality and how brands are vying to be vanguards in the present-day marketplace, it is important to contextualize such accounts, including by reflecting on cultural, social, and political shifts in recent decades. As outlined in Alex Niven's introduction to the second edition of *Capitalist Realism: Is There No Alternative?*, the much-read work of writer, music critic, and political and cultural theorist Mark Fisher: "After a flare-up of anti-capitalist protest in the very early part of the decade (the heyday of Naomi Klein's anti-globalisation screed *No Logo*), there was a drastic settling-down in much of the world in the mid- to late Noughties. At some unspecified point during these years, a mood of depressive apathy came to predominate above all else" (Niven 2022, xviii).

While previous decades have been marked by the swell and then decline of visible and direct forms of anti-capitalist protest, it is important to recognize that even during those perceived times of decline, there were still many forms of anti-capitalist community organizing and collective liberationist efforts, including work led by Black, working-class, and in the context of the US, Indigenous people, who tended to the interconnected nature of the oppressive impacts of capitalism, colonialism, imperialism, racism and xenophobia. Thus, indeed, the mid- to late 2000s was marked by "a drastic settling-down" (Niven 2022, xviii) of some forms of anti-capitalist protest, but it was not a time completely devoid of anti-capitalist struggles and efforts.

Moreover, such anti-capitalist work is not always visible, including for reasons related to protecting the safety of those involved in it and attempts to elude forms of "elite capture" that Táíwò (2022) insightfully conceptualizes and analyzes. Still, as the writing of Niven (2022) and Fisher ([2014] 2022) points out, the mid- to late 2000s became fertile ground from which brands could continue to sow their seeds of profit-making and do so in ways that were relatively undisrupted by anti-capitalist resistance. Fisher's ([2014] 2022) *Capitalist Realism* demonstrates "how the supremacy of the market had in fact led to the total subjection of citizens remodelled as consumers" (Niven 2022, xxxix). Hence, brands may now be turning toward much 2000s nostalgia, precisely because it was a time during which aspects of anti-capitalist struggles were perceived to be defanged, and a commercial product such as a film (e.g., *Wall-E* in Fisher's [2014] 2022 analysis) "perform[ed] our anti-capitalism for us, allowing us to continue to consume with impunity" (Fisher [2014] 2022, 12). New millennium (aka 2000s) hyperconsumption, materialism, and digital technology is now being repackaged and marketed as nostalgia (e.g., the surge in Mattel toy-related films in the works), in aid of brand messaging and calls to action that facilitate datafication, monitoring, tracking, and surveillance processes.

WATCHING THE WATCHER

In August 2022, a plethora of headlines highlighted contentious claims that TikTok's in-app browser could monitor people's keystrokes (Fowler 2022). But TikTok is not the only brand that may be watching you, nor will it be the last. The relationship between agency, privacy, morality, collective struggles, and social media has been under scrutiny for decades, as has the broader dynamic between surveillance and digital technology. For these reasons and countless others, the world of Big Tech is often in the spotlight. However, many businesses beyond the Big Tech industry also research, monitor, and respond to people in numerous ways that constitute how *Big Brands Are Watching You.*

Although the questions, themes, and topics discussed in this book are eclectic, what ties them together is how they demonstrate some of the many ways that morality is (re)defined and negotiated in the marketplace, and how they illustrate various shaky bridges and boundaries between brands, activism, digital culture, and pop culture. The future of advertising, branding, and marketing will continue to be marked by deep-seated and changing expectations of the actions of brands in relation to matters of morality and the construct of "the consumer-spectator" (Fisher [2014] 2022, 4).

The 1990s and early 2000s were never free from forms of brand targeting, tracking, monitoring, and measuring. But the germinal nature of social media then has contributed to certain perceptions of that time as being a "golden age" of both the internet and consumer culture. Big Brands were watching then (Klein 2000), and they are certainly watching now, so I am intrigued about the ways that the future of branding might involve a (re)narration of recent decades as part of efforts to portray past eras as a more "moral" and/or "freeing" time, or a time that involved more evasion of being watched. Long before now, matters such as feminism, (anti)racism, reproductive rights, and anti-capitalist activism and organizing were treated as "hot topics" by brands, but the Big Brother culture that has been amplified by surveillance technologies staged as social media has changed how brands engage with, and disengage from, politics and protest. As Alessandro—a retail and consumer rights expert—expressed his concerns regarding these matters during his interview:

> Especially in recent months, with regards to the way laws were changed for the police to handle physical protests, I think social media stuff—*and it already has*—is going to become ever more so important to people. Because people are going to be less motivated to physically

protest, whether that be against a brand, a company, a political issue, or a social issue.

Exasperated by what he views as being the empty platitudes of brands on social media, Alessandro said:

> I feel like there's such a lack of responsibility and accountability when it comes to these things. Like any brands, whether it's H&M, Nike, Adidas, even cleaning companies like Johnson & Johnson, or whatever, that they just throw out these #this, #that, picture this, picture that, and it's like, wait a minute, great, but are you actually [doing work to contribute to social change]? We don't know, like where's the actual proof, where's the substantial, "here's the thing"? Some brands will say that it's a five-year project or it's a ten-year idea, and it's like, but we need the here and *now*. You can't tell me, we did the # and then in ten years, we'll see what happens. No, if it's going to be ten years fine, but *every year*, they have to be able to come out and show us physically and not some rush-job that, in a day, they scramble together, where they go, "we did this though."

In the aftermath of feeling burned by the backlash against their (in)actions in relation to social, political, and moral matters, some brands have enlisted the informal, fan-like, and knowing tone of digital remix culture to try to soar like a phoenix from the ashes, or at least bury critiques of them. Other brands have tried to cool tense situations by altering their brand image through partnerships that position them in proximity to celebrities, activists, or people who may be considered both. As Lekakis (2022, 133) notes, influencers have the capacity to "impact consumer culture in novel ways, from the modes and messages of promotion to the ethics and actions advocated." But increasingly influential criticism of celebrity and influencer culture—as opposed to just critiques of individual celebrities and influencers—points toward a future that might involve more brands turning away from collaborations with the rich and/or the (internet) famous.

Consequently, although virtual/CGI/AI models may continue to be an appealing marketing device for brands, the creation and use of such models in the future may involve less of a focus on culti-vating a digital presence and personality for them. In other words, their construction as influencers in their own right might dwindle, and such virtual/CGI/AI models may be engaged with more as mere visual tools rather than brand personalities to collaborate with. The following claim by Levi's (Levi Strauss & Co. 2023) about the poten-tial benefits (e.g., "efficiencies") of its planned use of AI models is perhaps suggestive of moves toward this approach: "The Lalaland. ai partnership may deliver some business efficiencies that provide consumers with a better sense of what a given product looks like but should not have been conflated with the company's diversity, equity and inclusion commitment or strategy."

As Schudson (1984, 210) argues in a 1980s account of advertis-ing's "dubious impact on American society": "Advertising is part of the establishment and reflection of a common symbolic culture. Advertising, whether or not it sells cars or chocolate, surrounds and enters into us, so that when we speak we may speak in or with ref-erence to the language of advertising and when we see we may see through schemata that advertising has made salient for us."

Although the examples discussed throughout my book are dif-ferent in many ways, each reflects aspects of the tone and tenor of present-day consumer culture, including the ubiquity of advertising and branding that has seeped into many aspects of people's daily lives. As governments continue to crack down on the right of people to protest, businesses continue to court commodified concepts of social justice, and brands continue to construct an online voice by positioning themselves as one of "us," distinguishing between who is the watcher and who is the watched may become both clearer *and* more clouded. It is difficult to determine exactly what the future of branding and the marketplace will look, feel, and be like. But one thing is certain: how brands negotiate and (re)define matters of morality will still be shaped by structural-looking relations and power regimes that they may try to conceal, but which are often simply hidden in plain (white) sight.

References

Abidin, Crystal. 2015. "Micromicrocelebrity: Branding Babies on the Internet." *M/C Journal* 18(5). https://journal.media-culture.org.au/index.php/mcjournal/article/view/1022.

———. 2017. "#familygoals: Family Influencers, Calibrated Amateurism, and Justifying Young Digital Labor." *Social Media + Society* 3(2). https://doi.org/10.1177/2056305117707191.

———. 2021. "Mapping Internet Celebrity on TikTok: Exploring Attention Economies and Visibility Labours." *Cultural Science Journal* 12(1): 77–103. https://doi.org/10.1177/20563051231157452.

Alcántara, Ann-Marie. 2022. "Why Many Brands Have Kept Their Voices Down on Roe v. Wade (So Far)." *Wall Street Journal*, May 29. www.wsj.com/articles/why-many-brands-have-kept-their-voices-down-on-roe-v-wade-so-far-11652140246.

American Association of Advertising Agencies. 1992. "This Is a Recording." *Agency: A Publication of the American Association of Advertising Agencies* 3(1): 11. Available at Smithsonian Institution Archives.

Aniftos, Rania. 2022. "Everything the Stars Said about Roe v. Wade at the 2022 BET Awards." *Billboard*, June 26. www.billboard.com/lists/roe-v-wade-overturned-stars-react-2022-bet-awards/.

Aronczyk, Melissa. 2013. *Branding the Nation: The Global Business of National Identity*. Oxford: Oxford University Press.

Arsel, Zeynep, David Crockett, and Maura L. Scott. 2022. "Diversity, Equity, and Inclusion (DEI) in the *Journal of Consumer Research*: A Curation and Research Agenda." *Journal of Consumer Research* 48(5): 920–33. https://doi.org/10.1093/jcr/ucab057.

Bååth, Ingrid. 2022. "Intersectionality, Mapped." Climate Culture. www.climateculture.earth/5-minute-reads/top-10-intersectional-influencers.

Bagby-Williams, Atticus, and Nsambu Za Seukama (and edited by Fauwkes, Shannon, and Howard Waitzkin). 2022. *Black Anarchism and the Black Radical Tradition: Moving beyond Racial Capitalism*. Quebec: Daraja Press.

Bailey, Moya. 2021. *Misogynoir Transformed: Black Women's Digital Resistance*. New York: New York University Press.

Bakhtiari, Kian. 2022. "Gen-Z Demand Racial Justice, Not Just Diversity, Equity and Inclusion from Brands." *Forbes*, June 5. www.forbes.com /sites/kianbakhtiari/2022/06/05/gen-z-demand-racial-justice-not-just -diversity-equity-and-inclusion-from-brands/?sh=699306431781.

Banet-Weiser, Sarah. 2018. *Empowered: Popular Feminism and Popular Misogyny*. Durham, NC: Duke University Press.

Banks, Patricia A. 2022. *Black Culture, Inc.: How Ethnic Community Support Pays for Corporate America*. Stanford, CA: Stanford University Press.

Barr, Naomi. 2013. "'Happy Ending, Right?'" *Slate*, October 30. https:// slate.com/business/2013/10/victorias-secret-founding-roy-raymond -had-a-great-idea-but-les-wexner-was-the-one-to-see-it-through.html #:~:text=Raymond%20imagined%20a%20Victorian%20boudoir,%E2 %80%9Csecrets%E2%80%9D%20were%20hidden%20beneath.

BBC. 2022a. "The Truth about BrewDog." *Disclosure*. Series 4. BBC One. www.bbc.co.uk/programmes/m0013yfj.

BBC. 2022b. "The Jubilee Pudding: 70 Years in the Baking." BBC One. www.bbc.co.uk/programmes/m00178bg.

BBC Food (@BBCFood). 2022. "ALL HAIL THE WINNING PUDDING! Outcompeting 5,000 competition entries, this regal delight will go down in history as the OFFICIAL Queen's Platinum Jubilee pudding." Twitter, May 12. https://twitter.com/BBCFood/status /1524844656227405869.

Ben & Jerry's. 2019. "Introducing NEW Justice ReMix'd limited batch!" September 3. www.benjerry.com/whats-new/2019/09/introducing -justice-remixd.

Berger, John. 1972. *Ways of Seeing*. London: British Broadcasting Corporation and Penguin Books.

Birhane, Abeba. 2021. "Algorithmic Injustice: A Relational Ethics Approach." *Patterns (N Y)* 12(2): 100205. https://doi.org/10.1016/j.patter.2021.100205.

Bishop, Sophie. 2018. "Anxiety, Panic and Self-Optimization: Inequalities and the YouTube Algorithm." *Convergence* 24(1): 69–84. https://doi.org/10.1177/1354856517736978.

Black Lives Matter. 2022. "We Want to Talk to You about the Creator's House in California." May 13. https://blacklivesmatter.com/we-want-to-talk-to-you-about-the-creators-house-in-california/.

Bradshaw, Alan, and Linda Scott. 2018. *Advertising Revolution: The Story of a Song, from Beatles Hit to Nike Slogan*. London: Repeater.

Brown, Symeon. 2022. *Get Rich or Lie Trying: Ambition and Deceit in the New Influencer Economy*. London: Atlantic.

Cafolla, Anna. 2022. "Molly-Mae Hague Just Exposed Influencer Culture for the Thatcherite Poison It Is." *Novara Media*, January 7. https://novaramedia.com/2022/01/07/molly-mae-hague-just-exposed-influencer-culture-for-the-thatcherite-poison-it-is/

Campbell, Sean. 2022. "Black Lives Matter Secretly Bought a $6 Million House: Allies and Critics Alike Have Questioned Where the Organization's Money Has Gone." *New York Magazine*, April 4. https://nymag.com/intelligencer/2022/04/black-lives-matter-6-million-dollar-house.html.

Chang, Ailsa, Jason Fuller, and Kathryn Fox. 2022. "Secret $6 Million Home Has Allies and Critics Skeptical of BLM Foundation's Finances." *NPR*, April 7. www.npr.org/2022/04/07/1091487910/blm-leaders-face-questions-after-allegedly-buying-a-mansion-with-donation-money.

Chartered Institute of Marketing. 2020. "When Brands Go Woke, Do They Go Broke?" February 3. www.cim.co.uk/content-hub/editorial/when-brands-go-woke-do-they-go-broke/.

Clancy, Laura. 2021. *Running the Family Firm: How the Monarchy Manages Its Image and Our Money*. Manchester: Manchester University Press.

Clark, Kendra. 2022. "Bumble, Ben & Jerry's, OkCupid and Yelp on Why They're Defending Roe v Wade." *The Drum*, May 5. www.thedrum.com/news/2022/05/05/bumble-okcupid-and-yelp-why-they-re-defending-roe-v-wade.

Clark, Meredith D. 2014. *To Tweet Our Own Cause: A Mixed-Methods Study of the Online Phenomenon "Black Twitter"*. Chapel Hill:

University of North Carolina at Chapel Hill Graduate School. https://
doi.org/10.17615/7bfs-rp55.

———. 2020. "DRAG THEM: A Brief Etymology of So-Called 'Cancel
Culture.'" *Communication and the Public* 5(3–4): 88–92. https://
journals.sagepub.com/doi/10.1177/2057047320961562.

Clein, Emmeline. 2019. "Branding Fake Justice for Generation Z." *Nation*,
June 28. www.thenation.com/article/archive/social-justice-cgi
-advertising-brud/.

Cohen, Ben, and Jerry Greenfield. 1997. *Ben & Jerry's Double-Dip: Lead
with Your Values and Make Money, Too.* New York: Simon and Schuster.

Cole, Patrick. 2011. "Hilfiger Foundation Backs $120 Million Martin L.
King Memorial." *Bloomberg*, August 17. www.bloomberg.com/news
/articles/2011-08-17/hilfiger-foundation-helps-launch-120-million
-martin-luther-king-memorial#xj4y7vzkg.

Collins, Becks. 2020. "Black Lives Matter: Brands Who Are Doing It
Right." *The Marketing Society*, www.marketingsociety.com/blog-post
/black-lives-matter-brands-who-are-doing-it-right.

Combahee River Collective, The. 1977. "The Combahee River Collective
Statement." In *The Black Feminist Reader*, 2000, edited by Joy James
and T. Denean Sharpley-Whiting, 261–70. Oxford: Blackwell.

The Connexion. 2023. "Why France Is More Resistant Than Many
Countries to Wokeism." *The Connexion*, April 4. www.connexionfrance
.com/article/Comment/Opinion/Why-France-is-more-resistant-than
-many-countries-to-wokeism.

Connolly, Rachel. 2022. "Be Warned: For Influencers, Social Justice Is No
More Than a Branding Device." *Guardian*, February 9. www.the
guardian.com/commentisfree/2022/feb/09/influencers-online-social
-justice-branding.

Cottom, Tressie McMillan. 2020. "Where Platform Capitalism and Racial
Capitalism Meet: The Sociology of Race and Racism in the Digital
Society." *Sociology of Race and Ethnicity* 6(4): 441–49. https://doi.org
/10.1177/2332649220949473.

Craft, Ethan Jakob. 2020. "5 Key Takeaways from Ad Age's Town Hall on
Racism." *Ad Age*, August 20. https://adage.com/article/ad-age-events
/5-key-takeaways-ad-ages-town-hall-racism/2275071.

Crenshaw, Kimberlé. 1989. "Demarginalizing the Intersection of Race
and Sex: A Black Feminist Critique of Antidiscrimination Doctrine,
Feminist Theory and Antiracist Politics." *University of Chicago Legal
Forum* 1989(1): 138–67.

———. 1991. "Mapping the Margins: Intersectionality, Identity Politics, and Violence against Women of Color." *Stanford Law Review* 43(6): 1241–99. https://doi.org/10.2307/1229039.

Crockett, David. 2022. "Racial Oppression and Racial Projects in Consumer Markets: A Racial Formation Theory Approach." *Journal of Consumer Research* 49(1): 1–24. https://doi.org/10.1093/jcr/ucab050.

Daniels, Chris. 2022. "The Silence Is Deafening from Corporate America on Roe v. Wade: Why So Many Companies Are Staying Quiet." *Campaign Live*, May 13. www.campaignlive.co.uk/article/silence-deafening -corporate-america-roe-v-wade-why-so-companies-staying-quiet /1755958.

Daniels, Jessie. 2021. *Nice White Ladies: The Truth about White Supremacy, Our Role in It, and How We Can Help Dismantle It.* New York: Seal Press.

Davies, Rob. 2021. "Brewdog Co-Founder Apologises to Ex-staff over 'Toxic' Working Environment." *Guardian*, June 11. www.theguardian .com/business/2021/jun/11/brewdog-co-founder-apologises-to-ex-staff -over-toxic-working-environment.

Davis, Judy Foster. 2018. "Selling Whiteness?—A Critical Review of the Literature on Marketing and Racism." *Journal of Marketing Management* 34(1–2): 134–77. https://doi.org/10.1080/0267257X.2017 .1395902.

Demianyk, Graeme. 2022. "'Profit Is Not a Dirty Word': Liz Truss Dismisses Windfall Tax as 'Bashing Business.'" *Huffington Post*, August 11. www.huffingtonpost.co.uk/entry/liz-truss-windfall-tax-profit-is-not-a -dirty-word_uk_62f55af3e4b045e6f6abd51e.

Demopoulos, Alaina. 2023. "Computer-Generated Inclusivity: Fashion Turns to 'Diverse' AI Models." *Guardian*, April 3. www.theguardian .com/fashion/2023/apr/03/ai-virtual-models-fashion-brands.

Dess, G. D. 2022. "Cultural Dopes." *Los Angeles Review of Books*, April 8. https://lareviewofbooks.org/article/cultural-dopes/.

Dinnie, Keith, ed. 2008. *Nation Branding: Concepts, Issues, Practice.* Burlington, MA: Butterworth-Heinemann.

Doherty, Kelly. 2023. "How AbsolutePunk.net Helped Emo Fans Find an Online Community from the Early '00s-2010s." *Alternative Press*, February 14. www.altpress.com/absolute-punk-dot-net-history/.

Dowell, Erin, and Marlette Jackson. 2020. "'Woke-Washing' Your Company Won't Cut It." *Harvard Business Review*, July 27. https://hbr .org/2020/07/woke-washing-your-company-wont-cut-it.

Duffy, Brooke Erin. 2015. "The Romance of Work: Gender and Aspirational Labour in the Digital Culture Industries." *International Journal of Cultural Studies* 19(4): 441–57. https://doi.org/10.1177/1367877915 572186.

———. 2017. *(Not) Getting Paid to Do What You Love: Gender, Social Media, and Aspirational Work.* New Haven, CT: Yale University Press.

Duffy, Brooke Erin, and Emily Hund. 2015. "'Having It All' on Social Media: Entrepreneurial Femininity and Self-Branding among Fashion Bloggers." *Social Media + Society* 1(2). https://doi.org/10.1177/2056305 115604337.

Duffy, Brooke Erin, and Jefferson D. Pooley. 2017. "'Facebook for Academics': The Convergence of Self-Branding and Social Media Logic on Academia.edu." *Social Media + Society* 3(1). https://doi.org/10 .1177/2056305117696523.

Dunfee, Thomas W. 1998. "The Marketplace of Morality: First Steps toward a Theory of Moral Choice." *Business Ethics Quarterly* 8(1): 127–45. https://doi.org/10.2307/3857525.

Durney, Ellen. 2022. "Kim Kardashian, Kris Jenner, and More Celebrities Said the 4th of July Should Be Canceled Due to a 'Shortage of Independence' for Women after Roe v. Wade Was Overturned." *Buzzfeed News*, July 5. www.buzzfeednews.com/article/ellendurney/celebrities-speak -out-on-independence-day-after-roe-v-wade.

Fabry, Merrill. 2015. "The History behind the 'Victoria' in Victoria's Secret." *Time*, December 8. time.com/4140242/victorias-secret -fashion-show-history/.

Fashion Law. 2022. "How Abercrombie Ended up Being Sued by 250,000 Employees." April 21. www.thefashionlaw.com/how-abercrombie -ended-up-being-sued-by-250000-employees/.

Fathallah, Judith May. 2020. *Emo: How Fans Defined a Subculture.* Iowa City: University of Iowa Press.

Fisher, Mark. (2014) 2022. *Capitalist Realism: Is There No Alternative?* Winchester: Zero Books.

Fowler, Bree. 2022. "TikTok's In-App Browser Can Monitor Your Keystrokes, Researcher Says." *CNET*, August 22. www.cnet.com/tech /services-and-software/tiktoks-in-app-browser-can-monitor-your -keystrokes-researcher-says/.

Frank, Thomas. 1998. *The Conquest of Cool: Business Culture, Counterculture, and the Rise of Hip Consumerism.* Chicago: University of Chicago Press.

Fraser, Nancy. 2022. *Cannibal Capitalism: How Our System Is Devouring Democracy, Care, and the Planet—and What We Can Do about It*. London: Verso.

Gaca, Anna. 2017. "Emo Festival Announces Lineup Consisting Almost Entirely of Men." *Spin*, February 7. www.spin.com/2017/02/when-we -were-young-festival-lineup-2017-morrissey/.

Garfinkel, Harold. 1967. *Studies in Ethnomethodology*. Cambridge, UK: Polity Press.

Gee, Erin. 2021. "The Performative Faux Feminism of *Succession*'s Kendall Roy." *Harper's Bazaar*, November 18. www.harpersbazaar.com /culture/film-tv/a38253573/kendall-roy-succession-performative -male-feminism/.

Gelles, David. 2023. "How Environmentally Conscious Investing Became a Target of Conservatives." *New York Times*, February 28. www.ny times.com/2023/02/28/climate/esg-climate-backlash.html.

Glatt, Zoë. 2022. "'We're All Told Not to Put Our Eggs in One Basket: Uncertainty, Precarity and Cross-Platform Labor in the Online Video Influencer Industry." *International Journal of Communication* 16(2022): 3853–71.

Glatt, Zoë, and Sarah Banet-Weiser. 2021. "Productive Ambivalence, Economies of Visibility, and the Political Potential of Feminist YouTubers." In *Creator Culture: An Introduction to Global Social Media Engagement*, edited by Stuart Cunningham and David Craig, 39–56. New York: New York University Press.

Goldsmith, Jill. 2022. "Elon Musk Tweets 'the Woke Mind Virus Is Either Defeated or Nothing Else Matters' after Being Booed at a Dave Chappelle Show." *Deadline*, December 12. https://uk.sports.yahoo.com /news/elon-musk-tweets-woke-mind-182522320.html.

Gray, Kishonna L. 2020. *Intersectional Tech: Black Users in Digital Gaming*. Baton Rouge: Louisiana State University Press.

Greenwald, Andy. 2003. *Nothing Feels Good: Punk Rock, Teenagers, and Emo*. New York: St Martin's Griffin.

Grier, Sonya A., Kevin D. Thomas, and Guillaume D. Johnson. 2019. "Re-imagining the Marketplace: Addressing Race in Academic Marketing Research." *Consumption Markets & Culture* 22(1): 91–100. https://doi.org/10.1080/10253866.2017.1413800.

Habbouchi, Hayley. 2022. "All the Celebrities Who Have 'Cancelled' 4 July Celebrations amid Roe v Wade: From Kim Kardashian to Katy Perry." *Capital FM*, July 5. www.capitalfm.com/news/fourth-july-cancelled -roe-v-wade/.

Haig, Matt. 2011. *Brand Success: How the World's Top 100 Brands Thrive and Survive.* London: Kogan Page.

Hall, Stuart. 2013. Introduction to *Representation: Cultural Representations and Signifying Practices*, edited by Stuart Hall, Jessica Evans, and Sean Nixon, xvii–xxvi. London: Sage.

Hamilton, Amber M. 2020. "A Genealogy of Critical Race and Digital Studies: Past, Present, and Future." *Sociology of Race and Ethnicity* 6(3): 292–301. https://doi.org/10.1177/2332649220922577.

Hampton, Rachelle. 2019. "The Black Feminists Who Saw the Alt-Right Threat Coming." *Slate*, April 23. https://slate.com/technology/2019/04/black-feminists-alt-right-twitter-gamergate.html.

Hanbury, Mary, and Áine Cain. 2023. "The Rise, Fall, and Comeback of Victoria's Secret, America's Biggest Lingerie Retailer." *Business Insider*, July 30. www.businessinsider.com/victorias-secret-rise-and-fall-history-2019-5?r=US&IR=T.

Harris, Angela P. 2021. Foreword to *Histories of Racial Capitalism*, edited by Destin Jenkins and Justin Leroy, vii–xx. New York: Columbia University Press.

Harrison, Anthony Kwame. 2013. "Black Skiing, Everyday Racism, and the Racial Spatiality of Whiteness." *Journal of Sport and Social Issues* 37(4): 315–39. https://doi.org/10.1177/0193723513498607.

Harrison, Robert L., Kevin D. Thomas, and Samantha N. N. Cross. 2017. "Restricted Visions of Multiracial Identity in Advertising." *Journal of Advertising* 46(4): 503–20.

Heath, Joseph, and Andrew Potter. 2006. *The Rebel Sell: How the Counterculture Became Consumer Culture.* Sussex, UK: Capstone.

Henderson, Geraldine Rosa, Anne-Marie Hakstian, and Jerome D. Williams, eds. 2016. *Consumer Equality: Race and the American Marketplace.* Santa Barbara, CA: Praeger.

Hess, Aaron. 2017. "The Speaking Machine: Surveying the Field of Digital Rhetoric." In *Theorizing Digital Rhetoric*, edited by Aaron Hess and Amber Davisson, 1–16. New York: Routledge.

Hesse, Barnor, ed. 2000. *Un/settled Multiculturalisms: Diasporas, Entanglements, Transruptions.* London: Zed Press.

Hieatt, David. 2014. *DO/PURPOSE: Why Brands with a Purpose Do Better and Matter More.* n.p.: Do Book Company.

Holt, Brianna. 2023. "Levi's Announced They'd Use AI-Generated Models to 'Increase Diversity': Black models Say It's a Step Backward and They Should Book Real People Instead." *Insider*, April 4. www.insider.com/levis-ai-generated-company-models-diversity-backlash-2023-3.

Holt, Douglas. 2016. "Branding in the Age of Social Media." *Harvard Business Review*, March. https://hbr.org/2016/03/branding-in-the-age-of-social-media.

Holt, Douglas B. 2004. *How Brands Become Icons: The Principles of Cultural Branding*. Boston: Harvard Business School Press.

hooks, bell. 1984. *Feminist Theory: From Margin to Center*. Boston: South End Press.

———. 1992. *Black Looks: Race and Representation*. Boston: South End Press.

Horgan, Amelia. 2022. *Lost in Work: Escaping Capitalism*. London: Pluto Press.

Horton, Adrian. 2022a. "'Discrimination Was Their Brand': How Abercrombie & Fitch Fell out of Fashion." *Guardian*, April 19. www.theguardian.com/film/2022/apr/19/abercrombie-fitch-netflix-documentary-fashion-discrimination.

———. 2022b. "From Severance to The Bear: Why Some of the Best TV Focused on Work in 2022." *Guardian*, December 22. www.theguardian.com/tv-and-radio/2022/dec/22/best-tv-shows-workplace-drama-severance-the-bear-industry.

Hund, Emily. 2023. *The Influencer Industry: The Quest for Authenticity on Social Media*. Princeton, NJ: Princeton University Press.

Irving, Emma. 2021. "Tony's Chocolonely: The Risks of Being a Woke Brand." *Economist*, April 14. www.economist.com/1843/2021/04/14/tonys-chocolonely-the-risks-of-being-a-woke-brand.

Jackson, Lauren Michele. 2018. "Shudu Gram Is a White Man's Digital Projection of Real-Life Black Womanhood." *New Yorker*, May 4. www.newyorker.com/culture/culture-desk/shudu-gram-is-a-white-mans-digital-projection-of-real-life-black-womanhood.

Jackson, Sarah J., Moya Bailey, and Brooke Foucault Welles. 2020. *#HashtagActivism: Networks of Race and Gender Justice*. Cambridge, MA: MIT Press.

Johnson, Azeezat, Remi Joseph-Salisbury, and Beth Kamunge, eds. 2018. *The Fire Now: Anti-Racist Scholarship in Times of Explicit Racial Violence*. London: Zed Books.

Johnson, Cedric G. 2022. *The Panthers Can't Save Us Now: Debating Left Politics and Black Lives Matter*. London: Verso.

Johnson, Guillaume D., Kevin D. Thomas, Anthony Kwame Harrison, and Sonya A. Grier, eds. 2019. *Race in the Marketplace: Crossing Critical Boundaries*. Cham: Palgrave Macmillan.

216   REFERENCES

Joseph, Tanya. 2022. "Brands Have a Duty to Defend Women's Rights as Roe v Wade Is Overturned." *Marketing Week*, June 29. www.marketing week.com/brands-have-a-duty-to-defend-womens-rights-as-roe-v -wade-is-overturned/.

Kanai, Akane, and Rosalind Gill. 2020. "Woke? Affect, Neoliberalism, Marginalised Identities and Consumer Culture." *New Formations: A Journal of Culture/Theory/Politics* 102: 10–27.

Kanesaka, Erica. 2023. "The Mixed-Race Fantasy behind Kawaii Aesthetics." *Catapult*, January 17. https://catapult.co/stories/the -mixed-race-fantasy-behind-kawaii-aesthetics-japanese-post-racial -cute-licca-chan-erica-kanesaka.

Kho, Charlotte. 2022. "How Major Fashion Brands Are Responding to the Roe v. Wade Ruling." *PopSugar*, June 30. www.popsugar.co .uk/fashion/fashion-brands-for-abortion-rights-48873399?utm _medium=redirect&utm_campaign=US:GB&utm_source=www .google.co.uk.

Kilander, Gustaf, and Andrew Buncombe. 2022. "Black Lives Matter Apologizes after $6M California Mansion Purchase." *Independent*, April 12. www.independent.co.uk/news/world/americas/black-lives -matter-apologies-mansion-b2056313.html.

Kilikita, Jacqueline. 2021. "What It's Like to Work at the 'Cult of Lush' (by an Ex-Lush Employee)." *Refinery29*. https://www.refinery29.com/en -gb/working-at-lush-experience

Klein, Bethany. 2020. *Selling Out: Culture, Commerce and Popular Music.* London: Bloomsbury.

Klein, Naomi. 2000. *No Logo: No Space, No Choice, No Jobs.* New York: Picador.

Krutrök, Moa Eriksson, and Mathilda Åkerlund. 2022. "Through a White Lens: Black Victimhood, Visibility, and Whiteness in the Black Lives Matter Movement on TikTok." *Information, Communication & Society*, April 29. https://doi.org/10.1080/1369118X.2022.2065211

Kunda, Lily. 2020. "Ben & Jerry's, Black Lives Matter, and the Politics of Public Statements." *Flow Journal*, July 6. https://www.flowjournal.org /2020/07/ben-and-jerrys-blm/.

Kwittken, Aaron. 2022. "Brands and Agencies Should Stand with Ukraine—Silence Is Violence." *The Drum*, February 28. www.thedrum .com/opinion/2022/02/28/brands-and-agencies-should-stand-with -ukraine-silence-violence.

Lang, Michael. 2010. *The Road to Woodstock: From the Man Behind the Legendary Festival.* New York: HarperCollins.

Leal, Melanio L. 2022. "Moral Obligation or Moral Imposition: Which Moral System Works Better during COVID-19 Pandemic?" *Journal of Public Health* 44(4): e635–36. https://europepmc.org/article/MED/34487186.

Lees-Marshment, Jennifer. 2004. *The Political Marketing Revolution: Transforming the Government of the UK.* Manchester: Manchester University Press.

Lekakis, Eleftheria J. 2022. *Consumer Activism: Promotional Culture and Resistance.* London: Sage.

Lentin, Alana. 2020. *Why Race Still Matters.* London: Polity.

Levi Strauss & Co. 2023. "LS&Co. Partners with Lalaland.ai [Editor's Note]." Levi Strauss & Co., March 28. www.levistrauss.com/2023/03/22/lsco-partners-with-lalaland-ai/.

Lewis, Rebecca. 2020. "'This Is What the News Won't Show You': YouTube Creators and the Reactionary Politics of Micro-Celebrity." *Television & New Media* 21(2): 201–17. https://doi.org/10.1177/1527476 41987991.

Littler, Jo. 2008. *Radical Consumption: Shopping for Change in Contemporary Culture.* Maidenhead, UK: Open University Press.

Lush. 2021. "Lush Is Becoming Anti-social." https://weare.lush.com/press-releases/lush-is-becoming-anti-social/.

Mardon, Rebecca, Hayley Cocker, and Kate Daunt. 2023. "De-influencing: How Online Beauty Gurus Get Followers to Trust Them by Posting Negative Reviews." *The Conversation,* February 15. https://theconversation.com/de-influencing-how-online-beauty-gurus-get-followers-to-trust-them-by-posting-negative-reviews-199223.

Markarian, Taylor. 2019. *From the Basement: A History of Emo Music and How It Changed Society.* Miami, FL: Mango Media.

McBride, Dwight A. 2005. *Why I Hate Abercrombie & Fitch: Essays on Race and Sexuality.* New York: New York University Press.

Milmo, Dan. 2021. "Twitter Admits Bias in Algorithm for Rightwing Politicians and News Outlets." *Guardian,* October 22. www.the guardian.com/technology/2021/oct/22/twitter-admits-bias-in-algorithm-for-rightwing-politicians-and-news-outlets.

Miquela. 2021. "I'm Miquela, a Real Life Robot Mess." YouTube video. February 23. www.youtube.com/watch?v=6bn3tUUtj2M.

Mirzoeff, Nicholas. 2023. *White Sight: Visual Politics and Practices of Whiteness.* Cambridge: MA: MIT Press.

Miyake, Esperanza. 2022. "I Am a Virtual Girl from Tokyo: Virtual Influencers, Digital-Orientalism and the (Im)materiality of Race and

Gender." *Journal of Consumer Culture* 23(1): 209–28. https://doi.org/10.1177/14695405221117195.

Montell, Amanda. 2021. *Cultish: The Language of Fanaticism*. New York: HarperCollins.

Moorhead, Joanna. 2021. "Caked Crusaders: How The Great British Bake Off Took over the World." *Guardian*, September 19. www.theguardian.com/tv-and-radio/2021/sep/19/caked-crusaders-how-the-great-british-bake-off-took-over-the-world.

Morgan, Lucy. 2022. "Netflix's *Trainwreck: Woodstock 99* Is Being Called out for Seriously Downplaying Rape and Sexual Assault." *Glamour*, August 25. www.glamourmagazine.co.uk/article/woodstock-99-netflix-sexual-assault.

Mudde, Cas. 2023. "What Is behind Ron DeSantis's Stop-Woke Act?" *Guardian*, February 6. www.theguardian.com/commentisfree/2023/feb/06/what-is-behind-ron-desantis-stop-woke-act#:~:text=In%20addition%20to%20his%20Stop,or%20national%20origin%2C%20he%20has.

Mukherjee, Roopali, and Sarah Banet-Weiser, eds. 2012. *Commodity Activism: Cultural Resistance in Neoliberal Times*. New York: New York University Press.

Museum of Brands. 2020a. "Memory Trail." https://museumofbrands.com/wp-content/uploads/2020/10/MoB_Memory_Trail.pdf.

Museum of Brands. 2020b. "When Brands Take a Stand." https://museumofbrands.com/brands-stand/.

Myers, Joshua. 2021. *Cedric Robinson: The Time of the Black Radical Tradition*. Cambridge, UK: Polity Press.

Ng, Kate. 2022. "Which Celebrities Have Spoken Out against the Supreme Court's Decision on Roe v Wade?" *Independent*, June 28. www.independent.co.uk/life-style/roe-v-wade-celebrities-supreme-court-justices-b2111182.html.

Niven, Alex. 2022. Introduction to *Capitalist Realism: Is There No Alternative?*, by Mark Fisher, xiii–xxviii. Winchester: Zero Books.

Noble, Safiya Umoja. 2018. *Algorithms of Oppression: How Search Engines Reinforce Racism*. New York: New York University Press.

Noble, Safiya Umoja, and Brendesha M. Tynes, eds. 2016. *The Intersectional Internet: Race, Sex, Class, and Culture Online*. New York: Peter Lang.

Ogilvy, David. (1963) 2004. *Confessions of an Advertising Man*. London: Southbank Publishing.

Oremus, Will. 2023. "Musk Defends 'Dilbert' Creator, Says Media Is 'Racist against Whites.'" *Washington Post*, February 26. www

.washingtonpost.com/technology/2023/02/26/elon-musk-scott-adams
-dilbert-racist/.

O'Sullivan, Sadhbh. 2022. "Molly-Mae Exposes the Problems at the Heart
of Influencer Culture." *Refinery29*, January 7. www.refinery29.com/en
-gb/molly-mae-backlash-influencer-culture.

Otnes, Cele C., and Pauline Maclaran. 2015. *Royal Fever: The British Monarchy in Consumer Culture*. Oakland: University of California Press.

Ozzi, Dan. 2021. *Sellout: The Major-Label Feeding Frenzy That Swept
Punk, Emo, and Hardcore (1994–2007)*. New York: Dey Street Books.

Payne, Chris. 2023. *Where Are Your Boys Tonight? The Oral History of
Emo's Mainstream Explosion 1999–2008*. New York: Dey Street Books.

Perkins, Anne. 2017. "It's More Than Just a TV Show: Bake Off Is a
Window on the Nation's Soul." *Guardian*, November 1. www.the
guardian.com/commentisfree/2017/nov/01/great-british-bake-off
-national-values-identity.

Phillips, Justin. 2023. "Levi's Is Using AI to Generate 'Diverse' Models:
Here's Why That's a Fashion Fail." *San Francisco Chronicle*, April 5.
www.sfchronicle.com/bayarea/justinphillips/article/levi-diversity
-artificial-intelligence-17866765.php.

Phipps, Alison. 2020. *Me, Not You: The Trouble with Mainstream
Feminism*. Manchester: Manchester University Press.

Prins, Annelot. 2022. "On Good Girls and Woke White Women: *Miss
Americana* and the Performance of Popular White Womanhood."
Celebrity Studies 13(1): 102–7. https://doi.org/10.1080/19392397.2021
.2023852.

Ransby, Barbara. 2018. *Making All Black Lives Matter: Reimagining
Freedom in the Twenty-First Century*. Oakland: University of California Press.

Rauchberg, Jessica Sage. 2020. "TikTok's Digital Eugenics: Challenging
Ableism and Algorithmic Erasure through Disability Activism." *Flow*,
September 28. www.flowjournal.org/2020/09/tiktok-digital-eugenics/.

———. 2022. "#Shadowbanned Queer, Trans, and Disabled Creator
Responses to Algorithmic Oppression on TikTok." In *LGBTQ Digital
Cultures: A Global Perspective*, edited by Paromita Pain, 196–209.
London: Routledge.

Ray, Victor. 2019. "A Theory of Racialized Organizations." *American
Sociological Review* 84(1): 26–53. https://doi.org/10.1177/0003122418
82233.

Reilly, Nick. 2019. "Millie Bobby Brown Responds after Being Accused of
Defending Joe Goldberg from 'You.'" *NME*, January 17. www.nme.com

/news/millie-bobby-brown-has-a-controversial-take-on-joe-goldberg
-from-you-2432248

Rhodes, Carl. 2022. *Woke Capitalism: How Corporate Morality is Sabotaging Democracy*. Bristol: Bristol University Press.

Richmond, Michael, and Alex Charnley. 2022. *Fractured: Race, Class, Gender and the Hatred of Identity Politics*. London: Pluto Press.

Ritson, Mark. 2022. "Brands Take Note: The Purpose of Purpose Is Purpose." *Marketing Week*, September 16. www.marketingweek.com/patagonia-purpose-of-purpose/.

Robinson, Alex. 2022. "Which Companies Are Taking a Stand on Roe v. Wade?" *Corporate Knights*, May 24. www.corporateknights.com/leadership/which-companies-are-taking-a-stand-on-roe-v-wade/.

Robinson, Cedric J. 1983. *Black Marxism: The Making of the Black Radical Tradition*. London: Zed Press.

Rosa-Salas, Marcel. 2019. "Making the Mass White: How Racial Segregation Shaped Consumer Segmentation." In *Race in the Marketplace: Crossing Critical Boundaries*, edited by Guillaume D. Johnson, Kevin D. Thomas, Anthony Kwame Harrison, and Sonya A. Grier, 21–38. Cham: Palgrave Macmillan.

Rosa-Salas, Marcel, and Francesca Sobande. 2022. "Hierarchies of Knowledge about Intersectionality in Marketing Theory and Practice." *Marketing Theory* 22(2): 175–89. https://journals.sagepub.com/doi/abs/10.1177/14705931221075372?journalCode=mtqa.

Rosen, Christopher. 2020. "Progressive Dramedy *The Bold Type* Has a Diversity Problem, Says Its Star." *Vanity Fair*, July 16. www.vanityfair.com/hollywood/2020/07/the-bold-type-aisha-dee-diversity.

Ross, Loretta J., and Rickie Solinger. 2017. *Reproductive Justice: An Introduction*. Oakland: University of California Press.

Saunier, Greg. 2021. "Woodstock '99, or How to Do a USA in Late Capitalism." *Talkhouse*, August 10. www.talkhouse.com/what-woodstock-99-doesnt-say-about-human-nature/.

Schudson, Michael. 1984. *Advertising, the Uneasy Persuasion: Its Dubious Impact on American Society*. London: Routledge.

Schwingle, Nadia. 2021. "8 Black, Intersectional Vegan Influencers You Need to Follow and Support Immediately." *One Green Planet*. www.onegreenplanet.org/human-interest/8-black-intersectional-vegan-influencers-you-need-to-follow-and-support-immediately/.

Sedgman, Kirsty. 2023. *On Being Unreasonable: Breaking the Rules and Making Things Better*. London: Faber & Faber.

Shadijanova, Diyora. 2022. "Molly-Mae, Influencer Culture, and the Myth That Hard Work Reaps Rewards." *Dazed*, January 7. www.dazeddigital .com/life-culture/article/55197/1/molly-mae-influencer-culture-and -the-myth-that-hard-work-reaps-rewards.

Sharp, Gemma, and Ysabel Gerrard. 2022. "The Body Image "Problem" on Social Media: Novel Directions for the Field." *Body Image* 41:267– 71. https://doi.org/10.1016/j.bodyim.2022.03.004.

Sligh, Casta, and Crystal Abidin. 2022. "When Brands Become Stans: Netflix, Originals, and Enacting a Fannish Persona on Instagram." *Television & New Media* 24(6): 616–38. https://doi.org/10.1177/15274 764221134778.

Slupska, Julie, and Laura Shipp. 2022. "What You Need to Know about Surveillance and Reproductive Rights in a Post Roe v Wade World." *The Conversation*, July 6. https://theconversation.com/what-you-need -to-know-about-surveillance-and-reproductive-rights-in-a-post-roe-v -wade-world-185933.

Sobande, Francesca. 2017. "Watching Me Watching You: Black Women in Britain on YouTube." *European Journal of Cultural Studies* 20(6): 655–71. https://doi.org/10.1177/13675494177330.

———. 2018. "Digital Diaspora and (Re)mediating Black Women in Britain." PhD thesis, University of Dundee.

———. 2019a. "Woke-Washing: 'Intersectional' Femvertising and Branding 'Woke' Bravery." *European Journal of Marketing* 54(11): 2723–45. https://doi.org/10.1108/EJM-02-2019-0134.

———. 2019b. "Constructing and Critiquing Interracial Couples on You-Tube." In *Race in the Marketplace: Crossing Critical Boundaries*, edited by Guillaume D. Johnson, Kevin D. Thomas, Anthony Kwame Harrison, and Sonya A. Grier, eds., 107–20. Cham: Palgrave Macmillan.

———. 2019c. "Memes, Digital Remix Culture and (Re)mediating British Politics and Public Life." *IPPR Progressive Review* 26(2): 151–60. https://doi.org/10.1111/newe.12155.

———. 2020. *The Digital Lives of Black Women in Britain*. Cham: Palgrave Macmillan.

———. 2021a. "Spectacularized and Branded Digital (Re)presentations of Black People and Blackness." *Television & New Media* 22(2): 131–46. https://doi.org/10.1177/1527476420983745.

———. 2021b. "CGI Influencers: When the 'People' We Follow on Social Media Aren't Human." *The Conversation*, September 30. https://the conversation.com/cgi-influencers-when-the-people-we-follow-on -social-media-arent-human-165767.

———. 2022a. *Consuming Crisis: Commodifying Care and COVID-19.* London: Sage.

———. 2022b. "The Celebrity Whitewashing of Black Lives Matter and Social Injustices." *Celebrity Studies* 13(1): 130–35. https://doi.org/10.1080/19392397.2022.2026147.

———. 2022c. "Welcome to When We Were Young's Big Tech Parade." *Paste Magazine*, October 27. www.pastemagazine.com/tech/when-we-were-young/when-we-were-young-festival-big-tech-netflix-googl/.

———. 2022d. "Why Emo Endures: The Comforting Nostalgia of Emo on Vinyl." *Vinyl Factory*, November 9. thevinylfactory.com/features/emo-on-vinyl/.

———. 2023a. "Arts Marking, Social Justice Activism, and Government Messaging in the Age of Social Media." In *Marketing the Arts: Breaking Boundaries*, edited by Finola Kerrigan and Chloe Preece, 12–24. London: Routledge.

———. 2023b. "Succession and Scotland: Logan Roy and the Art of 'Nation Branding.'" The Conversation, May 15. https://theconversation.com/succession-and-scotland-logan-roy-and-the-art-of-nation-branding-204962.

———. 2023c. "Netflix's You: The Real Monster of Series Four Is 'Dark Academia.'" *The Conversation*, March 9. https://theconversation.com/netflixs-you-the-real-monster-of-series-four-is-dark-academia-201022.

———. Forthcoming. "White and gendered aesthetics and attitudes of #pandemicbaking and #quarantinebaking." *European Journal of Cultural Studies.*

Sobande, Francesca, and Emma-Lee Amponsah. Forthcoming "Demands, Displays, and Dreams of 'Black Joy' during Times of Crisis." *Ethnic and Racial Studies.*

Sobande, Francesca, David Hesmondhalgh, and Anamik Saha. 2022. "Black, Brown and Asian Cultural Workers, Creativity and Activism: The Ambivalence of Digital Self-Branding Practices." *Sociological Review.* https://doi.org/10.1177/00380261231163.

Sobande, Francesca, Akane Kanai, and Natasha Zeng. 2022. "The Hypervisibility and Discourses of 'Wokeness' in Digital Culture." *Media, Culture & Society* 44(8): 1576–87. https://doi.org/10.1177/01634437221117490.

Sobande, Francesca, and Bethany Klein. 2022. "'Come and Get a Taste of Normal': Advertising, Consumerism and the Coronavirus Pandemic."

European Journal of Cultural Studies 26(4): 493–509. https://doi.org /10.1177/13675494221108219.

Steele, Catherine Knight. 2021. *Digital Black Feminism*. New York: New York University Press.

Stewart, Rebecca. 2020. "'It's Not a Marketing Exercise': Ben & Jerry's on Dismantling White Supremacy." *The Drum*, June 23. www.thedrum .com/news/2020/06/23/its-not-marketing-exercise-ben-jerry-s -dismantling-white-supremacy.

Stokel-Walker, Chris. 2019. *YouTubers: How YouTube Shook up TV and Created a New Generation of Stars*. Surrey, UK: Canbury Press.

———. 2021. *TikTok Boom: The Inside Story of the World's Favourite App*. Surrey, UK: Canbury Press.

Táíwò, Olúfẹ́mi O. 2022. *Elite Capture: How the Powerful Took Over Identity Politics (and Everything Else)*. London: Pluto Press.

Taylor, Keeanga-Yamahtta. 2021. *From #Blacklivesmatter to Black Liberation*. Chicago: Haymarket Books.

Temple-West, Patrick, and Brooke Masters. 2023. "Wall Street Titans Confront ESG Backlash as New Financial Risk." *Financial Times*, March 1. www.ft.com/content/f5fe15f8-3703-4df9-b203-b5d1dd01e3bc.

Thomas, Kevin D., Guillaume D. Johnson, and Sonya A. Grier. 2023. "Perspectives: Race and Advertising; Conceptualizing a Way Forward through Aesthetics." *International Journal of Advertising* 42(3). https://doi.org/10.1080/02650487.2023.2167365.

Todd, Sarah. 2020. "If Everybody Hates Wokewashing, Why Do Companies Still Do It?" *Quartz*, October 20. https://finance.yahoo.com /news/everybody-hates-wokewashing-why-companies-080104113.html.

Tony's Chocolonely. 2021. "Tony's Chocolonely Annual FAIR 2020/2021 Report." *Respect*. https://respect.international/wp-content/uploads /2022/05/Tonys-Chocolony-annual-report.pdf.

———. 2022. "Tony's Chocolate Bar Is Closing . . . ." *Toney's Chocolonely*, November 30. https://tonyschocolonely.com/nl/en/our-mission/news /making-positive-impact-in-the-cocoa-industry-is-always-number-1.

Tounsel, Timeka N. 2022. *Branding Black Womanhood: Media Citizenship from Black Power to Black Girl Magic*. Newark, NJ: Rutgers University Press.

Towns, Armond R. 2022. *On Black Media Philosophy*. Oakland: University of California Press.

Turow, Joseph. 2008. *Niche Envy: Marketing Discrimination in the Digital Age*. Cambridge, MA: MIT Press.

———. 2012. *The Daily You: How the Advertising Industry Is Defining Your Identity and Your World*. New Haven, CT: Yale University Press.

———. 2017. *The Aisles Have Eyes: How Retailers Track Your Shopping, Strip Your Privacy, and Define Your Power*. New Haven, CT: Yale University Press.

———. 2021. *The Voice Catchers: How Marketers Listen In to Exploit Your Feelings, Your Privacy, and Your Wallet*. New Haven, CT: Yale University Press.

Vincent, Isabel. 2021. "Inside BLM Co-founder Patrisse Khan-Cullors' Million-Dollar Real Estate Buying Binge." *New York Post*, April 10. https://nypost.com/2021/04/10/inside-blm-co-founder-patrisse-khan -cullors-real-estate-buying-binge/.

Warren, Danielle E. 2022. "'Woke' Corporations and the Stigmatization of Corporate Social Initiatives." *Business Ethics Quarterly* 32(1): 169–98. https://doi.org/10.1017/beq.2021.48.

Warrington, James, Hannah Boland, and Giulia Bottaro. 2022. "'Ben & Jerry's Tendencies' of Woke Businesses Attacked by Kemi Badenoch." *Telegraph*, July 12. www.telegraph.co.uk/business/2022/07/12/ftse -100-markets-live-news-rail-strike-amazon-twitter/.

Warzel, Charlie. 2022. "Elon Musk Is a Far-Right Activist." *Atlantic*, December 11. www.theatlantic.com/technology/archive/2022/12/elon -musk-twitter-far-right-activist/672436/.

Weatherbed, Jess. 2023. "Levi's Will Test AI-Generated Clothing Models to 'Increase Diversity.'" *The Verge*, May 27. www.theverge.com/2023/3 /27/23658385/levis-ai-generated-clothing-model-diversity-denim.

Webb, Bella. 2021. "Lush Is Quitting Social Media: The Start of a Trend?" *Vogue Business*, November 22. www.voguebusiness.com/consumers /lush-is-quitting-social-media-the-start-of-a-trend-facebook -instagram-snapchat-tiktok.

Weinstein PR. 2022. "Say Hello to Intersectional Influencers." https:// weinsteinpr.com/say-hello-to-intersectional-influencers/.

Wellman, M. L. 2022. "Black Squares for Black Lives? Performative Allyship as Credibility Maintenance for Social Media Influencers on Instagram." *Social Media + Society* 8(1). https://doi.org/10.1177/20563 051221080473.

Wingate, Sophie. 2022. "Rishi Sunak Vows to Tackle 'Woke Nonsense' and 'Left-Wing Agitators.'" *Independent*, July 29. www.independent.co .uk/news/uk/rishi-sunak-liz-truss-british-conservative-party-english -b2134501.htmlfr.

Yesiloglu, Sevil, and Joyce Costello. 2020. *Influencer Marketing: Building Brands Communities and Engagement*. London: Routledge.

Zach Sang Show. 2019. "Miquela Talks Being a Robot, Her Song 'Money', Kissing Bella Hadid & Collabs." *YouTube* video, December 9. www.you tube.com/watch?v=S6wnHsEoTmc.

Zheng, Lily. 2020. "We're Entering the Age of Corporate Social Justice." *Harvard Business Review*, June 15. https://hbr.org/2020/06/were -entering-the-age-of-corporate-social-justice.

Index

Founded in 1893,
UNIVERSITY OF CALIFORNIA PRESS
publishes bold, progressive books and journals
on topics in the arts, humanities, social sciences,
and natural sciences—with a focus on social
justice issues—that inspire thought and action
among readers worldwide.

The UC PRESS FOUNDATION
raises funds to uphold the press's vital role
as an independent, nonprofit publisher, and
receives philanthropic support from a wide
range of individuals and institutions—and from
committed readers like you. To learn more, visit
ucpress.edu/supportus.